Exporting

OTHER BOOKS BY CARL NELSON

Your Own Import–Export Business:
Winning the Trade Game

Import/Export: How to Get Started in
International Trade

Global Success: International Business
Tactics for the 1990s

Managing Globally: A Complete Guide to
Competing Worldwide

Protocol For Profit: A Manager's Guide to
Competing Worldwide
(Global Manager Series)

International Business: A Manager's Guide to
Strategy in the Age of Globalism
(Global Manager Series)

■ GLOBAL MANAGER SERIES ■

Exporting
A Manager's Guide to the World Market

Carl A Nelson

INTERNATIONAL THOMSON BUSINESS PRESS
I(T)P® An International Thomson Publishing Company

London • Bonn • Johannesburg • Madrid • Melbourne • Mexico City • New York • Paris
Singapore • Tokyo • Toronto • Albany, NY • Belmont, CA • Cincinnati, OH • Detroit, MI

Exporting: A Manager's Guide

Copyright © 1999 Carl A Nelson

Business Press is a division of Thomson Learning
The Thomson Learning logo is a registered trademark and used herein under license.

British Library Cataloguing-in-Publication Data
A catalogue record for this book is available from the British Library

First published 1999 by International Business Press

Reprinted by Thomson Learning 2000

Typeset by J&L Composition Ltd, Filey, North Yorkshire
Printed in the UK by TJ International, Padstow, Cornwall

ISBN 1–86152–316–5

Thomson Learning
Berkshire House
168–173 High Holborn
London WCIV 7AA
UK

http://www.thomsonlearning.co.uk

Contents

Preface

Exporting is as old as trade itself—it is international trade and it is a universal process. There are exporters in every nation and the process from place to place is exactly the same. The only thing that differs is the interface with government, that is, the country-specific laws, procedures, and regulations.

Exporting: A Manager's Guide To The World Market is targeted for a universal audience, it is for every business person in every land.

So what's new?

What is new is that in the current era of globalism, cross-border trade is big time—everyone is getting into it because there are great opportunities and excellent profits.

Products are everywhere just waiting to be sold into a foreign market. International trade brings profits to the smallest of businesses as well as to the greatest corporations in the world.

Think about this! By best estimates, global economic output in 1945, following World War II, was less than $1 trillion, but by 1996 the global economy was more than $35 trillion in gross world product (GWP). During that same period world output grew by just less than four percent, but world exports grew by over six percent, thus demonstrating international trade's importance. Not withstanding this success, the global economy is still in its infancy. Some estimate GWP could be greater than $100 trillion by the middle of the twenty-first century and world exports could exceed 25 percent of that.

Besides making a lot of money and profits, what are the benefits of exporting?

- Do you want an exciting career?
  Why not?
- Do you like to to travel?
  Why not?
- Do you like to meet the interesting people of the world, have fun, and go to beautiful, romantic places?
  Why not?

Exporting requires only a low capital investment. It is a business with only moderate risk. The criteria for exporting are world-class products, a willingness to do business with foreigners, and an eye for selling in different cultures. Unlike other means of exchanging goods and services national governments encourage exporting between firms and peoples of other countries.

Why?

Because exporting creates jobs, brings in hard currencies and is a major element of economic development. For the small business there is plenty of financing available because governments show their encouragment with financial support.

Things are becoming even more interesting as a result of modern communications. Television, facsimile, and the Internet introduce our products around the world without us leaving our offices.

Exporting is a product marketing process easily learned by people in any land. The approach of *Exporting: A Manager's Guide To The World Market* is to explain in an easily understandable way how exporters can compete in the age of global interdependency.

The theme of the book is that the business function called "exporting" is universal, is not difficult to learn, and is growing at unprecedented rates worldwide. Businesses with exportable products can expand significantly by taking advantage of the globalization process.

Exporting: A Manager's Guide To The World Market is for all forward-thinking people interested in international trade: entrepreneurs, managers and decision makers. But, the book is particularly useful for those small and medium-sized manufacturing and service companies that are ready for new challenges.

Exporting: A Manager's Guide To The World Market covers every aspect of the exporting process including negotiations, the contract, terms of sale, pricing, insurance, the market plan, how to use intermediaries, and much, much more. It explains how to get started for those who are venturing into the global arena for the first time. It is also for those businesses, large or small, already in international business that want to learn how to expand.

Acknowledgements

I accept full responsibility for any faults of this book and gratefully share any praise for its virtues with the following persons who gave freely of their time to critique and otherwise offer comments to make the book as good as it can be: Mr. John Bushnell, U.S. Department of Commerce (Western Regional Bureau of Export Administration); Ms. Cassandra D. Stiles, Senior Vice President, International Banking, Imperial Bank; Ms. Julie Osman, International Trade Specialist, U.S. Department of Commerce; Mr. Craig B. Barkacs, Partner, Barkacs & Barkacs; Ms. Elizabeth M. (Goldman) Cushinsky; Editors Julian Thomas and So-Shan Au, and Marketing Manager Jacqui Baldwin of International Thomson Business Press.

About the Author

With eight published books in his field, this former CEO/CO of five public and private organizations, with over 40 years in public and private enterprise experience, has become known as "Mister Global Trade Strategist." Dr. Carl Nelson is currently Professor of International Business at the School of International Management in San Diego, California, and president of Global Business Systems (GBS) an international business consulting and training company. He has conducted workshops and seminars about global strategy, export/import operations, international development, Mexican Maquiladora operations, and economic integration (NAFTA).

He earned his Doctorate in Business Administration, (International Finance and Trade) from the United States International University in San Diego (USIU), California, where his research focused on U.S. small business export problems. He was recognized by USIU with its 1989 outstanding alumni award. Dr. Nelson is also a graduate of the Naval War College, holds a Master of Science degree in Management (Economics/Systems Analysis) from the Naval Post Graduate School in Monterey, California, and an engineering degree from the U.S. Naval Academy at Annapolis, Maryland.

PART ONE

How to export

Introduction

Nothing happens until you sell something, and conversely until something is bought.

Anon

There is a substantially increased opportunity to find buyers, with money, worldwide.

Feast your eyes on Figure 1!

Why are the curves so dynamically upward?

Because the post World War II recovery, particularly in Europe and Asia brought masses who are better off. The opportunities for sales in foreign marketplaces has never been better.

After all, more than five billion people inhabit the earth and unless you live in China or India only a fraction of the world's buyers live in your country.

Not withstanding Asia's financial problems during the late 1990s, four decades of balanced development positioned these once booming economies to bounce back with sustained growth driven by swelling middle classes who are enterprising, have money, and want world class things.

Today, organizations worldwide are taking advantage of this explosion in trade by selling in the global marketplace.

Competition between domestic and foreign firms in local markets is dynamic. Products from businesses all over the world have invaded other countries markets.

Managers of small and medium-sized firms who recognize the change are saying, "Hey! I'm going to get into your market, too. I'm going to challenge you on your own turf."

The wealth exchange bridge

Exchanging products and services across international borders can be visualized as a bridge between nations spanning land, sea, or air. The bridge has three levels, each level increasingly more complex than the one below. The transaction level can be viewed as the mechanics of

Figure 1 World exports of merchandise, goods and services
Source: Constructed by the author from 1998 statistics provided by the World Bank

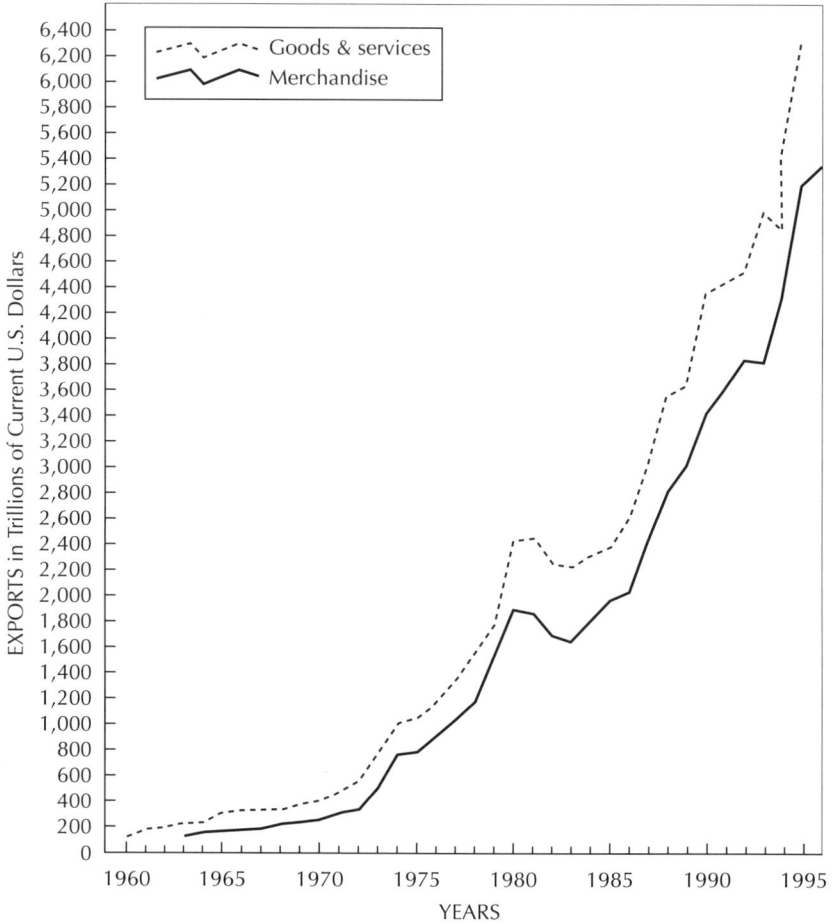

everyday cross-border operations. Tactics is the next highest level and therefore more complex. It is the organizational means whereby exchange takes place. The highest and most complex level are the strategies and policies that overlay and govern the lower two levels of the bridge.

As shown in Figure 2 the bridge levels are bounded at national borders by interstate controls, i.e. "incentives" and "barriers", which stimulate trade at the same time as they sometimes diminish it.

Figure 2   The wealth exchange bridge

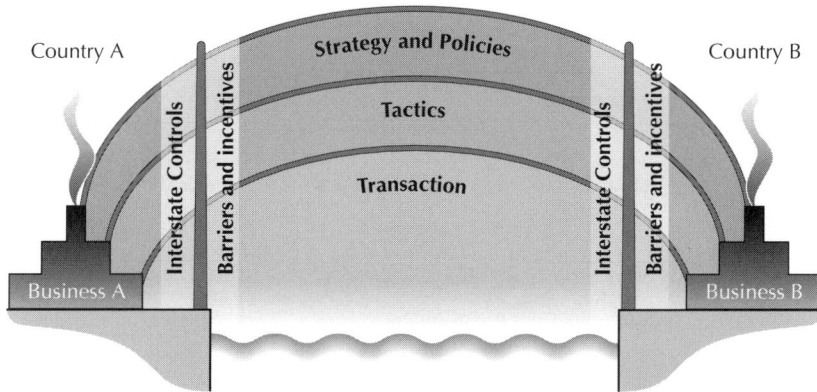

What is exporting?

For purposes of this book the term "exporter" is synonymous with the term "seller." The buyer is an importer. *Exporting: A Manager's Guide to the World Market* explains exporting as a universal business tactic that permits manufacturers and service companies in one nation to sell their products across borders to a foreign country.

Exporting is just one method among a long list of ways by which we exchange wealth between nations. Other tactics imply a greater commitment and capitalization in order to do business as an "insider" or "risk sharing/learner" in a foreign country. A fuller discussion of the various other means of exchanging wealth across borders can be found in the Global Manager Series book *International Business: A Manager's Guide to Strategy in the Age of Globalism*.

Exporting is the most important tactic for the small to medium-sized firm because it requires less capital investment and permits the business to remain as an "outsider," that is, at arm's length from national boundaries, particularly when interstate controls such as tariffs and other local laws require such a tactic.

Insider–outsider tactics

What do we mean by being an insider or outsider? Figure 3 shows that a firm may vary its tactics country by country, depending on each nation's approach to international trade and its perceived political risk. Outsider tactics are those which permit the wealth exchange of one company to be at arm's length from businesses and consumers of another nation because that country's strategic approach is inward looking, protectionist

Figure 3 Insider–outsider tactics

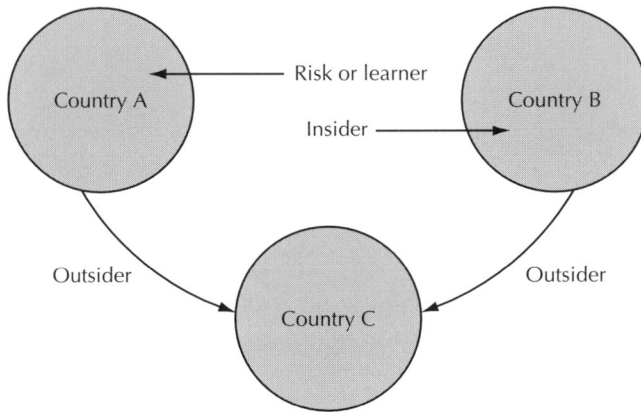

and independent of the global economic system. Outsider tactics include: exporting, forming associations, using intermediaries, licensing, and direct mail.

Insider tactics are those that gain a local position in a national economy which welcomes foreign competition and where country risk is low. Insider tactics include: starting a firm, acquiring a firm, mergers, partnering (joint ventures), and franchising.

Caution is the watchword when entering countries that have confused or mixed strategic approaches or where country risk is moderate to high. In those cases wealth exchange through risk sharing buys time to learn business methods and culture. For instance, *perestroika* (restructuring) and *glasnost* (openness) brought surprising market opportunities. Needless to say, restructuring from Marxism to capitalism has not happened overnight. During the shake-out period many companies are carefully assessing methods of developing this eventual consumer explosion using the dominant risk sharing/learning tactics of production sharing and joint ventures.

Government support

The interesting thing about exporting is that most nations support it as a tactic because when home products are exported jobs stay at home and foreign currency is induced which has a positive effect on the nation's balance of payments. Exporting is the process of selling a product or service from a manufacturing base in one country to customers in another country. This tactic is most successful when:

- home currency (exchange rate) is weak against the importing country's currency;
- product life cycle can be extended;
- the importing country has low tariff barriers;
- consumers are inclined to buy foreign;
- there is encouragement to import by a foreign government;
- there is high country risk;
- diversification of financial risk across a broader market is important.

Complexity at the borders

Exporting does not exist freely across borders. Private businesses experience conflict at the borders of other countries in the form of cultural differences, conflicting trade theories, competing development theories, and opposing political policies. Figure 4 shows the elements of conflict among nations that causes business complexity.

The concept that charity begins at home is alive and well. A nation's economy is under the care of economic physicians called politicians who determine what happens as things and people cross political borders. The health of a national economy comes into conflict with that of the over-laying global business system when the welfare of those within a nation is at issue.

Development is the primary concern of every national government and is the summation of those complex factors of infrastructure, human health and education, as well as capital, which permits people to achieve higher living standards.

Interstate controls are the laws, regulations, procedures, and practices *between* nations or economic unions of nations that inhibit or stimulate

---

Figure 4   Complexity at the borders

Border

Business A → Diverse Cultures
Language, Laws, Education, etc.

Business B → Conflicting Theories
Capitalism, Socialism, Communism,
Free Trade, Comparative Advantage

Business C → Competitive Economies
Creation Incentives
Barriers

Business D → Opposing Political Policies
Trade and Investment, Nationalism,
Protectionism

"free trade." Some controls are *barriers* which cause significant distortions to free trade while at the same time others are stimulants in the form of *incentives*. Thus controls may be visualized as having a part in driving economic growth.

All sovereign nations, to some extent, control the flow of goods, thought, services, funds, freedom of movement, etc. across their borders. Not all barriers are bad; not all stimulants are good. For instance, public health conditions in one nation may dictate certain barriers to free trade that may differ from another.

For purposes of explanation, *incentives* are the various laws and rules, exceptions to laws and rules, and financial "carrots" offered by governments to stimulate or create global business and trade. These schemes are designed to encourage foreign businesses to operate in a given country for purposes of economic development and growth.

Purpose for writing the book

Exporting: A Manager's Guide to the World Market was written to provide a practical reference and teaching tool—an operational guide which has worldwide application. Exporting takes place every day in every country in the world and except for differences in government laws and procedures the methods are the same. Yet many more businesses could sell the goods and services across borders if they wished, but are deterred often by irrational doubts and fears. This book is intended to reduce that anxiety and show that the process is reasonably simple and particularly useful for small and medium-sized companies.

What sets this book apart

The thing that sets *Exporting: A Manager's Guide to the World Market* apart from other books of its ilk is the universality of its approach. The book focuses on service companies as well as manufacturers and covers a wide range of specific information brought together for the first time in one book. Such things as how to:

- choose the right export method;
- select the right people;
- organize your firm for export;
- develop a coherent export strategy and plan;
- take legal recourse;
- export services;
- avoid costly behavioral mistakes when doing business in different national cultures;
- deal with the cultures of the newly independent states of the former Soviet Union;

■ use a trading intermediary;
■ band together to form a trading association;
■ take advantage of tricks of international trade;
■ compete in trade blocs, i.e. European Union and NAFTA;
■ profit by using Free Trade Zones;
■ improve profits through production sharing;
■ understand the laws and legal environment;
■ get help from your government.

How the book is organized

Exporting: A Manager's Guide to the World Market is organized into two parts: How to Export and Tricks of Trade.

Part One explains how to make the decision whether to export by "doing it yourself," or by using various intermediary options. This part of the book shows how to select the right people, organize them, develop an international market plan, and execute that plan. If your product is a service, it shows how to export that service. Finally the first part explains how to either use existing intermediaries or band together to set up your own trade association.

Part Two offers a menu of tricks known only to the "professionals" of international trade. It explains how to negotiate a contract and complete the transaction, how to finance the deal, organize for tax advantages, and use countertrade. The chapter titled "Dos and Don'ts of World Behavior" is particularly valuable because it explains the key elements of marketing and negotiating within diverse cultures. The book explains how to take maximum advantage of Free Trade Areas such as NAFTA and the EU trade bloc, and how to use Free Trade Zones (FTZs) and bonded warehouses to transform products and save money. It also explains how to improve profits through overseas production sharing. The final chapter offers a wealth of information about the international legal system and how to get government help.

Summary

Vast amounts of goods are shipped every year to buyers in foreign countries. In general, this process called "exporting" has the support of home governments because it is linked to economic development. Exporting requires a low investment and can be undertaken by almost anyone who has a product or service to sell and the willingness to do business with foreigners.

The next chapter is about getting started—the readiness of the firm to export.

CHAPTER ONE

Getting started

We become just by performing just actions, temperate by performing temperate actions, brave by performing brave actions.

Aristotle

It is not enough to be aware of the growth of international trade. To do something about it—to go beyond interest—requires an understanding of the changes that have taken place.

What has changed

Globalization is not something that will happen in the future, it has happened. Decision makers now visualize the marketplace in multi-national terms. Modern manufacturing companies, small, medium, and large-sized have adjusted to the realities of global competition. Marketplaces are full of consumer products from other nations, the less expensive the better. Women, who do most of the world's household consumer product buying, no longer inspect where a product was made. They respond to "pocketbook" economics. They want world-class products for less.

Modern service companies are adjusting to the same global competitive realities. Many have local overseas operations and compete for government contracts all over the world. Firms such as McDonald's are everywhere, fulfilling the wants and desires of people in worldwide consumer marketplaces.

Modern salespersons fly around the world meeting distributors and developing networks of contacts. They attend major trade shows and strategically target advertising programs. Capital equipment and raw materials purchasers are searching for the best value—worldwide. A growing number of companies have overseas manufacturing and assembly operations and "outsource" raw materials and components from all over the world.

What we make

Industrial nations are in the "high-tech post-industrial era." That means smokestack industries have been replaced by "clean industries," the incubators of new technology. Modern firms are users of high-technology. That means big changes in terms of what we make, how we trade, and what we consume. The best example is America's electronics industry which is 70 percent small business and is now the country's largest manufacturing industry—three times bigger than the auto industry, and ten times the steel industry. Services in the U.S.A. account for ⅔ of Gross National Product (GNP) and about 70 percent of employment.

How we trade

Products can generally be characterized in four broad sectors. Those quadrants, as identified in Figure 1.1 are:

■ Quadrant 1—high volume commodities such as grains.
■ Quadrant 2—high volume, highly differentiated products such as auto-mobiles, computers, and TV sets.
■ Quadrant 3—low volume commodities.
■ Quadrant 4—low volume highly differentiated products and services.

Major international trading companies typically trade in quadrant 1.

The IBMs of the world are in quadrant 2—they need little help to export.

Those that trade in quadrant 3 often form associations, simply because profit margins are small—economies of scale are essential.

The lower right quadrant in the diagram is almost as difficult to export

Figure 1.1 What we trade

	Commodities	Differentiated Products (Technical Systems)
High Volume **Textiles** **Raw Materials**	QUADRANT #1 Typical Trading Company	QUADRANT #2 Large Firms Do it themselves
Low Volume	QUADRANT #3 Too expensive to do alone therefore use Associations	QUADRANT #4 Small and medium-sized manufacturing and service companies What U.S.A. wants to sell

as quadrant 3, yet it is in this quadrant that 90 percent of manufacturing and service firms are offering their products. "Quadrant 4" companies are the thousands of small (from five to 250 employees) and medium-sized (between 250 and 1000 employees) firms that are interested yet have not got into the global market. Quadrant 4 is also the sector where there have been the greatest changes. It is the quadrant of innovation—where high-tech products are spawned. It is also the quadrant where thousands of smaller firms are not yet participating in international trade.

What we consume

World trade is not just about exports, it is about two-way trade—imports and exports, and the reality of interdependence is that consumers the world over respond to basic pocketbook economics, not to emotion, or patriotic slogans.

People's attitudes about the origin of product content have changed. Once upon a time "Made in U.S.A." meant know-how and quality, unsurpassed in the world. At another time, "Made in Japan" meant cheap, low-quality copies. Then came "The Origin of Content Phenomena." In the 1970s and 1980s products with labels "Made in Hong Kong," "Made in Japan," "Made in Germany," or "Assembled in Singapore," began penetrating world markets and content took on less and less importance to the consumer. The reality of today is that few products have the pure content of one nation. Product content is more often a mixture of labor, raw materials, capital, and know-how— whatever it takes to provide the best product, at best price, for the consumer who cares little about how or where it was made. What does count is global name identification: Kodak, Fuji, Mercedes, IBM, etc.

Most business persons and economists believe that to retain purity of national content at the expense of competition is protectionism and economic suicide. They believe content is a business decision not a political decision—what is good for the consumer is good for business.

World class

Consumers want that which is considered "world class." That is, the things with the level of quality that people in other countries are enjoying. In other words, because of television and the Internet, the world market instead of the domestic market is determining what consumers want to buy. World class is often a perception that a product is the best of the best. That perception is sometimes influenced by good advertising often using world-class people for promotion purposes. The use of Michael Jordan, the exceptional American world class professional basketball player to represent a line of sports equipment is intended to convey that that company's recreational products are therefore world class.

Quality standards

Even standards have become world class. The Japanese led the way to higher levels of quality when they adopted Dr. W. Edwards Deming's concepts of statistical quality control. People want quality products, so most manufacturers worldwide have joined the International Standards Organization (ISO) in Geneva, which has established global guidelines. Companies who wish to be certified must follow rigid instructions and be examined by a team of independent auditors. In order to sell into world markets ISO certification is practically a must.

Is the firm ready?

In today's interdependent world a company must consider marketing on a global scope, but whether your company is in services or manufacturing you must assess your growth pattern and your company's potential for success.

Ask yourself. What are your long-range growth goals? Does your firm have maturity? Has it been in the marketplace long enough to sustain entry into new markets? These questions relate to commitment, attitudes, plant capacity, personnel, finances, and environment. See Appendix A for the ten most common exporting mistakes.

The decision

The key to winning the export game is the decision to commit resources, and a long-term strategy to maintain long-term competitiveness.

It's a misconception that the only successful international businesses have their own branch offices and plants in foreign countries. Certainly many do, but the vast majority of exporters are just successful domestic manufacturers or service companies.

Many smaller firms are not waiting. When asked about the benefits of international trade, the president of a small electronics outfit explained it this way:

> For most companies, expanding the firm's market area to consider the entire globe can only benefit the overall sales picture. Some foreign markets will not be as rich or as promising as others. But the potential for even modest sales gains outweighs the associated costs or risks. An increase in volume usually means rising profits as well as an opportunity to utilize excess production capacity. For some products it can often extend the life cycle that was otherwise on the decline.

That's not to say there will not be barriers in the path of the decision. Faced with a formidable list of apprehensions, some perceived, some real, the misinformed will think of every conceivable reason not to get started. This book is about reassuring you and assisting you to overcome the real barriers.

In spite of the perceived stones in their path, many quadrant 4 firms have overcome the obstacles. One of those is a small electronics firm near San Diego, California that does about $9 million in annual volume, has 65 employees, and almost 100 percent of its sales are in the international market.

Does a firm have to sell 90–100 percent to foreign countries? Of course not. A firm that exports 15–50 percent of total sales has an aggressive program. On the other hand a company that is selling totally overseas is probably missing sales opportunities in their domestic market.

It is important to recognize in today's interdependent business setting that marketing is a global activity, and domestic marketing by itself no longer has meaning.

Aggressive international companies are not deterred by lack of cash flow or inability to form their own foreign department. They search for alternative business arrangements.

It starts at the top

Motivation of top managers is the prerequisite to foreign market entry and many join hands with competent trading companies, because they know there is more than one way to compete internationally.

This issue starts at the top. Is management resolved to enter the international market with staying power? Or is the effort lukewarm, just waiting to wilt at the first resistance?

The internationalization process begins when top management becomes committed and motivated. The need for profitability improvement, the receipt of over-the-transom orders, the gaining of special knowledge about foreign opportunities, and the prestige of international operations are all factors in stimulating the decision to move into global operations.

Reasons to export

Of course commitment to enter foreign markets must be backed up with common business sense and logic. Here are several reasons why you should consider marketing internationally as a business tactic:

■ **Profit**. Some say that a strong dollar prevents the taking of reasonable profits, yet the relative value of currencies is only one factor in the calculation of profit. Quality, service, and consumer acceptability are often better measures of product sales success than price.

■ **Break ground for hardware**. Software offered by service and consulting firms often breaks ground for subsequent improvements and the entry of high-technology hardware.

■ **Develop trust**. Service companies gain ancillary sales based on relationships and trust developed by having a presence in and knowing the capabilities of foreign nations.

■ **Expansion of marketing base**. Expanding your firm's market area can only benefit the sales picture and although some foreign markets are not as rich, they are often quite profitable. Some overseas markets provide for greater profit margins than the sale of the identical product in the domestic market and in many cases provide an increased market share by beating the competition to the foreign country. A wider base of sales distribution can also minimize fluctuations in domestic conditions. Expanding into foreign markets can be a source of growth for your company if it is facing a domestic market which has matured and is trending toward a down turn.

■ **Extension of product life**. Often, as a result of less-developed technology in foreign countries, your firm can, by exporting, extend the life cycle of a product that may have reached the obsolescence stage in domestic market.

■ **Excess capacity**. By expanding your market to foreign countries your production can increase beyond the limits set by the domestic market. The benefits of this are obviously better utilization of labor and capital by reducing unit production costs, more effective use of management and technology, and lower overall operating costs. Thus exports can increase volume, amortize overhead, and absorb excess capacity.

■ **Sales stability**. Where your company's product line is subject to seasonal demand, exporting to a foreign market can counterbalance that seasonality, thus stabilizing sales, generating efficiencies in production, cash flow, and employment.

■ **Diversify risk**. There are different perceptions of what is considered the risk of doing business overseas. Some explain it as a financial risk while others might say it's the risk of producing then finding out that the market dried up simply because of political changes. Another might explain the risk as the ever-changing global economic and political environment. Competing in only one economy can make your firm dependent on that economy. By diversifying into more than one economy you can insulate yourself from the dangers of that single dependency. This is particularly true when foreign markets are in earlier stages of product life cycle than the domestic market.

■ **Defend the domestic market**. By competing in the international market against other multinational firms your company may improve its marketing skills and thereby be in a better position to protect your own domestic market in the long term.

■ **Penetrate trade barriers**. Establishing production and marketing operations overseas may allow your firm to enter markets that are not otherwise open competitively.

■ **Lower off-border production costs**. By taking advantage of lower off-border labor rates and raw materials costs, products can be made more competitive in world markets.

■ **Encouragement of imports and foreign investment by some foreign governments**. As a way of developing their own economies, many host governments welcome foreign operations and trade. Often these are joint ventures or technical arrangements serving to gain markets within the country.

■ **Tax and other incentives**. Most governments offer distinct advantages for companies that sell or lease their goods to customers in foreign countries.

Time horizon and profit attitudes

Does the firm have the staying power and mental toughness to make a foothold and grow in a foreign culture; even to sustain losses in the short run to gain long-term profits? This is an internal problem and unique to each company. Internationalization requires a longer time horizon than many investors prefer. In the international scene expect profits and certainly excellent growth, but it takes longer.

For exporters, costs and profit margins are less important than total long run profit potential. For example, it may be smarter in the long run for your company to sell more at a smaller profit margin than to sell a few at a higher margin but only be in the market for the short haul. Japanese and Korean firms have used the "long haul" concept over and over to gain entry into foreign markets.

Plant capacity

Don't plan expansion into a new market based on a heavy outlay for capital equipment. Instead, calculate the number of additional units your firm can produce from the existing fixed costs over and above average sales. Your loss due to production is then only the per-unit cost of materials and man hours.

Personnel

Are key people willing to put in the time and investment? Do you have a pool of creative and experienced marketing personnel and a research staff?

Size and financial position

More than any other obstacle, the size of the firm and finances, determine ability to make international market entry. A company's financial picture in the domestic market frequently determines its capability to make the initial investment. You should have sufficient reserves or see sufficient cash flow to satisfy borrowing the necessary working capital to kick-off an international department and begin market penetration.

High cost is a frequent perception of exporting. Obviously it is more expensive to fly to Germany from Colorado to establish a market for goods than to fly to New Jersey. On the other hand the long-run profit opportunity could be greater in Germany. Each situation is different. But as one executive of an excellent international company said, "Expense scares off the beginner, but it is trivial compared to the potential market."

All business ventures require a financial commitment in terms of investment. In the case of entering a foreign market the primary costs are management, travel, overhead, promotion, advertising, and administration. A rule of thumb for expansion into any new venture is to have a steady profit margin trend for a period of one to three years. Each export project undertaken by the firm should consider the likelihood of attaining better than bank interest rates ("cost of capital") otherwise the investment should not go forward.

Getting started

In the past, most firms worldwide entered the global market only as a sequence of events over time. In other words, companies came to the business of exporting only as an after-thought. This staged process, often taking many years, generally began only when smaller firms were successful in the domestic market. The stages of entry typically followed a pattern similar to this:

1 At some point in the firm's life it became engaged in extra-regional expansion, widening its experience and "market consciousness." For some it began with a search for cheaper raw materials or components. During this period the small firm began to fill some unsolicited (over-the-transom) orders but still had not engaged in a serious international plan.
2 Soon the firm began to investigate exporting. If the investigation was successful, the small firm began to experiment. At first it was interested only in overseas sales of its surplus products but was without resources to fill overseas orders on an ongoing basis.
3 If the experimentation was successful the firm became an experienced exporter by actively soliciting overseas sales. Therefore, it was willing to make limited modifications to its products and marketing procedures to accommodate the requirements of overseas buyers.

4 The exporting firm eventually made major modifications in its products as well as its marketing practices in order to reach more buyers.
5 Finally, the firm developed new products for existing or new overseas markets and diversified its markets to other countries.

Choosing the right exporting method

Today the firm that considers entering international business does not have to wait for the slow, step-by-step process to take place. Starting a new department can be expensive as well as time consuming, but you can get into the international market without investing a large sum of capital.

There are three roads to get your products overseas.

1 One is the "do-it-yourself" road. This is the most expensive but the one that affords the most control.
2 Another road lets a trading intermediary export for you. This is the fastest and least expensive way to start, but you give up control.
3 Forming an association of firms and thereby sharing costs and control is yet another road.

Each of the methods have merit and each have limitations. Do not discard any choice until you have done a solid analysis. In fact a mix of these methods may be your best bet.

Do-it-yourself (direct)

Your firm uses the direct method when you develop your own market plan and set up your own international sales department to deal with foreign distributors, agents or overseas marketing subsidiaries. Using this method your company is responsible for shipping its own products overseas. Typically the do-it-yourself method requires the full-time effort of a trained department manager, a sales representative, and suitable administrative support.

Use trading companies (indirect)

The quickest way to get into the global market is also the least expensive. Many companies in quadrant 4 also use this method to get started.

This approach means dealing through an international trading firm that acts as a sales intermediary (middleman). The trading company develops the market plan and acts as the manufacturing company's international department. These intermediaries normally assume responsibility for moving products overseas. Chapter 3 discusses trading intermediaries such as general trading companies (GTCs), import–export management companies (EMCs), and even piggybacking your products with some multinational corporations (MNCs).

Form a marketing association

Many quadrant 4 companies are forming associations with other firms in their industries. Chapter 4 explains this method whereby you might join with competitors (other manufacturers or service companies) to penetrate foreign markets.

The decision factors

How does a smaller firm decide whether to do-it-themselves, work with an intermediary or form/join an association? Here is a list of considerations:

Global market reach

Global market reach is the term used for the organization, offices, and contacts in other countries to support the gathering of intelligence and execution of a foreign sales effort. Market reach would be considered "limited" if a firm or intermediary has contacts in only one or two foreign countries. On the other hand, a "comprehensive" global reach would be defined as capability to market a given product in every country where that product has logical buying potential.

International marketing personnel

Does your firm have trained international marketing personnel? The consideration here is the expense of hiring experienced employees versus having an intermediary do the marketing.

Team spirit (control)

This factor involves the question of how well your firm can accept a hands-off approach to the marketing of your products by an intermediary. This can become a major factor in the case of a high-technology product where an engineering background is essential to providing after-sales support.

Studies have shown that the relationship between an intermediary and its clients is critical. Given a long-term investment in an intermediary's expertise, team spirit is that intangible belief that the agent is at all times working in the manufacturer's best interest, even though in specific instances it may not seem so. The relationship is even more difficult when one realizes that international marketers are not door-to-door salesmen. Because the time horizon for doing business internationally is by its very nature longer than for domestic business there are often long periods when nothing seems to be happening. International business generally takes a great deal of patience, as a result, confidence and a team spirit is more difficult to sustain.

Occasionally a manufacturer signs on an intermediary to market the company's product, but after some time has the temptation to go around the middleman. This is self-defeating and contractually dangerous. On the other side of this matter, because there are no professional standards for qualifying or licensing, the small manufacturer should exercise due care in selecting the proper intermediary. If your firm cannot accept a middleman as an equal, do it yourself.

The financial decision

The critical decision is the financial decision.

The major fixed cost of your own international department is the personnel. At least three employees working full time are usually required to market products in several countries. At a minimum, a foreign sales department will require an export sales manager, an export sales representative, and an administrative person. Table 1.1 shows these typical costs on an annual basis:

Table 1.1 Typical export sales department costs (Annual)

Function	Cost
Export Sales Manager	$40,000
Sales Representative (Bonuses not included)	$30,000
Administration (Secretary)	$24,000
Travel & Entertainment	$20,000
Promotion & Advertisement	$35,000
Admin costs (Telex, etc.)	$30,000
Benefits Package (at about 15% of salaries)	$11,000
Market Intelligence	$10,000
*Traffic manager	
*Communications Manager	
*Engineering Services	
*Promotion Assistant	
*Additional Sales Personnel	
	‗‗‗‗
Total costs	*$200,000*
*Expansion personnel	

The total costs in this example were chosen for convenience and are considerably understated.

Case analysis

The following analysis is designed to show you how to make the financial decision, assuming the firm considers the international marketing
department is a profit center.

Assume company X sells its product for $10.00 a unit, but it only costs
$2.50 to make. An intermediary will buy at 50 percent off recommended
retail price (not unusual) or at $5.00 a unit and resell it overseas. If com-
pany X had developed its own export department it could sell the product to an overseas distributor at only 30 percent off list price or at $7.00
a unit.

For this example profit is defined as retail price times unit sales minus
trade discounts, direct production costs, and fixed costs. The break-even
decision is described graphically in Figure 1.2.

The dotted line represents company X profits at $4.50 ($7.00 − $2.50)
selling through the firm's own export department. Note that 44,445 units
must be sold before the firm generates enough revenue to overcome the
annual export department costs of $200,000.

In contrast, assuming no up-front fees (which is sometimes the case),
the solid line represents company X profits at $2.50 ($5.00 − $2.50). At

---

Figure 1.2 Break-even analysis
Source: Becker and Porter

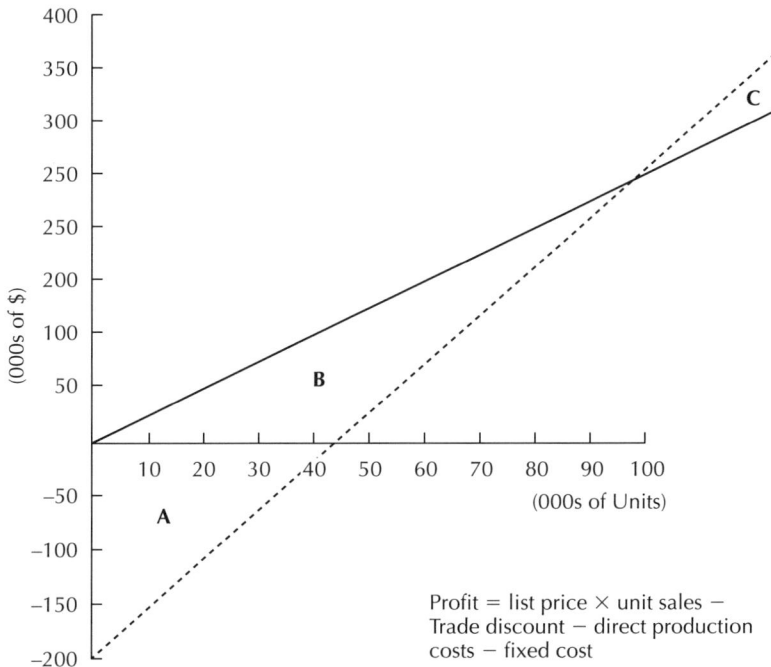

Profit = list price × unit sales −
Trade discount − direct production
costs − fixed cost

the break-even point the middleman has already generated profits of greater than $100,000. Of course at the intersection of the two curves (100,000 units) the company's own export department would generate more profit. Everything in area A would be losses. Everything in area B would be early profits, and everything in area C would be the advantage of company X having its own international department provided that several other factors such as market reach, international know-how and market knowledge is available.

Summary

Assuming your firm has the finances, a viable product, and definite long-range goals, your own foreign sales department can eventually generate sufficient revenues to support the costs. If the firm's financial situation can sustain losses for the short run, it should use the "do-it-yourself" method.

On the other hand, if your company does not have foreign market knowledge nor the immediate finances, yet has international goals, you are better off to go the intermediary route or join with others to form an association.

The next chapter explains how to "do-it-yourself."

■ CHAPTER TWO ■

Do-it-yourself exporting

Our products now are known in every zone,
Our reputation sparkles like a gem,
We've fought our way thru
And new fields we're sure to conquer too,
For the ever onward IBM

IBM company song

Expanding to have your own international department will be a function of commitment, capitalization, and personnel. The firm can build from within by expanding the duties and responsibilities of a few personnel who show an interest in exporting or it can recruit already trained personnel from the outside the firm.

Building from within

It is not unusual that one or more members of the firm's domestic marketing organization have the inclination and ambition to begin forming the new department. Slowly, over time, allow those personnel to become the international department. The key to success is finding a leader personality who is capable of developing and executing a plan, being responsible for training the staff and generally functioning as the export manager. Sometimes a firm will bring in an outside consultant, one who is a seasoned manager and who has had experience with start-ups.

Other duties related to export marketing, finance and traffic are spread among the various domestic departments and integrated with their normal activities.

Advantages

Personnel who already know the firm's products, organization, and key employees in other departments bring initial stability to the development of a new department. There is a built-in level of trust that is never there initially when outsiders are hired for a new function. In reality this method of developing from within brings with it some cost savings in the short run. Often only the job descriptions of "old hands" are enriched not their salaries.

Disadvantages

The flip side to this method of growing from a base of employees from within is that the present staff will have their time diluted and the development of the new department will often take a "back seat" to their normal duties. Two things can suffer: first, the current job, with the inevitability of errors, omissions, and delays that a new exporter can ill afford; and second, the timely start-up of the new department. For the same reasons, when an outside consultant is hired, that person sometimes has a difficult time getting the attention of the current staff due to their overload condition.

Recruit a staff

The second option is the recruitment of a staff that is already trained and has developed a track record at other companies. In this case you would create a separate export department by hiring several key employees to concentrate on the development of export business. The first to be hired would, of course, be the export manager who, with your support, would hire the remainder of the staff using the schedule developed in your strategic plan as modified by the actual growth pattern of world sales activity.

Advantages

By having a separate export department, in charge from the beginning, management can get better data and a feel for the development process. Recruited personnel often have established contacts and relationships with support organizations. The company's image will be enhanced and employee morale within the department should not become a problem.

Disadvantages

Top management of the company must be cautious of new management for international operations that bring with them approaches that are too optimistic, interjecting utopian sales projections based on their experiences with other established firms. This method will require a period of familiarization for new employees to learn how your company operates, and about your products.

The right people

The most important aspect of the growth of your international sales effort will be the selection of the right people to carry out your plan. The dominant personal characteristic of these employees will be the ability to work on a team in a multicultural environment.

A typical international marketing department when fully developed, would include an export manager, a traffic manager, a communications manager, an engineering services manager, credit and finance personnel, a sales manager, a promotion assistant, and sales personnel. Of course, not all of these positions are filled at once, instead most companies let their organization develop as their sales and activities increase, hiring only as cash flow will allow their expansion. In the early stages many of these functions can be farmed out to such support organizations as a reliable freight forwarder, or your banker who will review your documentation and give you advice. Fleshing out an entire international marketing department may take several years, nevertheless from the start you should have an understanding of the responsibilities of the key personnel.

Export manager

The single most important position to be filled in any exporting organization is the export manager. The person in this key leadership role will have control, planning, and profit/loss responsibility. He or she will be the person in your organization who, based on interpretation of market intelligence, will set the marketing objectives, coordinate with production, design, service, inventory planning, finance, credit, and will develop the overseas contacts. Needless to say, the export manager should be well trained and fully competent in the fundamentals of international marketing and market planning, including adapting to sensitive cultural differences as they relate to product and market decisions. Above all, the person hired for this job should be an able leader who can work effectively with and motivate the international staff, yet have good rapport with other corporate officers.

Traffic manager

The job description of the traffic manager includes processing all incoming orders, and supervising collection, documentation, packing, insurance, and shipping. In other words, he or she is responsible in general for all preparation and expediting of goods to fill orders. When searching for someone experienced for this position look for someone who has familiarity with documentation, foreign transportation processes, freight forwarders, packing requirements, shipping regulations, and payment methods. Obviously this employee must be someone the export manager can completely depend upon, because the position is so important to executing the transaction.

Communications manager

This position is critical to "sound" relationships with overseas markets, and the proper execution of this job often can reflect well on the company. The communications manager should, as a minimum, understand how to prepare correspondence. While not a requirement, a good working knowledge of several languages is also useful. He or she should have the nicest sense and concern for the nuances of language as they affect the sale of products. Hands-on experience with long-distance communications equipment such as telex and facsimile is essential. Another important, and a more recent requirement, is appreciation of video and other special sales training methods.

Engineering and services manager

As the department grows and sales activity increases, the need to coordinate critical technical design and engineering assistance becomes vital. This is a critical issue! In-country service, response time, and logistic (supply) support is essential to serving an export market. This person must be top drawer because he or she is often the link to protecting the company's reputation in distant markets. This position often serves as the link between the marketing and the international sourcing organizations.

Promotion assistant

Although the export manager acts primarily as a sales manager, the need to follow through on details related to media campaigns, catalogs and coordination of overseas trade fairs often requires an assistant. This should be a high energy, details-oriented person, willing to travel and put in long hours in support of the overseas sales effort.

Sales representatives

Personal relationships are most important in international trade. Therefore, export salespersons should be the kind of person who has a "feel" for finding the key that converts or closes a sale through personal contact with overseas buyers. The relationship between buyer and seller is often more important than price. Most companies are hiring foreign nationals for these positions, because they know and understand the local customs and the language.

Administration personnel

Like any other business operation, there is a basic need to keep order in the house. If nothing else, administrative personnel—secretaries, and clerks—serve to allow others freedom to think and not be tied to the office. In the case of an international organization, where the travel time of managers is often much greater than for domestic operations, the office personnel become a major reflection of the company and as such should be multi-lingual and culturally sensitive as well as proficient in their tasks. It is not unusual that administrative entry-level personnel "step-up" to management positions after suitable experience.

Evaluating sales personnel

In as much as your sales staff is so vital to you, from the outset you should have an image of the ideal international salesperson in mind. Among other things they should:

1 Want to sell!
2 Enjoy travel.
3 Have a desire to deal in a foreign environment and language.
4 Be able to adapt to other cultures.
5 Have a track record or at least exhibit behavioral instincts for the bottom line—the ability to close.
6 Show bounce-back characteristics, the ability to regroup and recover from rejection.

Foreign nationals

As your success in international sales grows it's inevitable that you will be faced with reorganization. At the outset you should be aware there's no best method, no standard model. Each business must design the organization that works best for its product line and global application.

During this growth period you should carefully watch your costs and selling patterns. An export department is primarily a sales department and if a major part of your business originates from one country or a specific area of the world you should consider forming an overseas subsidiary. This subsidiary could only be for marketing (export), i.e. handling distribution, or it could serve a combination of processes such as exporting, sourcing (import), and coordination of assembly and/or manufacturing operations.

Sooner or later you will want to hire foreign personnel, because they offer advantages over the exclusive use of domestic hires that you send across borders. The most usual reason to hire locals is when a firm establishes their own marketing subsidiary instead of using a local distributor.

Foreign personnel offer excellent advantages. For instance they:

1 Allow you to do business. In many countries, a foreign firm cannot operate unless they use native agents or representatives.
2 Are often less expensive in terms of both salaries and travel costs.
3 Give your company a home country identity.
4 Can help you avoid cultural and legal barriers.
5 Have an easier time managing other foreign nationals.
6 Are less vulnerable to threats of terrorism.

On the other hand, foreign nationals can be difficult to shed once they become settled into a job. Some foreign laws require severance pay or specific causes prior to firing. Typically they are hired through an employment contract which unless carefully worded can become binding and expensive to break.

Turnover

Personnel turnover in international marketing is more important than turnover in other aspects of your business. The limited number of people involved and the distances can cause catastrophic implications. Make certain top executives visit overseas distributors and foreign employees often to ensure continuity, should the unexpected happen. Back-up international data and information so that your market effort will not lose a step due to change of key personnel. Replacement personnel should be hired for their contacts, and having had experience promoting related goods.

Organizing to export

At the outset you should be aware there is *no*, repeat, no standard organization model. Each firm must design the organization that works best for its product line and global application.

Your expansion may grow to be in many countries on many continents with many products. When that happens you will have several organizational options available, depending on selling patterns, sales growth and significant legal or tax advantages recommended by your lawyer or accountant.

In selecting the proper organization for your firm the critical elements are:

■ Avoid duplication, i.e. divisions or departments doing the same function.
■ Avoid suboptimization, that is, treating international business as a separate segment of corporate business thus preventing their optimal use in the best interest of the total organization.

Intelligence, the prerequisite

Organizing for international marketing is all about organizing for selling and that effort requires creativeness and determination not experienced in some aspects of business operations.

The prerequisite for any successful international business venture is intelligence. Before your international effort can move forward you must invest in market research, either by your own personnel or with the assistance of a firm that specializes in the field.

Organization models

There are several ways to organize your firm to accommodate changes as it grows in the international arena. While there is rigid pattern, most global companies are organized geographically, functionally or by product line. For a fuller discussion of organization see, in this Global Manager Series, the book titled *International Business: A Manager's Guide to Strategy in the Age of Globalism.*

Start-up organization

The first organization will either be split off from the domestic marketing or organized as a new entity. The initial effort is generally focused on one or two high-priority target countries.

Organizing geographically

You may find early on that your firm is serving several countries in a region that are close to one another yet far from your home base. This is the typical beginning of restructuring the organization by geographical area.

By organizing a headquarters or a "marketing subsidiary" in the region there is a common base for management and it becomes easier to communicate, thus optimizing marketing know-how.

Functional organization

A functional organization lends itself to a firm that has very homogeneous lines of products and line executives have global responsibilities.

Organizing by product

Another way to organize is to give each line product its own international sales organization. This is the world-company approach where product groups are responsible for global marketing. This method is typical for firms with several unrelated product lines for which their marketing tasks vary more by product than by region.

Marketing subsidiary

If a major part of your business originates from one country or a specific area of the world you should consider forming an overseas subsidiary. Marketing subsidiaries are either wholly owned or joint ventures organized to support direct exporting by providing information and a successful tactical entry and sales effort. Instead of exporting through a foreign importer, the establishment of a subsidiary represents a physical presence and a greater commitment. In other words, your home company exports to itself.

When using this technique, you should consider positioning centrally the foreign organization such that it remains in continual communication with the marketing department of the parent company. By this means it can pass on local experience and respond to market feedback with regard to image and protectionist maneuvers.

Summary

Many firms undertake to export their products by forming their own export department. Often this transformation takes place slowly over time as their products become known in foreign markets. Just as many companies, learning of the potential profits to be earned across border, invest for the future by researching then organizing a new department whose task it is to penetrate new national markets.

The next chapter explains how to use export intermediaries.

CHAPTER THREE

How to use export intermediaries

We buy and sell everything under the sun, except people and coffins.
Japanese Sogo Shosha executive

In Chapter Two you learned how to make the rational business decision: should you enter export trade by the "do-it-yourself" method or go the indirect route by using an "intermediary?"

This chapter explains what export intermediaries are, how to find them, and how to use one to best advantage.

What is an export intermediary?

Defining the various intermediaries that operate in international trade is difficult. In general, a trading company is a firm that acts to market or broker goods manufactured in one country to companies and governments in another.

There are several arrangements available to the smaller firm that decides to use the indirect method:

■ **General trading companies (GTCs).** These firms, as their name implies, import and export a broad range of goods, cutting across many product lines and marketing to many countries. There are both foreign and American GTCs operating in the United States.
■ **Export Trading Associations.** These are organizations formed to market goods for several companies. They can be bank or non-bank owned and have broad anti-trust benefits. They may be creatively organized to stimulate exporting, but they may import goods as well.
■ **Import/Export Management Companies (I/EMCs).** These are the world's traditional intermediaries. Most often referred to in the literature as EMCs, they are usually smaller firms that specialize by: (a) exporting or importing, (b) product/industry, and (c) market areas.
■ **Brokers.** These organizations buy for their own account then resell the products.

- **Agents.** Like EMCs agents seldom take ownership, rather they work for a commission on things they sell.
- **Piggybacking.** This is a method of exporting whereby a company with complementary products convinces a larger firm, often multinational corporations (MNCs), to act as intermediary. Most of these very large corporations compete on a global basis and will take on, as an additional business unit, the exportation of goods for others.

What can they do for you?

Intermediaries are independent organizations which often act as the exclusive sales department for non-competitive manufacturers. Although there is some loss of control, these organizations come very close to behaving like your own export department. Even the loss of control can be tempered by asking for frequent performance reviews.

These firms work simultaneously for a number of manufacturers for a commission, salary, or retainer plus a commission. They work through their own overseas network of distributors and market your products overseas along with other allied but noncompetitive product lines. Most intermediaries provide a wide range of services including:

- strategic market planning;
- market research;
- shipping;
- advertising;
- documentation;
- channel distribution selection;
- insurance;
- financing;
- exhibit your products in trade shows.

In short, the intermediary essentially domesticates your overseas sales by taking full responsibility for the export end of your business, relieving you of all the headaches of doing it yourself. A good intermediary takes a personal concern in your company, managing the entire scope of the international marketing effort for long-term development and profit.

These firms will solicit orders from foreign clients, correspond on your stationery, and sign off on letters or telexes and invoices in the name of the principal (manufacturer), as your export manager. The manufacturer bears the risk of non-payment, but the intermediary assists the manufacturer with the details of the transaction and gets paid a commission on the export sale.

Most sales initiated by the intermediary need the approval of the client company. This way manufacturers retain greater control of the marketing of their product overseas, especially when they maintain their own brand names.

What the manufacturer wants

In the early stage, the manufacturer should search for the right intermediary, that is, one that handles similar product lines. Having narrowed the search to several that can do the job, the final selection should be based on finding the company which has/will:

- develop strategic market plans similar to those suggested in Chapter 5;
- international experience;
- product knowledge;
- overseas network;
- geographic coverage;
- no conflict of interest;
- make progress reports (no less than every 90 days), showing status based on the market plan.

What the intermediary wants

A manufacturer should not be surprised to learn that many large, successful intermediaries have more to say about who selects who than the manufacturer. What manufacturers and intermediaries want and get are two different things. Everything is negotiable and no one works for nothing. Here is a list of what intermediaries want:

- a product that has a ready market;
- a product that has staying power;
- an advance (some call it retainer) against time spent doing research and developing a strategic market plan;
- sufficient margin to cover handling costs and make a reasonable profit;
- freedom to develop a strategic plan and execute the plan, hands-off;
- products in the intermediary's area of expertise;
- a trustful relationship with the manufacturer, i.e. to be perceived as member of the team;
- realism in expectations;
- free marketing support, i.e. samples, advertising, trade show participation, etc;
- kept informed about company progress, policy changes, or production delays.

Compensation

Basically, the intermediary offers two things: (1) time, and (2) expertise, and the manufacturer should expect to compensate fairly and reasonably for these services.

The way an agent is compensated depends primarily on how "bullish" the intermediary feels about the product. If the intermediary believes the product is unique and very salable, the intermediary will probably work for the manufacturer on a straight percentage of sales basis. On the other hand if the middleman firm feels there will be a lot of development work required, it will ask for a retainer and you pay the extraordinary expenses of market entry.

In return for their services the intermediary will usually want your best domestic commission. The agent receives a commission that is generally based on invoice cost of the products being represented. This could range from 10 percent for consumer goods to 15–20 percent for industrial products. The commission can also vary between 7.5 percent and 20 percent of the wholesale distributor price. In this method the intermediary is like an internal export department. The manufacturer invoices the foreign customer directly and carries out the financing required.

Example

Product cost:	$5.00/unit
Retail price:	$20.00/unit
Distributor Price:	$10.00/unit @ 50% Discount
Intermediary @ 20% off:	$2.00 (comm. + handling costs)
Manufacturer's Profit:	$3.00

Overseas distributors want your best discount, plus as much as an extra 15 percent discount, especially if they are handling high-technology electronics.

In addition to commissions some intermediaries ask their clients to share 50:50 on trade show costs, others require a three-way cost split between the middleman, the client, and overseas agents. It is not unusual for intermediaries to ask for contributions towards advertising and promotion. This is usually at least equal to the proportional amount the manufacturer spends for domestic sales. The agent should match the contribution.

Retainers are required by many intermediaries, particularly when the introduction of a new product must have heavy advertising and promotion to gain market share.

Why use an intermediary

The primary reasons for using intermediaries are:

■ They conserve financial resources (out-of-pocket cash flow) that would otherwise be consumed during the years your firm took to develop its own international marketing department.
■ Export sales come quicker because intermediaries already have agents,

distributors and customers in place.
- You learn by observing the professionals in order to eventually develop your own international department.
- Intermediaries save you time by concentrating their effort on your overseas sales thus allowing you to concentrate on your domestic market.

General trading companies (GTCs)

The term general trading company (GTC) is used in two ways in this book:

- A trading firm that regards itself, or is regarded by others, as a general trading company whatever its definition might be.
- Those firms that have extensive overseas networks and offer one-stop diversification by product, market area, and function.

In the broad sense, the term applies to a firm that buys goods in one national market to resell at a profit in foreign markets. In this context, trading company has an identical meaning with trading house, although the latter has the historical connotation of the European export merchant while the former does not.

In a more specialized sense, the term has been used to describe a handful of Japanese trading companies called *Sogo shoshas* that have extensive marketing networks all over the world. Of course many Japanese firms export their own products, but most deal through their *Sogo shosha*. The Japanese have other trading companies (some have estimated there are as many as 5,000, similar to our EMCs) of varying sizes. But the dominant ones, the *Sogo shosha*, are large and handle a great range of products and turnover of goods.

Intermediaries have been the backbone of Japanese international trade success. The giant *Sogo shoshas* trade more than $350 billion of goods each year. Now the Koreans, Taiwanese, Europeans, as well as countries in South America, depend more and more on the expertise of trading companies. Few foreign manufacturers try to market their goods internationally by themselves because they need the economies of scale and marketing expertise intermediaries provide.

Today, the major difference between the average intermediary and the largest general trading companies in the world is annual sales. The largest export management companies (EMCs) have annual sales of about $60 million while the largest Japanese *Sogo shosha* have sales of about $60–100 billion. *Sogo shosha* are truly among the most significant phenomena of contemporary world commerce.

Since the mid-1970s the importance of large general trading companies has grown rapidly. Japan's success has caused the concept to spread around the world. Since about 1975, the Korean government has encouraged their establishment. By the early 1980s, 11 giant enterprises, called *Chonghap-mooyeok-sangsa* were in place. Most, like Samsung, Hyundai, and Daewoo are closely affiliated with groups of large Korean corporations called *Chaebol* (similar to Japanese *Zaibatsu*) and are competing as general international trading companies. Like the Japanese *Sogo shoshas*, they have become highly prestigious companies and already account for about half of their country's exports.

The Brazilian government helped set up both private and public trading companies in 1976. Their progress has been slower than that of Korea, but by the early 1980s accounted for more than 20 percent of Brazilian exports.

The Chinese word for these economic concentrations is *Caifa* and they are developing them industry by industry. Although the *Sogo shoshas* are the largest and best known, multi-product general trading companies also exist in Finland, Canada, Hong Kong, Sweden, Switzerland, Singapore, and Taiwan.

History of Trading Companies

There have always been trading companies since early Egyptian days, and even before. The earliest English overseas trade organization, the Merchants Staple, was organized in the fourteenth century as a way to replenish the royal treasury. The Company of Merchant Adventurers was formed in 1505, the Russia Company in 1553, and Levant Company in 1581. All were traders in search of spice. Home governments not only gave the companies exclusive right to trade, but also protected them with armies and naval forces. The East India Company conquered a subcontinent, ruled over 250 million people, raised and supported the largest government and standing army in the world. They even deployed 43 warships. American history books are full of tales about the Virginia and Plymouth Trading Companies—they discovered the New World.

America's export trading companies (ETCs)

Prior to 1982, the United States did not have a law that allowed business arrangements to be formed to avoid antitrust for the joint exportation of products and services or that permitted banks to take an equity position in trading companies. Before that time, export management companies (EMCs), Webb-Pomerene associations and a few large general trading companies (GTC) were the only intermediaries available to assist manufacturers.

Now there is a new kind of American middleman called export trading companies (ETCs). These special kinds of trading intermediaries can even form their own association of companies using a new law which enhances their global marketing competitiveness and gives them excellent protection from antitrust.

There is a special office in the Department of Commerce, the sole purpose of which is to assist Americans to know who the current export trading companies (ETCs) are and help you form one.

Since its passage two new types of trading companies have been formed. In the first instance bank holding companies have developed what are now known as export trading companies (ETCs). Most of these fit the generic definition of general trading companies (GTCs) in that they handle a wide range of products, buy and sell in their own right, assist in financing, and act as a one-stop export–import organization.

In the second instance, associations have formed under the same law to handle a narrower grouping of products. These are also called export trading companies, yet have used the law expressly to minimize their exposure to U.S. anti-trust laws.

Export management companies (EMCs)

Export management companies, or EMCs as they are popularly called, are also sometimes known as import/export management companies (I/EMCs), combination export managers (CEM) or export distributors.

The term export management company is used to describe a trade intermediary which is usually small, privately held, sometimes under-capitalized, and product or area-specific. More importantly, most EMCs neither take title to the goods they export nor provide a "one-stop" exporting service, although that is not the case among the larger ones.

Export management companies are currently the predominant means for the smaller firm to enter the international trade arena, and the most common form is the commission agent.

Some are relatively large, with annual sales as high as $50 million, and handling as many as 50 to 100 manufacturers. These companies cut across a wide swathe of industries and export to most of the world's markets.

Another group is smaller with annual sales ranging from $500,000 to $5 million. These EMCs represent a few carefully selected clients.

Because, in most countries, there is no licensing requirement, there are an untold number (thousands) of very small companies (often home based) with fewer than five employees handling goods on their own account and maybe those of one or two smaller manufacturers.

EMC as an agent

Sometimes the EMC works as a commission agent for the manufacturer and uses the manufacturer's name. For this method all correspondence, invoicing, and literature use the logo and stationery of the manufacturer being represented.

These companies are usually only interested in specific lines of goods. These "commission houses" as they are also called will not buy your merchandise, but are capable of matching buyer and seller. For this service, the agency receives a fee from their foreign clients. See the sample agency agreement in Appendix B.

THE TEN MOST IMPORTANT QUESTIONS TO ASK A POTENTIAL AGENT

1 How long have you been in business?
2 How big is your agency (one man or multi-person) and what territory do you cover?
3 How many lines do you currently handle?
4 What are some of your other products and how will mine fit in?
5 Do you have any references?
6 What is your commission rate and when do you expect to be paid?
7 What do you expect in the area of literature and/or sales aids?
8 What level of sales of my product do you anticipate achieving over the next 12 months?
9 How often do you usually see or speak with your principles?
10 What terms would you like written into our agreement?

Remember: They are also choosing you!

Country controlled export agents

These are foreign government agencies with a quasi-governmental role, which locate and purchase goods.

EMC as a distributor

EMCs can also act as independent distributors, buying and selling the products, but marketing in the name of their principal. When an overseas order is received, it places the order with the manufacturer, pays cash to the manufacturer, resells the goods to foreign buyers, and invoices them directly. Usually the EMC buys at domestic net wholesale prices less a percentage that approximately equals the manufacturer's domestic-sales overhead. The EMC then marks up the price sufficiently for it to cover handling costs and make a satisfactory level of profit. The EMC pays its overseas distributor or representative a commission and carries the cost of credit required by foreign buyers. Most EMCs acting as distributors work closely with their manufacturers with regard to pricing and customer relations, especially if the product is technical and requires installation and/or after sales service.

EMC as a consultant

Sometimes EMCs act only as consultants to a manufacturer, providing their international marketing expertise to the company's international department. For this they receive a retainer/fee or a combination retainer/commission. Often they are rewarded on a project basis.

Import/export management companies are not without weaknesses. Most of these weaknesses are found in the export firms themselves but they sometimes have problems in their relationship to clients. Most often this relates to lack of trust on the part of the manufacturer. Other causes of ineffectiveness on the part of EMCs have been high unit costs, deficient personnel depth, and inability to provide market services beyond selling. Needless to say, picking the right Export Management Company is critical, but it is a two way street. Trust and team work is the answer.

Finding an EMC

EMCs are hands-on experts, but finding the right one for your product can sometimes be a chore in itself. The first stop in your search for an EMC would be your local international trade association.

Other sources of information might be trade publications, or your local government representative.

Once you have identified several EMCs which have experience with your product or at least products that are complimentary, gain an appointment or write to explain your situation. EMCs are always looking for new lines, but don't be surprised if they select you instead of you selecting them. They don't waste time on something that doesn't show profit potential or a firm that won't give them adequate backup support.

Other EMC arrangements

Besides the dominance of the export management companies, and a smaller number of general trading companies, there are several other options open to the manufacturer wishing to expand into overseas markets. Each option represents a link in the market channel and each has inherent advantages and limitations.

Export brokers

Like the export commission agent, the broker will not buy your goods, but they will smooth the groundwork because of their knowledge of markets and contacts. They will save you money and time by locating and putting you in direct contact with interested buyers, but for that your broker will receive a commission on sales. Some brokers have a wide network of contacts both commercially and geographically, while others focus on narrow industrial and geographic segments of the world.

Export consultants

By their nature, consultants bring expertise you need only on an occasional basis. The firm that is inexperienced in international trade would do well to employ a consultant in the initial stages of entry. Once you have established your own international organization the consultant has lost value. The consultant's importance derives from experience in every facet of a project particularly market analysis, personnel selection, product evaluation, promotional strategies, tax implications, and legal considerations. Consultants work on a fee-based retainer or commission, or a combination. Their seasoned experience and judgment more than pay for their fee.

Export merchants

This is the old, established term to describe a trader, usually serving as an agent for the manufacturer, who plays the role of the principal in transactions with foreign customers. In the 1800s, European export merchants took over most of the responsibilities of the manufacturers by providing a wide range of services in trading, and the term *export merchant* was gradually replaced with *trading house*. As a result of this evolution, the trading house now offers multiple services related to trading, such as providing the manufacturer with cash to cover the cost of the goods, giving credit to the customer on its own account, and taking on the financial risks by assuming the title of the transactions.

Think of an export merchant in the same sense you would of any other domestic sale. These companies simply buy your goods at the door and you know little about the eventual marketing or shipping. Most often there are no ties between you and this international entrepreneur; therefore, they may buy once and never be seen again. For you it only means additional sales volume without the problems of overseas documentation, or coordination.

Webb-Pomerene associations

In the United States, the Export Trade Act of 1918, better known as the Webb-Pomerene Act, was passed by Congress in order to allow manufacturers more flexibility to cooperate for international sales. Under this legislation, trade associations can be registered with the Federal Trade Commission for the sole purpose of engaging in export trade of "goods, wares, or merchandise" so long as they do not restrain trade within the United States.

Simply put, the Webb-Pomerene Act allowed American firms to team up to form cartels and fix prices for foreign trade goods without violating the United States anti-trust laws.

The Webb-Pomerene Act is still on the books and is an exception to antitrust laws that prohibit competitors from acting jointly. The intent of the act is to help smaller firms acquire economies of scale by combining to compete more efficiently against foreign cartels. By working together they can conduct market research of foreign markets, and reduce unit costs of international distribution with higher volume than going it alone. WPAs can fix prices and set up quotas for overseas markets.

The limitations of the Webb-Pomerene Act are:

- It is only applicable to the export of goods or merchandise and does not apply to the exporting of services or licensing transactions.
- There is no binding anti-trust pre-clearance.
- Not limited to single damages—could be assessed treble damages for an anti-trust violation.
- Must engage solely in exports.
- Does not provide for the payment of attorney's fees by plaintiff, should plaintiff lose the case.

Between 1918 and 1965, a total of 176 associations were registered in the United States, of these only 130 ever functioned. Until about 1930 these associations accounted for approximately 12 percent of total United States exports. By mid-1978 the number of WPAs had declined to 30 and the share of exports had fallen to only 1.5 percent. For the past 10 years these trade associations have remained stalled. There were only 36 active WPAs in 1981.

Joining a Webb-Pomerene Association should not be overlooked because it is still an option for the new-to-export firm, however the numbers of WPAs that have survived are small and they are predominantly in the areas of agriculture and raw materials.

Piggybacking

Several major multinational corporations (MNCs) have their own trading companies which handle large volumes of goods for themselves and others. Larger companies with excess marketing capacity or a desire for a broader product line take on additional products for international distribution. The generic term for such activities is "complementary marketing," but the common name is "piggybacking."

There are several reasons why large firms may be interested in piggybacking your products:

- These firms look for those products that are noncompetitive and add to the basic distribution strength of the large company itself.

- Exports to existing markets can be increased at little additional expense.
- Relationships with foreign clients can be improved by satisfying their requests for additional products.
- Expansion of foreign markets may be easier with a more complete line
- Most piggyback arrangements are undertaken when a large manufacturer wants to fill out its product line or keep its distribution channels for seasonal items functioning throughout the year.

Piggybacking can work well for products that are complementary to the exporting firm's line, for example sports carrying bags might be a good piggyback with a company that manufacturers racquets.

Companies may work together either on an agent or merchant basis, but by far the greatest volume of piggyback business is handled on an ownership (merchant), purchase-resale arrangement. Most will be satisfied to work with you at your best distributor price. Some exporting manufacturers ask for an extra discount above your best distributor price and extra time to pay. Such requests are not out of line if the exporter is going to strongly promote your product or if they need extra time due to foreign customers delay in paying. In every case it is recommended that a formal contract or letter of understanding exist between you and the exporter.

Finding a piggybacker

Your search should begin in your own industry by contacting your industry association or trade magazines. Your governmental representative can sometimes be helpful, but don't be surprised to learn that information is limited about who is or who is not piggybacking. Your search may require a company by company inquiry before you find the right firm.

Piggyback limitations

Piggybacking has its drawbacks and is not for every product. Because margins are so narrow in most basic commodities, it seldom works well in those industries. Another problem is that some international firms look at piggyback products as an add-on to the basic distribution strength of their own company. In other words the small firm is at the mercy of the major manufacturer. Don't link up in a piggyback arrangement outside your own business area without some excellent reason. If you cannot find a piggybacking manufacturer, it is better to go with an EMC or GTC.

Negotiating an intermediary agreement

It is recommended that you always enter into a written agreement with an intermediary. Appendix C is an agency/distributor form, and the following are the main elements of an agreement:

A. Basic Component
   1 Parties to the agreement.
   2 Duration of agreement.
   3 Territory: Extent of the geographical territory to which the agreement is to apply.
      (a) exclusive;
      (b) non-exclusive;
      (c) manufacturer's right to sell direct at reduced or no commission to local government and old customers.
   4 Products covered. Range of products offered and any possible modifications to the product line covered.
   5 Order and delivery terms
   6 Which party is responsible for product warranty, liability and indemnification.
B. Manufacturer's Rights and Duties
   1 Arbitration.
   2 Jurisdiction.
   3 Governing law of the contract and relevant arbitration bodies that the contract should be the sole agreement to apply.
   4 Termination conditions.
   5 Clarification of tax liabilities.
   6 Payment and discount terms.
   7 Conditions for delivery of goods.
   8 Rights to change prices, terms, and conditions at any time.
   9 Right of manufacturer or his agent to visit territory and inspect books.
   10 Training of distributor personnel.
   11 Rights of the exporter to add further representatives to the agreement, both within and without the specified territory.
   12 Duties of the exporter in the following areas:
      (a) provision of adequate support services;
      (b) marketing support;
      (c) maintenance of good communications;
      (d) method and terms of payment;
      (e) delivery of the product.
C. Distributor's Limitations and Duties
   1 No disclosure of confidential information.
   2 Position as legal agent of manufacturer.
   3 Penalty clause for late payment.

4 Limitation on right to handle competing lines.
5 Distributor to publicize his designation as authorized representative in defined area.
6 Requirement to remove all signs or evidence identifying him with manufacturer if relationship ends.
7 Information to be supplied by distributor:
   (a) sales reports;
   (b) names of active prospects;
   (c) government regulations dealing with imports;
   (d) competitive products and competitor's activities;
   (e) price at which goods are sold;
   (f) complete data on other lines carried on request.
8 Accounting methods to be used by distributor.
9 Requirement to display products appropriately.
10 Duties concerning advertising and promotion.
11 Clarification of responsibility arising from claims and warranties.
12 Responsibility of distributor to provide repair and other services.
13 Responsibility to maintain suitable place of business.
14 Responsibility to supply all prospective customers.
15 Requirement that certain sales approaches and literature be approved by manufacturer.
16 Prohibition of manufacture or alteration of products.
17 Requirement to maintain adequate stock, spare parts.
18 Requirement that inventory be surrendered in event of a dispute which is pending in court.
19 Marketing activities and sales levels expected.
20 Respect of patent and proprietary rights.
21 Product installation and qualifiying level of maintenance required for the distributor's staff.
22 General level of service expected.

Note: Sometimes agreements are required to be written in the languages of all parties involved.

Summary

There are several alternatives for the firm that doesn't want to export on its own. The choice is not complicated, but does require some analysis. The intermediary you choose can help you analyze the problem and serve as your getting started partner. Trust is a major factor—the manufacturer wants it, as does the intermediary, and the process works well when the two work as a team.

The next chapter is about how to form winning export associations.

CHAPTER FOUR

Form winning export associations

A rich country makes for a strong army.

Old Chinese proverb

Instead of each company supporting the overhead of its own export department, they may join together, even forming cartels, thus benefiting from economies that affect the bottom line. A common staff with one international distribution network can make a large profit difference.

Export associations

An export association is a firm organized and operated principally for purposes of providing one or more export trade services to multiple unaffiliated companies or persons. There is no binding definition or configuration of such a trading association. It may be used in many creative and ingenious ways, and is often just what the doctor ordered to allow small service and manufacturing companies to join together to compete and be profitable in international trade. Some export trading associations are formed with banks, shipping firms or insurance companies as partners.

An export trade association can provide a framework for innovators and risk takers who step forward to coordinate a smaller firms participation in the international trade game.

Advantages

The export association concept affords smaller firms several advantages, all of which come by way of joint export activities.

- **Barriers**. Firms can end-run non-tariff trade barriers by sharing costs of difficult foreign government labeling, packaging, and quality requirements.
- **Bidding**. By teaming-up, firms can respond to foreign orders which might exceed the capacity or capability of any single firm.

- **Capital**. Greater funds in the form of equity can be brought to export activities by bank participation.
- **Economies of Scale**. Joint venture agreements between domestic companies to compete internationally bring increased efficiency.
- **Immunity**. By gaining advanced approval from the government, joint activities, even price setting can gain immunity from criminal and civil prosecution for export activities.
- **Market Research**. Firms that join together can share the costs of foreign market research, and travel.
- **Market Entry and Development**. Firms with complementary products can achieve cost reductions of advertising, trade shows, missions and other joint activities.
- **Shipping**. Carriers will negotiate lower discounts and longer rate contracts because joint arrangements can provide needed volume and scheduling guarantees.

Structuring an export association

There are an unlimited number of formation options. Groups interested in combining would do well to first consider these strategic implications:

- What is the environment for international trade related to their products or services?
- What are the objectives? Profit or economic stimulation?
- What does the investor expect to gain?
- Should products be sourced locally, regionally or nationally?
- Where will the products be marketed? The world, a continent, or a region?

Models

An export association can allow the formation of many imaginatively modeled trading companies. Some of which are presented below.

Combinations formed by banks

Many of the needed ingredients for a successful trading company are found in banks. Access to capital and the handling of international financial transactions are among the skills they possess. But bankers are not generally characterized as risk takers; therefore, this model requires careful development of some of the missing elements. Risk taking, the entrepreneurial nature of traders, must be blended into the equation with banking capital, access to products, and the ability to move goods from seller to buyer. Figure 4.1 shows what this organization might look like.

Figure 4.1   ETC combinations formed by banks

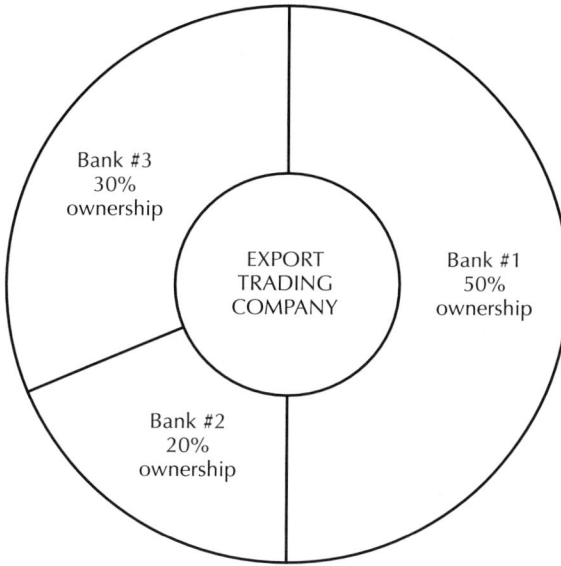

Figure 4.2   ETCs formed by combinations of small to medium-sized manufacturing firms

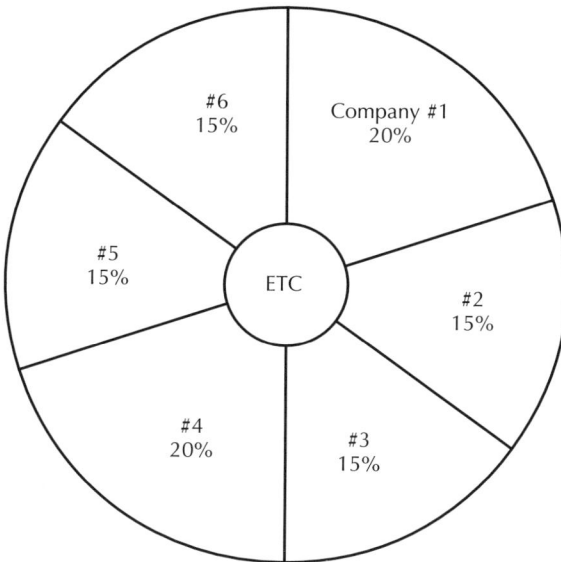

Combinations of quadrant 4 manufacturing firms

Figure 4.2 shows a model wherein firms have equal partnership and share a common staff for the export function. A fraternity of chief executive officers in a city or industry would most likely develop this kind of business relationship. In Japan, "Presidents Clubs" are often developed around the *Sogo shosha*. A close relationship of the decision makers is essential for any model.

Project-specific combinations of quadrant 4 service companies

This model holds great promise to take advantage of export trade associations. Most often these are not long-term business arrangements and therefore are suitable for smaller firms. A joint-venture partnership may be formed for the purpose of bidding for international projects. This model is most common for that kind of service company that offers management, engineering or construction. Figure 4.3 is an example.

Combinations of shipper's associations

A shipper's association is simply a group of shippers that consolidates or distributes freight of the members in order to obtain volume transporta-

---

Figure 4.3 Project-specific combinations of service companies

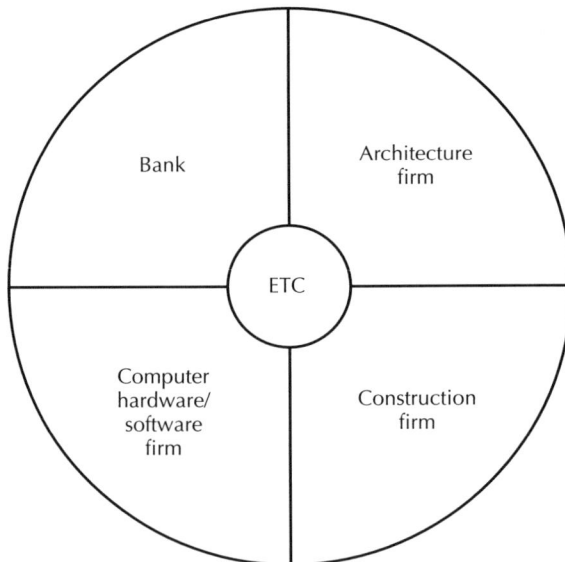

Figure 4.4 Combinations formed by Export Management Firms

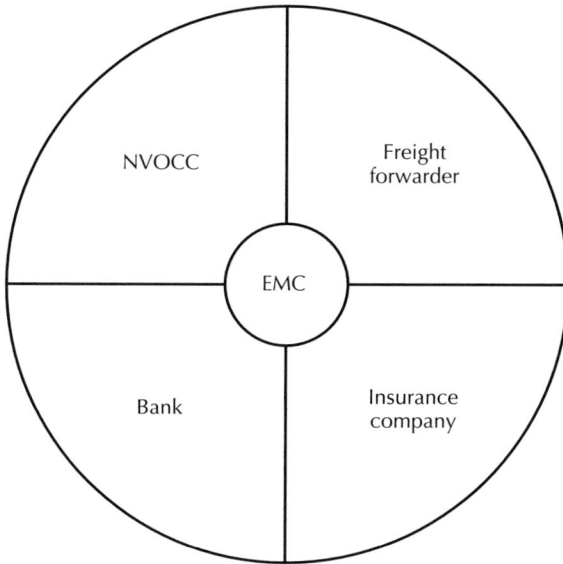

tion rates or service contracts. Shipper's associations can realize lower transportation costs previously available only to larger shippers.

Combinations formed by export management firms

The largest export management companies (EMCs) have offices through-out the world. They often take title to goods, and already operate essentially as full-scale trading companies. As a result of their expertise they are excellent candidates for combinations with other service firms, including banks or with groups of producers. Figure 4.4 offers a model of such combinations.

Combinations for technology licensing

The licensing of patents, trademarks, know-how, and technology are intangible economic outputs and as such are likely candidates for association. This makes licensing arrangements the best method for innovators to effectively exploit technological advances.

Public sector combinations

One model of an export association would be organized like a public utility serving a specified region. States and cities with jurisdiction over a sea or airport are likely to be interested. They have a vested interest in

Figure 4.5   Public Sector Combinations

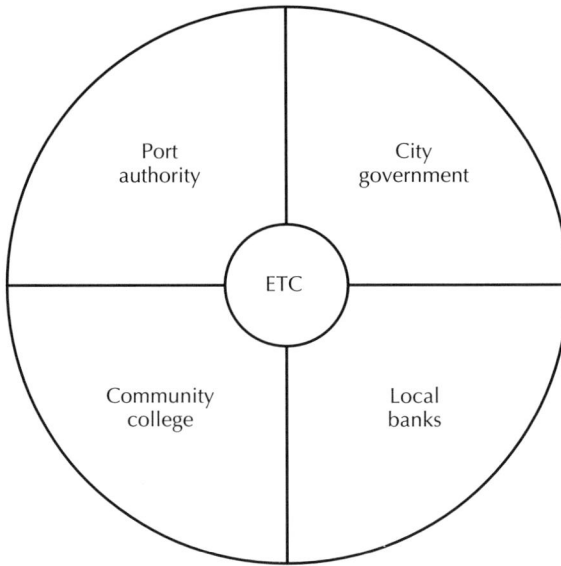

promoting the flow of goods through their facilities and often have the most to gain from this approach. Typically the objective of this model is to stimulate economic development by serving the small and medium-sized manufacturers and agricultural producers in the region. Figure 4.5 shows a way this may be done by combination of a city government, port authority, a community college, and several local banks. A sub-structure of associations of product specific firms might also take an equity position.

Combinations to form "Export" cities

This model functions as a showcase for exports. Buyers would be flown in from all over the world to see in one area, the goods a location has to offer. Figure 4.6 shows how those linkages could be formed.

Combinations through existing trade associations

This model would be a by-product of existing industry associations such as food, electronics or chemical manufacturers. Some of these organizations already provide market intelligence and research for their members. Buying and selling of goods overseas is a natural extension. An obvious advantage of this model is that the association has strong potential for attracting new-to-export firms.

Figure 4.6 Export City Combinations

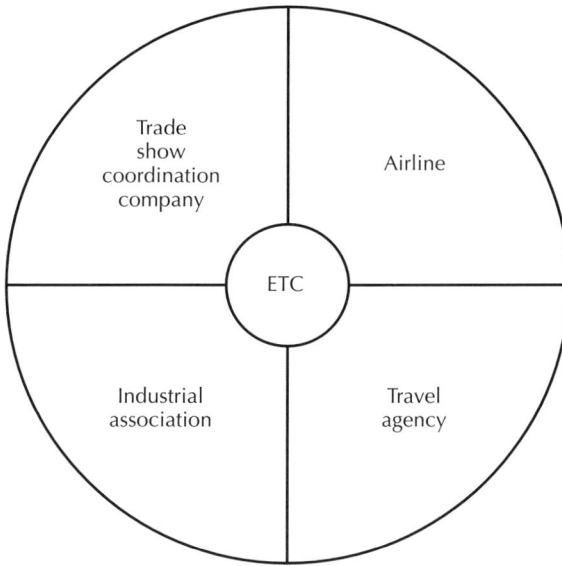

Organizing an export association

The key variable in developing an export association is the range of services to be offered. It can be a one-stop full service organization or it can be limited to specific functions. Three general forms of specialization or combinations were visualized:

- Perform all export marketing services. In other words be a "one-stop" operation.
- Buy and sell on their own account, thus achieving economies of scale.
- Specialize in foreign government procurement contracts. This company would put together the right mix of goods and services to fill large-valued foreign government contracts.

Products

Single-product associations such as cotton, grains, or poultry have traditionally been served. Multiple-product lines such as a combination of agricultural products, business equipment and electronics require a larger staff and increased training requirements.

Domestic coverage

Export trading associations could be organized to source products or provide trading services on a national, regional or local basis.

Global reach

The international focus and reach of its distribution network is a special strategic consideration. Export attention can be diverse. It can be on a worldwide basis or localized to a region like the Pacific basin or Latin America.

Activities

Selection of activities is a strategic decision and is a fundamental part of the start up and operation of an export association. An export trading company can export, import, enter into third country transactions, barter or countertrade, or conduct switch trade. The decision is related to those activities that will make the business profitable, and that will usually be those which have historically been offered to customers of a given region.

Investors

Like the start-up of any business, the first convincing step for investors is development of a comprehensive, professional business plan. Investors must believe through research that there is a market, that the concept is well thought through, and the very best management will be put in place. Potential investors, whether they be banks or manufacturers, want to hedge their risk by being assured that the venture has the best possible chance of success. Large money-center banks and other financially strong institutions like regional banks, insurance companies, and international trading companies are likely candidates. Short-term profits cannot be the objective for this investment. International trade takes time and progress must be measured against long-term objectives.

For the public sector, economic stimulation in terms of regional incomes and employment usually has greater consideration than profit.

Summary

The export association is a business arrangement that could, trustfully, attract small and medium-sized firms to international trade. It provides a powerful tool to extend global market reach through stronger capitalization and economies of scale. Smaller firms that don't consider taking advantage are missing an opportunity to become a "global business" at minimum risk. In other words the export association concept can be everything the general trading company (GTC) and the export management company (EMC) can be and more. In fact the only limitation of the concept is imagination and innovation.

The next chapter of the book explains how to build an export marketing plan.

CHAPTER FIVE

The export plan

The plan is nothing, planning is everything.

Dwight Eisenhower

Someone has to develop an export marketing plan, *in writing*. If your firm exports or forms an association, your own staff (or a consultant) should do the research and write the plan. If you decide to deal with an intermediary, they should write the plan.

No matter who does it, a plan *must* be written!

There are two phases to an international marketing plan. Phase I is the planning stage and phase II is the action stage. This chapter is organized to explain these phases.

Phase I: The planning stage

There are two major aspects of a written marketing plan: "strategy" and "tactics." These words have been adapted by the business world from military terminology and are used extensively in developing new markets, particularly global markets. Don't be intimidated by the terms strategy and tactics.

Strategy is the term for adopted policies. A strategic plan is the integration of smaller pieces (tactics) into a larger purpose.

The term tactic describes the art or skill of employing available means or specific actions leading to the accomplishment of the strategy.

Strategic planning

Modern marketing requires the development of a strategic plan, then isolating the tactical steps needed to implement the plan. This part of the international market plan is the data gathering and thinking stage. Allow plenty of time for this to include many staff meetings which encourage "blue sky" discussions.

Your marketing plan should be written as a distinct part of your firm's larger, overall strategic business plan and should define your company's international policy. Realistic goals and objectives should be set and a

A Executive Summary (written only after all other parts of the plan are complete)
B International Marketing Objective
  1 Leader, follower, challenger, or nicher (explained in the section titled International Marketing Objective)
C Intelligence
  1 Data gathering
  2 Kinds of information
  3 The target market
    (a) Segmentation
  4 The players
  5 Interstate (government) controls
  6 Strategic alternatives
D Market Tactics: The Six P's
  1 Pop
  2 Persistence
  3 Product
  4 Price
  5 Place
  6 Promotion
E Action Stage
  1 Budget
  2 Contingencies

suitable organization plan should be developed. Above all your plan should be put on paper.

Strategic planning and policy determines how your business fits into the marketplace. The strategic plan is simply the measurement of your company and its products and the likely prospects for success. A firm's total strategic plan has three sub-parts, the domestic commercial plan (for your country), the government plan, and the international plan. Don't make the same mistake many firms do by making two separate plans, one for the domestic and government market and one for the international market. Certainly the approach should be a separate investigation of each market, but the total plan should include all, because there is synergy, and there are many commonalties. This chapter deals mainly with the international marketing plan. The outline above explains the process. A similar outline may be used for the domestic and government plan.

Intelligence (market research)

The need to search and know (intelligence) is a prerequisite for any successful business venture. Before your international effort can move

forward you must invest in market research, either by your own personnel or with the assistance of a firm that specializes in the field. From this
search for broader markets will come a strategic approach.

In the past, all too many firms have migrated to a foreign market by
accident. But today, more and more companies are making strategic decisions and entering the international game with a well-thought-out plan.
The plan is developed from gathered intelligence.

Intelligence has great significance for you the modern manufacturer or
service company manager. The correct application and rationing of capital is dependent on information, otherwise it is wasted on bad decisions.
Once the decision is made to enter a given market, research should begin
to collect, select, assess, and pass on useful information to the decision
maker.

Most smaller firms do not have a corporate-level intelligence gathering
capability other than that which may have been developed in their
domestic marketing department. Even then, most marketing organizations are often no more than a personal sales effort. Salesmen often lack
the time or the opportunity to be isolated long enough to take on the
kind of research and analysis necessary to bring about thoughtful information for decision making.

Most often, the smaller firm is well advised to contract with a private
service company that specializes in international research. These firms
have the experience to not only gather and sift through the magnitude of
information, but also to tailor the analysis to the specific needs of the
client.

Don't overlook the many services provided by governments to
exporters. Most countries invest considerable tax dollars in export promotion and information. Chapter 13 explains how to get help from the
government.

Data gathering

Marketing research (intelligence) is the systematic gathering, recording,
and analyzing of data about problems relating to the marketing of goods
and services. In other words it is the process of supplying information for
marketing business decisions, and those decisions can be about planning,
problem solving, or control of performance.

Think of this as a building block process wherein the researcher starts
with a problem and ends with a presentation of the findings to top management. The methods have been perfected in modern business, and the
risk of not doing research is loss of profits and time.

Classically, the approach to gathering intelligence has seven steps:

1 define the problem;
2 develop a research plan;

3 identify data sources;
4 collect the data;
5 analyze the data;
6 interpret the data;
7 present the results for application (decision making).

Secondary data

Most research begins with secondary data, that is, publications, journals, periodicals, official government documents. etc. In general there is a wealth of material, but for some country markets there is a serious short-age of secondary data. Nations with low per capita income have commensurably smaller government budgets to collect and analyze statistical data. For example some countries have never taken a census. Others have few publications which deal in the kind of information you might need.

Primary data

Intelligence should be company specific, that is, you want to know what people think about your product, prices, and promotion. Primary data is gathered directly from the people who know—the consumer. But people in different countries react differently and have varying views about responding to collection of data. In some nations responses are driven by the culture where a polite answer is given no matter what a person's real feelings might be. In others the suspicion of government is very high, yet in others illiteracy is the significant barrier. An important way to gather primary data is through the International Chambers of Commerce abroad.

Language

In lieu of readily available information, researchers may have to design data collection instruments. The sequence for this effort is to lay out, translate, test, redesign, retest, conduct the study, then finally translate back to the parent language. Needless to say, communications and primary data collection is compounded when a country has several languages.

Communications

Probably the most frustrating condition for the international intelligence gatherer is the lack of modern communications in some countries. In many countries consumers don't have telephones, and mail systems that are unreliable. Data has to be developed from a street questionnaire or interviews gathered in popular metropolitan areas, then extrapolated for the country as a whole.

Kinds of information

In general before moving into the international marketplace, you the decision maker should look at three things:

- Which markets to enter (strategy).
- How to enter the markets (tactics).
- How to market in the target markets (tactics).

Your intelligence effort should focus on three different areas: the target market; the players, and interstate (government) controls. Let us explore each.

Target market

Learn to think like an admiral or a general, because the beginning step of this effort is the development of a strategy. A world map should be displayed in a room we will call, for lack of a better name, the intelligence center. Using pins, flags, or small magnets you can easily identify countries and cities which are to be your targets. Next an erasable board should be located nearby. On the board you will list by priority your targets. You might ask, "why not just do it all on a computer?" There's nothing wrong with using computers. It should be done, but there is something about displays that provide visibility to the intelligence process. The wall display still has its value and is recommended.

Targeting involves finding that part of the total market which a business feels it can serve most effectively. It's impossible for a given company to meet the needs and tastes of all consumers in a particular area. Most products must be aimed at only a segment of the total market population, principally because consumers like to feel that a product is produced for their particular needs. People tend to identify with a product when this psychological bond has been created. Of course there are several other reasons why target marketing is important:

- Targeting focuses the firm's efforts and encourages realistic goals.
- Aiming marketing efforts at everybody is like aiming at nobody.
- Focusing on target countries and consumer groups within that target country makes marketing less expensive and more effective.
- Targeting helps develop a market niche and differentiate the company from the competition.
- Buyers of consequence are not always the end users of a product. It is the buyers you are interested in.
- Segmenting the market into sub-targets helps in the identification of the competitors, both foreign and local.

Segmenting

Segmenting prospective markets in international market research requires a two-tiered approach.

First the researcher sorts the available information at a "macro" level.

Macro segmentation divides market by broad characteristics such as geography, demography, development level, host government involvement, personality, behavior, and competition.

- **Geography**. Think first in terms of continents, Europe, Asia, or Australia. Which major region offers the most sales appeal? Then segment countries within the continent, thinking of the people, where do they live—rural or urban, near oceans, mountains or plains?
- **Demography**. Consider the income, age, religion, nationality, and culture of potential customers.
- **Development level**. For instance certain services may be excluded from a country which has a low level of technology development, has a closed business environment, or low capital availability.
- **Host government involvement**. Some governments are directly involved with the negotiations between sellers and private sector buyers. The role of government should be analyzed on a country-by-country basis.
- **Personality**. Think in terms of *their* self-image; what are *their* psychological needs and tastes?
- **Behavior**. Who will benefit from your product?
- **Competition**. Who is the general competition? Is there any? Is it local or foreign? What is their market share?

The *second* tier of the segmentation approach is called micro segmentation. It is the determination of homogeneous customer groups within macro segments, that is, pinpointing the actual decision makers who buy the product. Factors that define micro segments might include procurement criteria, cultural aspects of buying, procedures employed by firms, the structure of decision-making units within firms, and competition's techniques. This information allows you to design a promotional strategy which caters to the decision making unit (DMU).

- **Procurement criteria**. In one company decisions may lie with a committee, in others only with the president. In some cities the mayor is the sole fiscal authority, while in others the city or planning manager may be the actual DMU for major procurements.
- **Cultural aspects of buying**. In some countries only the women of the family do the buying, while in others, for certain products, the young people decide for themselves what they will or will not buy.
- **Procedures employed by firms**. Buyers in some firms will only deal with their own national representatives. Some buy as a result of competitive bids developed from formal requests for proposal (RFP).

■ **Structure of decision-making units (DMU) within firms**. Some companies require presentations to committees of top management while others give autonomy at certain levels of management up to specific dollar values.

■ **Competition's techniques**. Call it industrial spying, call it research, no matter what it's called an appreciation of local competition and their methods is essential.

The players

Another display, in or out of the computer, should be a list of the customers, suppliers, competitors, government officials, and any others that can affect your program. This should be developed in detail, using names, addresses, background, and decision-making power. Remember, when you go international, your competitors now expand by a significant multiple, because you must now think in terms of foreign competitors, not just domestic.

Interstate (government) controls

Many of your tactical decisions will be based on how to maneuver around the obstacles or barriers presented by foreign governments, or how to take advantage of certain incentives those same governments offer to stimulate international trade. A rigorous analysis of tariff schedules, taxes, and non-tariff barriers should be developed. Analyze these barriers and incentives not only from your domestic point of view, but also from the point of view of nations that are adjacent to the target market country. Sometimes there are opportunities to flank a problem.

The need for in-depth market segmentation varies from company to company. Manufacturing companies may find their target DMU is a specific individual, much the same as in their own domestic market. On the other hand, a service company may find that the perceived risk of buying a piece of software is so high that only a top management committee can make the decision.

Ultimately the questions that must be answered are:

■ Who is the end user?
■ Who is the actual buyer?
■ What are the best methods of closing a sale?
■ How large a target market can your firm serve?
■ What is unique about your product or service?
■ What are the company's resources to serve this market?

International marketing objective

The very nature of capitalism ensures that if a business enjoys a monopoly position, and if that business is lucrative, there will, sooner or later, be competition. Therefore, if a new firm is entering the market with a standard product or service it is immediately faced with the question of how to obtain a market share. In any business environment, a firm must decide how to position itself in relation to the competition. This analysis applies in the international marketplace as well as the domestic market. Your company can be either a market leader, a challenger, a follower or a business that has its own "niche."

Based on the analysis of your intelligence, if your firm can identify a target market and pursue an effective marketing strategy to become a "nicher," bigger firms may not be attracted and the competition may be much less. Obviously, the niche must be large enough to be profitable.

Marketing tactics: the six "P's"

Few marketers think of their actions in terms of tactics; however, the success of your work is measured by your ability to adjust to the changes of the marketplace just as the tank commander or ship captain must change their tactics to the battle scene.

In academia, these methods are called the market mix or variables—the four "Ps": product, price, place and promotion. But in reality they are the tactics of the profitable trade game. This book offers a fifth and sixth "P", called "Pop!" and "Persistence" which will not be explained later, but rather by their nature will be discussed right now!

POP!

"Pop!" is the characteristic of being responsive to the customer. Action! Right now! It's that quality that makes one company win over others. It's the thing that wins contracts and sells products all over the world. It turns a "looky-loo" into a sale. It is the tone that pervades a company and gives the prospective client a feeling you really care about solving his or her problems. It's answering the mail, today! It's the way you answer the telephone and when you answer the telephone.

Persistence

Let there be no doubt, international business takes a little longer and the key to success is persistence. Product identification, and an eventual insider's position will take staying power. If your original intelligence showed that your firm had a good chance of success, then don't give up. Find out what works and do it!

Product

In general the same factors used to evaluate a product's potential in the domestic market will determine your success in a foreign market. Much of the common-sense business knowledge you have relied on in the domestic market will serve you well internationally. You must still offer a world class product at competitive prices that serve a need of a given population. However not all products marketed in one economy or environment can be marketed in another country at a profit. Such things as religion, and cultural preference can be major factors. Adapting your product culturally requires learning about your target market and what they like. What are their tastes? What turns them off in terms of attitudes, social differences, and language? Obviously there are a range of other business and engineering issues which should also be considered, such as product need, product standards, level of technology, durability/quality, technical specifications, and alternative uses.

Product need

To determine need in a new market, the prudent approach is to observe and examine known buying patterns. Climate, culture, history, and habits must be considered. There is universal appeal for leading-edge technology that is durable, adaptable, and requires little servicing, but purchasing power often overcomes appeal and need when the local population cannot afford to buy the products.

Product standards

Each country has its own product standards such as food and drug laws, safety standards, quality, and technical standards. While most countries are moving toward accepted worldwide practices prudence dictates that a firm entering a new foreign market must research the host country's regulations.

Level of technology

Typically, the most advanced products are developed in the most advanced countries. Hi-tech, as these products are known, are exported to the most favorable foreign markets first. Later, as the original countries lose some of the export market (when other advanced countries begin to produce the product locally) the product should be marketed in less developed countries. Eventually, lower production costs in these countries could reverse the process and the original country may begin to import their own product. This process, commonly known as "product life cycle" is well understood among international businesses and is used to extend sales life. Knowing where a product is in the product life cycle will help you to target markets.

Durability/quality

One of the most remarkable consequences of Japanese export success has been the importance of quality. After-sales service can be expensive, particularly when repair parts and technicians must travel an ocean away from the factory. Equipment operations under varying and demanding conditions strain the best engineered parts; therefore durability becomes a major issue in the design of products for overseas markets.

Technical specifications

Analyze your product in terms of adaptability to a particular foreign country. Each national government establishes and enforces technical standards to ensure products meet safety requirements and are compatible with or interchangeable with locally produced products. As an example, in the United States the electrical system is based on 120 V, 60 Hz, while the majority of the rest of the world uses 220 V, 50 Hz. Conversion to the metric system, technical specifications and codes is essential to market in foreign target markets.

Alternative uses

Products in one country are not always used for the same purpose in other countries. One of the most obvious examples is the bicycle. In the United States, they are used almost exclusively for recreation or physical fitness purposes, but in many foreign markets, where automobiles are not affordable to the general public, bicycles are a primary mode of transportation.

Price

The first step in setting a price for the overseas market is to establish the policy objectives. As discussed earlier, entering the international marketplace requires commitment. Most firms view foreign market entry as the first step of a long-term effort, so pricing must be consistent with maximizing long-run profits. On the other hand, prices must be attractive enough to stimulate interest by consumers and agents/distributors.

Market costs

Marketing across oceans and international boundaries adds costs to a product. The cost of doing business includes transportation, import duties, foreign taxes, overseas sales representatives, travel, lodging, and paperwork. Begin with your factory output cost, including profit margin, then add on:

- packaging for overseas shipment;
- average shipping costs (truck to port as well as ocean or air);
- insurance;
- documentation;
- banking charges;
- warehousing;
- commissions to foreign distributors;
- import duties;
- cost of currency differential;
- cost of warranty;
- cost of in-country product support.

Of course, some of these costs may be borne by the buyer, but it's better to over estimate your costs, than to later underquote and learn you have significant losses.

Market price

When determining your price for the overseas market it is essential to learn as much about the market price as possible, then compare that knowledge with your calculation of costs, usually cost-plus profit or (domestic price-plus).

This is called "pricing in—costing out". The comparison of the two, that is, market price minus actual costs-plus will determine where your product is in the market and whether you can make sufficient profit.

Market price can be deceiving, because it may be a reflection of foreign domestic manufacturing costs, or other features your competitors have built in, such as allowance for credit, or services. Make certain you compare apples to apples. Nevertheless, begin with competitive market pricing. Check catalogs, order a competitor's product, or review government price index reports.

The question to be answered is will your price be competitive overseas? Regardless of the method used, you are looking for the difference between market price and costs (price in-cost out). When the difference is positive you can begin export marketing secure in the thought that there are profits to be made. If the difference is negative you have two directions to go:

- Reduce the product's direct costs by employing cheaper materials or cut some of the product features.
- Position the product at the upper end of the consumer market, cut middlemen, or begin manufacturing or assembling the product overseas (see Chapter 12).

Market-entry prices

Market-entry pricing is still another matter. Taking a long-term view of pricing policy does not preclude gaining short term objectives. Gaining market share, recovering an initial cash investment, or forcing competitors, who are experiencing only marginal success, from the market may dictate rapid penetration.

Over the years Japanese and Korean companies have used this tactic. They often enter a market at a price under their nearest competitor, then after traditional buying patterns have been interrupted and market share is gained, they systematically raise the price until profit margins and shares are stabilized. This tactic helps explain why the Japanese and Koreans have established themselves as world class exporters.

If you decide on this tactic, be careful you are not guilty of what is known as "dumping" (see Glossary). This is the practice of placing a product in a market at prices much below fair market value (often below domestic manufacturing costs) in order to gain market entry.

Place

By place we mean the market channel and physical distribution considerations for a product or service. Market channels are the steps a product or service follows from the manufacturer to the final consumer, i.e. the means of getting the product before the public.

Earlier, in Chapter One, you learned how to decide which marketing method to use. If you had decided to let a trading company market your product you would expect the place considerations to be taken care of by the intermediary firm.

In general, overseas market channels are the same as those in the United States. There are agents, brokers, distributors, retailers, as well as the direct means of getting the product to the consumer such as the mailers or magazine advertisement.

Sales agents or independent representatives

These are commission representatives (export agents) who typically serve more than one related but non-competitive firm and are paid a commission based on actual sales. This is often the most cost-effective way for a firm that has a technical product or has limited marketing resources. Selling through these agents leaves the risks, responsibility of documentation, shipping, and payment arrangements with the seller. They do act as your representative to promote your firm's reputation, resolve problems and/or recommend solutions. A contract usually defines the respective rights and obligations for a specific period and can be exclusive or non-exclusive.

Brokers

Brokers usually bring buyers and sellers together by use of worldwide connections and special knowledge of the marketplace. In general, they deal in bulk commodities such as paper or sugar and are often an inexpensive way to dispose of surpluses.

Distributors

A distributor is a merchant who normally buys your product at a discount then stores, resells it, and collects using an established sales organization in a defined geographic region or territory. A distributor is particularly useful for those products that require after-sales service and/or repair and for products which are advertised heavily. It is usually the responsibility of the exporter to provide for the safe shipment to the distributor's warehouse and also provide promotional literature. The distributor in turn uses his means to advertise and/or distribute the materials and product. It is not unusual that the distributor and seller share the costs of advertising. As with the agent or representative, the length of the association is established by contract which is renewable provided the arrangement proves satisfactory.

Retailers

Foreign retailers are an important channel, particularly for mass-market consumer products. It is to your advantage to deal direct just as it is to their advantage to deal direct with the manufacturer. Often large-chain retailers will insist on their own house label but will buy in large quantities.

Direct marketing

As discussed later in this chapter under the heading of advertising, direct-mail marketing is a growing means of doing overseas selling, and often means working closely with a foreign advertising firm.

State controlled trading companies

This term applies to countries where business is conducted by a few government-sanctioned and controlled trading entities.

Contract protection

Whether you decide to go with an agent or distributor a contract should be carefully drawn up which describes the territories which will be covered and under what exclusive rights and authorities. Such an agreement is discussed in more detail in Chapter 7, and the important elements are listed in Appendix A.

Promotion

A series of well-prepared news releases about new products, entry into new markets, or the hiring of new personnel can often provide just as much recognition for the new-to-market company as an ad campaign. Of course the copy must use the short and easy-to-read "news" approach, and not appear to be a sales gimmick. Media will publish news free of charge, but they want you to pay for sales related advertising.

The purpose of your market research phase was to gain the necessary information to place your product in the marketplace in the most rational way to maximize sales. After all, communications between seller and buyer whether it be the international or domestic market has always been the essence of sales success, and the major tactical elements of promotion are advertising, direct mail, and trade fairs.

Advertising

Regardless of your method of marketing, direct or indirect, you will want to maintain some degree of control over the implementation of your marketing program. Advertising is a results-oriented business function, and you want the highest yield for your invested dollar.

Your selection of a target market was based on research evidence that there was indeed a large group of customers with needs, and the ability to pay. But before you can develop a budget to implement your market program you must answer several questions.

- Is your goal immediate sales or long-term customer relationship?
- Have you decided on rapid market entry or are you happy with a steady, modest share of the market?
- What is your market? Is it distributors and wholesalers or is it direct to the target-market segment?

Developing the message

Begin with the product. Develop a list of the features of your product. Next develop a table of its benefits, satisfaction or advantages. Then compare that information to your research about the target consumers in your market. What are the uses, prices, service considerations, varieties, and maintenance needs of your product? On the consumer side look at frequency of purchase, motivation of purchase, location of purchase, income, local culture, religion, sex, and age of your consumer. Thus the systematic matching of product and features with the target market becomes the structure of the message. Now you can begin to write the copy using these comparisons to formulate appeals to your target consumer.

Of course the message must, out of necessity, be translated into the language of the target market. This will be true even if the target language is the same as yours. For instance, American English is not British English, nor is it Australian English. You need better than a word-for-word translation. Only someone intimate with the culture and language can convert the inferences, nuances, punch, and flair needed to persuade. This is even more difficult when translation is into a completely different language. Remember, on market entry you may get just one chance. If your message has an error that insults the foreign consumer or makes your company the standing joke in the local bar, it may take a long time to recover. You must be just as careful with the instructions that accompany the product so that the user is not confused about how to safely operate the equipment or software.

Media selection

Don't fall into the trap of thinking that the same media you currently use in the domestic market will necessarily prove successful in your foreign market. The media of each overseas location has reached a different stage of maturity. Most developed and semi-developed nations have a full array such as billboards, bus and trolley posters, magazines, television, radio, newspaper, point-of-sales displays. On the other hand, in less-industrialized countries the print media will be less available so you may have to rely on trade exhibits or personal selling.

Buyers of different countries often have different ways of evaluating a product. Some need to touch and see the product first hand, others will act on the written word alone, yet others need to examine catalog literature. Because of low standards of literacy in many countries, pictures displayed on buses or outdoor billboards at sporting events and along major transportation routes are extensively used.

Choosing an advertising agency

Most countries have home-based advertising agencies which handle accounts in foreign countries. On the other hand there are local foreign firms and multinational agencies with which you may wish to work. The choice is sometimes a difficult one and often determined by whether you can live with an ad campaign similar to the ads you use in your domestic advertising or whether you need it tailored to the specific target market. Certainly your budget will be a major factor in your decision. A visit to the country, discussions with local business persons, distributors, or sales agents will help you decide.

Home based

The advantage of the choice of a home based ad agency gives you the comfort of convenient communications. You have no language problem so you can talk over progress and trade copy ideas in a quick give-and-take manner. Of course this lends itself to a campaign similar to that used in the domestic market. A disadvantage may be the high overhead costs required to keep overseas offices.

Local foreign firm

A local firm may be experienced in delivering material to the target consumer in their own culture. They may already have promoted a product similar to yours. If your objective is to develop your export activities in a concentrated territory, an agency primarily specializing in that region is the better choice for both economic and service reasons. Copy developed for one country could require only minor adjustment to serve an adjacent one, thus saving the cost of starting over with a new agency in your next target market. The disadvantages may be language barriers and distance factors.

Multinational agencies

If you have selected several countries as target markets you may wish to engage a multinational agency. These firms often have a greater international perspective. If you intend, as a long-range goal, to move into markets that are significantly separated and culturally different, the multinational is logical. By choosing one centralized agency you can establish a long-term relationship and avoid the management problem of coordinating among too many external agencies.

Cooperative approach

Rather than undertaking their own campaign, many successful exporters enter into agreements with their selected trading company or overseas distributor/agents to share the costs of advertising. The advantage of the co-op method is the shared cost, and immediate familiarity with local markets and media. The disadvantage is loss of budgetary control.

Direct mail

Do some companies market their products overseas by direct mail? You bet they do and this method is growing. In many ways, for the small, new-to-export business, posting can be superior because working capital requirements are often less and budgeted funds can be dispersed in a very rational way.

Direct mail is a medium of advertising and communicating through the postal service. Marketing through the mail is fundamentally the same whether it be domestic or international. The process involves identifying the potential consumer universe within the target country and soliciting a response based on presentation of the written word through the postal system. This method has two techniques, the one-step and the two-step:

■ **One-step**. This method is designed to generate an immediate sale. A response from a qualified (interested) consumer is developed from either an advertising appeal which includes a purchase coupon, or a message sent through the postal system to a highly qualified segment of the population which also includes an order form.
■ **Two-step**. With this method an initial message either an advertisement or a message is used to generate a response from qualified (interested) consumers within a larger "unqualified" population. A second or subsequent appeal is then used to close the sale.

The key words are "response" and "qualified," because if the message does not generate a response from prospects that have a high degree of interest (qualified), the process has failed.

Almost any product or service can be sold by direct mail, but your results depend on these elements: the mailing list; the offer; and the package.

The mailing list is the most important element because in order to make sales you must send your offer to interested prospects. It is estimated that because of population mobility, most lists of names in the United States will deteriorate 20–25 percent in a given year due to bad addresses. Other countries are generally less mobile.

Next, make your offer simple and clear. Seldom do you get a second chance to explain your points when you are communicating by mail. No letter is too long if it tells the whole story and keeps the reader's attention. Make certain you write and re-write your message until anybody can understand what you're selling. In this regard let a few disinterested people read the material before you mail it.

The package is the presentation of the material to the prospect. There are no hard and fast rules, but generally the package consists of a letter, a circular or catalog, an order form and a return envelope.

■ The letter should clearly explain your offer and entice the buyer to move and not procrastinate.
■ The circular or catalog should be uncluttered and show and explain the product's uses and qualities.
■ The order form should be easy to fill out and return to you in the return envelope.

The dominant skills required for direct mail are the ability to write persuasive, compelling copy, and an understanding of statistics. By its very nature, direct marketing is like fishing in a pond. First, the right pond must be selected. That is, the universe of interested, potential consumers in the foreign country must be identified. Then the campaign must continually test the message, including price, and description of the product, until the right bait is offered that produces a sale. It cannot be overemphasized that just like fishing, this marketing tactic requires testing, over and over, until the right formula is found, and this can be measured statistically. The success of direct marketing is directly related to statistical analysis.

The start-up of a direct marketing campaign typically begins with test mailings that are no larger than that required to give a statistically measurable response.

Needless to say, a firm using this technique for the first time should not attempt to "reinvent the wheel." An axiom of this method is: go where the competition has been and use the techniques they have already pioneered. On the other hand, the fact that competitors are not using this method should not necessarily be a deterrent, but one should be suspicious.

There are a number of reasons why you would not use direct mail. The relative acceptance of direct mail varies among countries, just as does the sophistication of their postal systems. Media availability can also be a problem as can finding a pool of talented direct marketing personnel.

A successful direct mail campaign should:

- be able to flourish on statistical percentages of as small as ½ to five percent of a mail offering;
- develop a technique to generate a current qualified mailing list;
- create mailing pieces (message) based on precise information about the target universe;
- run test mailings to verify the viability of the direct-mail approach;
- refine the mail package;
- have sufficient resources (funds) to stay with a viable concept until the refinement can be evaluated;
- expand the scale of the offerings once the right message, price point, product related appeals, and mailing lists are identified.

Internet marketing

Very much like direct-mail marketing, selling on the Internet is growing in popularity. Lists of Internet addresses are available from firms that collect and sell them. The key to Internet sales is to design the written or pictorial sales piece in order to quickly catch the attention of the net surfer. On the other hand, wide advertising of your firm's Internet address will bring the customer to your "home page" from which you can offer your products by way of innovative sales promotions.

Trade fairs

By their very nature some products need to be seen by potential customers. The flip side to that notion is no matter how much market research you do, it will not tell you everything you need to know about your product's reception in a foreign country.

There is no substitute for taking the product to the market. Advertising, sales letters, brochures, and other literature are helpful, but observation of the consumer reactions must be a major tactic in any marketing effort. Trade shows, fairs, and missions provide that opportunity. They are today's "window on the market." The concept is not new. Most Asian and European countries have been doing them for centuries. By their very nature they provide a unique opportunity for communicating with a large number of potential buyers in a personal, one-on-one environment. They also give you an opportunity to gather intelligence about competitors.

Trade shows, like advertising, are results oriented. From the beginning, because you want the highest yield for your invested dollar, you should develop a method of measuring results. The data you will need is:

- cost per visitor;
- number of leads;
- sales per lead;
- total sales at the show;
- sales as a result of the show;
- number of prospects invited versus those that attend;
- comments from attendees;
- a comparison of your effort vis-à-vis your competitors.

Planning for the show

Begin your efforts with result measurement in mind. The key elements of preparing for a trade show are:

- **Check it out**. When time permits, first attend a trade show as an observer.
- **Where to exhibit**. From your market research you will already know where your industry shows are held and which ones are most popular. Some specialize in specific products, others promote a range. Inspect lists of previous attendees to be certain your target market (decision-making units (DMUs)) are likely to be at the one you select.
- **Develop a timetable**. Include the dates for completion of: show space reservations; booth shipment; set-up date; carnet application; pre-show campaign; travel reservations; hotel reservations.
- **Pre-show campaign**. Advertise your participation several weeks before the show. Send press releases, flyers, and even formal invitations to potential customers.

- **Apply for a carnet**. This document, arranged through the Council for International Business, eliminates the need to pay tariffs or post bonds for the temporary importation of professional equipment and commercial samples. This should be done at least three weeks in advance. (see ATA carnet in Chapter 8).
- **Booth size**. Your investment in the design of a booth is for the long term. Be sure that it assembles, packs, and ships easy. When installed it should be large enough to comfortably accommodate several people.
- **Booth location**. Attempt to position your booth on main aisles and near the entrance where the traffic flow is the highest. These locations cost more but the return in terms of leads and sales contacts yield the highest results.
- **Literature development**. Keep your general literature simple, but informative. Use plenty of pictures and diagrams. Above all, make certain it is done in the local language.
- **Coordination with distributors**. When you can, bring your distributors into your booth. Make them feel a part of the team. As a minimum cut them in on your plans and get their input.

Results

The show is over and you're exhausted. You go immediately to the Riviera for several weeks rest. Right? No, wrong! Now the real work begins. The follow-up period is when sales are made. Get a list of the shows attendees. Compare that with the list of leads you developed at your booth. Needless to say every person your booth team made contact with needs to be contacted in some way, if only by a follow-up sales letter. However, many potential contacts on the attendee list never got to your booth, yet they may be the very people you should contact. Remind them of your presence at the show and send them the literature they missed.

Only after the follow-up period has been exhausted can you rest on your laurels and develop the statistical analysis to determine your success. go back to your original measuring method and lay out the numbers. Don't be blinded by the beauty of the venue. It's all about results.

Phase II: the action stage

Don't let your plan sit on a shelf where all your hard work never gets executed. Now the fun begins—executing the plan—your efforts should not be random.

The systems approach

The marketing process should be visualized as "system" wherein a set of predetermined inputs (market tactics) are measured and acted upon in such a way that the inputs are continually changed as conditions change. In the international marketplace these tactics are sometimes affected by external as well as internal conditions. The strongest of the firms participating in the international marketplace retain a flexibility about their efforts which allows them to react to these changing conditions. A systems approach is recommended so that when you are finished the results can be *measured*. To do this I recommend a four-step method:

1 budgeting;
2 measuring results;
3 correcting tactics;
4 contingency plans.

Budgeting

A strategic market plan is a "wish list" developed by your marketing staff, a consultant, or intermediary. It represents every method they would like to use to get the product to the target market. But few firms can satisfy all tactical elements in terms of resources. Marketing must stand in line alongside research and development (R&D) and production for its fair share of the company's funds. This is when the best planners prioritize the elements of their plan in terms of results. Select from your total plan those elements that you think will bring the greatest, fastest return—for cash flow. Don't give up on the rest of your plan. Execute it as funds come available.

Measuring results

The elements of every strategic plan must, from the beginning, be developed in such a way that they can be measured in terms of actual sales success. Statistical analysis should drive every step of the marketing plan. Every advertising campaign, every trade show, every distributor must have measurable, quantitative, statistical check points that determine sales success.

Correcting market tactics

Keep in mind that marketing tactics are never "locked in concrete." In fact the most important thing you should understand about success in winning the trade game, is that just like the battle field, the six Ps are in a state of almost constant change.

The development of any strategic market plan must have safety valves. That is, in case one marketing tactic doesn't work, where do we go from here? For instance if advertising doesn't bring in the desired sales results through the media, of one target market, there must be some thought to redirecting those funds to a distribution network or the hiring of agents.

Contingency plans

Every plan should have a set of contingencies or activities, based on a set of "what ifs." Those decisions will not be based on conjecture or emotion, but rather on hard statistical data related to income and profit over a predetermined time objective.

Examples of a contingency plan in international marketing might be:

- If sales in a certain country do not meet your return on investment criteria, turn your product over to a local agent.
- At a certain sales level you will consider severing your ties with an intermediary and establishing your own marketing subsidiary.

Summary

International marketing is, in the eyes of decision makers of many Quadrant 4 firms, an awesome mental picture—the major obstacle to tapping growing market opportunities. But if the activity is approached logically and rationally there are sufficient alternatives such that any company should be able to enter foreign markets.

The next chapter explains how to market services.

CHAPTER SIX

Export your services

The service sector is the fundamental keystone to the U.S. economy and our ability as a nation to compete.
John Reed, Chairman and CEO, Citicorp and Citibank

The international services market over the past 40 years has exploded. Worldwide it has grown to become a multi-billion dollar business. In many countries services has surpassed farming, manufacturing, and mining as the dominant employer. As an example, services, including government, now accounts for more than two-thirds of the United States' gross national product (GNP). Approximately 70 percent of all employment, let me repeat, 70 percent of all Americans, work in a service industry.

This chapter explains the kinds of service businesses that lend themselves to the international marketplace, and how to compete.

What services can be exported?

Almost all research and development (R&D) is done by the developed nations. Much of the professional and technical know-how emanates from the industrial nations and is in high demand for transfer to less developed countries. Many new products, concepts, and procedures being developed are directly applicable to the environments of these countries, particularly in food processing, medical services, agriculture, water resources development, education, and housing.

Your business could be technical consulting; management consulting; legal services; advertising; information; accounting; computer hardware or software; telecommunications; most kinds of insurance; construction and engineering, or several not on this list, which are being marketed on a global basis. To get your thinking juices flowing let's discuss a few.

Data services

Some call it the information age because data processing services are crucial to individuals and to the operations of businesses, governments and educational organizations. Data processing is used to deliver vital records such as census, death, birth, payroll checks, and the list goes on. Overseas, major data-processing companies have international operations, but smaller firms are moving to compete.

There are barriers to overseas growth that the data service company should be aware of, such as telecommunications regulations, and restrictions on the content of transborder information and data flows.

Health care

Coincident with post World War II industrial growth has come a rising standard of living and a demand for better private and public health care service. Commitment to upgrade medical and health care has brought an upsurge of modern medical equipment as well as buying the know-how to manage health delivery systems.

Venture capital

The story goes that the first venture capital project that affected the United States of America was when Queen Isabella of Spain financed Christopher Columbus. Since that time venture capital has become the instrument for much of the world's development and industrialization. The current boom developed during the 1970s and 1980s as a result of improved national tax laws and has proven to be the engine of new growth, particularly in high-tech industries. Recognizing venture capital as the locomotive of innovation, most countries have reached out to the venture capital industry. Consequently many venture capital supplying firms are looking into overseas opportunities where the rewards will match the risk.

Entertainment

Worldwide distribution of the pre-recorded music and motion picture industry, including feature entertainment, television films, video tapes, video cassettes, CDs, and video discs is dependent on foreign markets as valuable sources of income. Companies serving the entertainment industry should be aware of trade barriers such as import quotas, subsidies, excessive taxes, and a recent upsurge in piracy resulting from new technologies such as video recorders and cable and satellite television which make duplication and interception easy. Nevertheless, international competition is growing daily, especially digitized satellite and Internet delivery.

Life insurance

Foreign premiums for life insurers are expected to grow at double-digit rates in the decades ahead. Because insurance is a heavily regulated industry, it is critical to research each country's laws and attitudes. Nevertheless there are solid business opportunities for those who have patience and are innovative.

Management consulting

This category includes training and supervision of personnel, management of facilities, economic and business research, finance, market analysis, strategic planning, and other management services. Governments, private industry, and other organizations hire these firms for a fee or on a contract basis. The international activity of management and consulting services firms has grown rapidly in recent years and will continue to prosper. Net foreign receipts for consulting and technical services increased at an average annual rate of over 20 percent between 1978 and 1985. Like other service industries, expansion overseas is sometimes impeded by non-tariff trade barriers such as ownership restrictions, foreign exchange controls and discriminatory taxation policies, all of which require innovative business operations.

Franchising

The factors that have spurred the growth of franchising are new jobs, increased numbers of entrepreneurs, and fresh services. This has also propelled its movement into overseas markets. The future will see an increase in the variety and growth. In general, foreign laws and regulations have not been overly restrictive, since franchising tends to foster ownership and employment.

Travel and tourism

Tourism might already be the world's largest industry. Worldwide tourism receipts exceed $200 billion and for many countries it is a major source of foreign exchange earnings translating into a booming service industry in terms of travel, lodging and restaurant-related businesses as well as such spin-offs as rental cars, and foods and beverages .

Business services

Advertising, accounting, construction and engineering continues to show a surplus of export activity for firms operating overseas. In addition to a continuing growth projected in the developed world, there is much contract work available in Third-World nations and it is often financed with the help of international development organizations.

Breaking in

Given that a company is established in the domestic market and has the resources, the first step is some early "homework."

What is going to be offered overseas? Some minor working capital outlay and time should be allocated to determine the price, delivery, quality, warranty, and after-sales blended into a thoughtful desirable offering. Keep in mind that distances, communications, language, culture, and government regulations are some of the forces that play a part in the offered package.

As a rule of thumb, if a service is competitive in the domestic market, then it may have some overseas potential.

The excitement of entering "exotic" markets could push your service firm into the international arena before you are ready. As a general rule, a firm in a given service industry should be mature in the domestic market before attempting to go overseas. It is important to take a realistic view of the firm's financial, management, and personnel resources. Unless there is a reasonably stable foundation, the firm may not be ready. Unlike trading a mechanical product, often the costs to get a soft product into a foreign country are higher than in the domestic market.

How to organize

Large service companies, such as the accounting firms have been in the overseas market for many years. Nevertheless there is room for the growing smaller firm, and many go it alone. In order to compete it may be necessary to network a group of specialized companies into a cohesive organization. Many organizational forms can be used; however, for a group of local service companies, an export association (see Chapter 4) could be considered a valuable method to market services worldwide.

Personnel

In the early stages of developing an international service business most firms assign the responsibility to a project manager (PM) who becomes an expert in the new market and brings the information to the corporate organization and line managers.

The project manager is also usually assigned to be the manager of competitive proposals and as such sees the venture through to the successful end. PMs are often given profit and loss responsibility as well as the authority to select and assign employees.

It is not unusual that experienced personnel from the parent company kick-off a venture in a new country; however, soon after start-up, foreign hires are often brought into the operation. The benefits are market, culture, and language knowledge as well as the wise suggestion to the host country that the firm is a good citizen and intends a home identity.

The market plan

A market plan, based on sound market research, should lay out the country or countries the firm intends to penetrate, in terms of sequence, and market communications methods. For instance, your service may require procurement decisions. In one city decisions may lie with a committee, in another the decision-making unit (DMU) may be the mayor, i.e. he or she may be the sole fiscal authority. Sales people can gather this information from their own experiences in dealing with customers. In the international marketplace, unless the service firm already has a sales force presence, it may be necessary to include in the plan the development of a relationship with some local representative, client, or associate. The plan should follow the basic outline given in Chapter 5 and include some understanding of the competition, both domestic and by other international firms. The resultant plan will lead to an estimated budget, which will be necessary to gain top management approval.

Market research

Again, intelligence is the prerequisite for a plan designed for successful penetration of a new market. Service firms should have a clear understanding of foreign business environments and potential customers before committing themselves to the international marketplace. The need to invest time and money in market research cannot be over emphasized.

Step one

What are your goals?

Step two

Locate the regions and nations with the best potential to reach those goals. In other words where are the best market/buyer segments?

Step three

Analyze the international barriers and learn the DMUs of the service. To get the answers to these big questions, service companies often must piece together information gleaned from a number of different sources.

Unlike data about manufactured products, comprehensive data about services in many countries is often not available. Therefore, services must often use the concept called "derived demand."

Derived demand

Demand for a service buyer's industrial end product or consumer good determines that buyer's need and desire for those services and equipments, which enable the firm to produce the product.

Two methods are used to arrive at derived demand: "complementary" and "substitute." By examining trends in complementary or substitute product areas that are closely linked to their expertise, consultants and other service industry firms can often determine their best overseas markets.

Complementary

Examples of complementary product areas might be:

- A service company that provides clean overalls, rags, and smocks on a turn-around basis would examine machinery and hardware sales in order to find the DMU of the end-user market.
- Suppliers of computer software can utilize the trade statistics which show flows of computer hardware.
- An agricultural consultant dealing in farm management might analyze sales of tractors, farm chemicals, and irrigation equipment.

Substitute

Substitute product indicators are sometimes harder to find and may not always lend themselves to the services area. Examples might be:

- A company with a new industrial technology which negates the need for certain raw materials would search for markets where those raw materials are now being sold.
- Firms in a certain country are using obsolete methods, and it can be shown that your product can speed up the process and be more efficient and cost effective.

The bottom line of your research should be to answer the question: Is it feasible or desirable to expand into the overseas market?

Key elements to win bids

Much of the world's services are used by governments, and as a result of new WTO rules these kinds of contracts are becoming more competitive. There is a gamesmanship to winning government contracts and subcontracts no matter what country makes the offer.

Types of bid instruments

Most countries use procedures that are similar. They issue such advertisements as IFBs and RFPs.

IFB (invitation for bids)

These bid instruments are the simplest and fastest means for a government to make purchases of either manufactured goods or services. Awards are ordinarily made to the lowest bidder. Formal advertisement is made through one or more of the public publications described later.

RFP (request for proposals)

These are used when a government wants a contractor to design the product or service and depends heavily on the skills of the contractor. In these cases governments cannot afford to rely on only the lowest bid because there are often technical requirements which also must be met. Generally RFPs are in two parts: (1) the technical proposal; and (2) the cost proposal. Governments evaluate the technical proposal before cost is considered. Usually those contractors that are technically competent are then asked for a best and final offer.

Two-step procurements

This is the method used by some governments to get the most technically qualified bidder at the lowest price. It usually goes like this. A government first asks for technical proposals without pricing. Once those with the best technical proposals are determined, a second proposal is submitted as a sealed bid.

Sole source

Sole-source procurements bypass normal competitive bidding processes and allow a government agency to give the project to one contractor. These can be justified when:

■ There is only one source for a highly specialized product or service or it is proprietary.
■ The skills or qualifications are unique and no one else can do the job less expensively.
■ An emergency exists and a purchase must be made in less time than a normal offering would allow.

Unsolicited

Contractors can submit a proposal for a sole source award. These must be for things that are unique and proprietary.

Bidders mailing lists

In addition to monitoring publications where you might find advertisements for the service your firm offers, you can write to appropriate agencies in other governments and get on their bidders lists. Sometimes these lists represent those companies that have met some pre-qualification requirements, thus representing a "blue ribbon" list of contractors.

Strategy

The keys to winning contracts are: understand the bid process; then develop an appropriate strategy. The submission of a bid in response to an IFB or RFP is as much a sales effort as if you were selling a product in the market. As stated earlier, gamesmanship or proposalship wins bids, not through luck, but rather through an intelligent, persuasive effort.

Most of your competitors will be able to show that they can do the job, but to win the contract you must show, using compelling evidence, that you are the best contractor for the *client*.

The minimums

Your proposal must at least:

- **Be timely**. Bid must be to the agency that advertised no later than the exact time set to open the bids.
- **Conform** to the requirements and specifications of the offer. Don't impose new conditions.
- **Minimize clerical and technical mistakes**. Some governments allow for opportunities to correct, but for some, they are grounds for disqualification.

Beyond the minimums

Capturing the bid means more than just being able to do the job. Your proposal must be organized for the greatest impact to the reader, show how you are more technically qualified, must appear to be within the ball-park for cost, and must include a counter to what you believe will be the competitor's proposal. Above all, it must take into account cultural and language differences.

Summary

The services sector of every national economy offers big profits. As the globalization of business grows so will the opportunities to export services. Good intelligence, a well-drafted plan, and timeliness are the essentials.

The next chapter reveals the dos and don'ts of international business behavior country by country.

PART TWO

Tricks of trade

CHAPTER SEVEN

The transaction from A to Z

Ah, but a man's reach should exceed his grasp,
Or what's a heaven for?

Robert Browning

Transactions don't happen automatically. Even though you executed your export marketing plan and made your product or service available for a foreign sale, nothing is complete until the product is shipped and the money is in the bank.

The purpose of this chapter is to show the steps that take place from beginning to end, not necessarily in the order they always happen.

Quotations

Sales usually begin after your marketing effort has stirred interest in someone in a foreign country, someone who can say "YES, I'll buy." An inquiry could come by telephone, facsimile, letter, or e-mail or it may be in the form of a request for proposal (RFP), request for information (RFI), or a request for bid (RFB). This is an invitation to send more information about the service or product and leads to negotiations. On the other hand, you may be fortunate enough to receive a purchase order.

Bids

Sometimes the RFP, RFI, or RFQ is issued to more than one exporter (seller) and in that case your quote will be competing with others for the importer's (buyer's) best price, quality, and delivery criteria.

The proforma invoice

You, the seller, may make an offer in the form of a proforma invoice which describes the commercial qualities of the thing you wish to sell. The proforma does not always end up in a sale. The buyer, may, and often does, make a counter offer on some or all of the terms and so the negotiations begin, eventually leading to the contract. The terms and conditions of your proforma should include essentially the same elements that would be found in a contract which become the exact elements of a letter of credit, word for word:

- description;
- unit price;
- quantity;
- delivery;
- technical specifications;
- discounts;
- shipping costs;
- delivery time;
- payment terms;
- terms of sale;
- procedures such as deposits, and letters of credit requirements.

Checklist for preparing export quotations

The easiest, safest, most understandable means of submitting quotations to foreign customers is in the form of "proforma" invoices. As much of the following data as possible should be listed on the proforma invoice, or in your bid quotation, since in foreign trade a "quotation" is sometimes considered as a binding and valid contract.

1 Always show the exact name of the buyer.
2 Give a short, detailed description of the merchandise—state unit price per item & total price.
3 Indicate estimated pieces and weight of shipment.
4 Specify mode of transportation (air-ocean).
  A. Give destination—ocean port or airport.
  B. State whether trans-shipments and/or partial shipments are allowed.
5 State terms of payment (letter of credit, sight draft, etc.).
  A. If letter of credit:
    —advise through and negotiable at specified financial institution
    —place of reimbursable
    —all bank charges for buyer's account
    —state whether or not confirmation is required
  B. If sight draft, request draft be presented through specified financial institution.
  C. If to be paid by wire, contact your bank for appropriate instructions.
6 State terms of sale (FOB, EX WORKS, CIF, C&F, etc.).
7 Give approximate shipping date after receipt of confirmed order.
8 State time frame the proforma invoice is valid (30 days, 60 days, etc.).

Negotiations

Negotiations in cross-border trade are to be expected. There is no international fixed price system for goods or services. Keep in mind that you and the buyer want to "do business," why else would they inquire and why else would you offer? Never take a "rock hard" negotiating position—to the extent you wish to sell your product to the buyer, it is in your interest to keep negotiations active, open, and informal until there is agreement and the buyer says "yes." You may have to retreat on your terms and the buyer may also have to yield something. Keep in mind the other person's culture (see Chapter 9). Negotiations are complete when each feels "good" that they are achieving their ends. Then and only then should the contract be formalized.

The contract

Do people agree to informal contracts based on another person's word, a hand shake, or gentleman's agreement? Of course they do! But ... only when a level of "trust" has been achieved based on having done reliable business over a reasonable period of time. The word of an international trader has been, historically, a bond never to be broken. In our modern world where so much trade is done across borders, there are instances where the trader's bond has eroded. Flim-flam artists exist in every country. Back up your intuition with good research about those with whom you do business.

A formal contract may be a simple purchase order or a complex written document requiring a lawyer's review of each word.

Keep in mind that the contract serves several purposes. It is a record of the agreement to purchase. It is also the foundation document to establish a letter of credit, and serves as a legal document upon which disputes (heaven forbid) will be adjudicated. Don't sign a contract that describes the agreement in general terms—be precise. Spell out all the details of a commercial contract such as payment, delivery, terms of sale, etc. (see list given under proforma invoice section above). For those unfamiliar with cross-border transactions, the International Chamber of Commerce (ICC) offers an excellent model document for international sales contracts.

The extent to which an attorney, well grounded in international contracts, is needed for your transaction depends to a certain extent on the value of the sale. For a small transaction where the financial risks are minimal you may make the business decision to ship without advice and hope all goes well. On the other hand, should you be shipping a container or several containers full of very valuable goods, worth millions, it makes good business sense to let an attorney have a look. Of major importance is the applicable national law that is agreed to as an element of the

Figure 7.1 The Winding Road to Contract

contract. Based on this element, a court would first decide whether or not it has jurisdiction. Depending on the countries of the buyer and seller involved there may very well be entirely different legal theories (see Chapter 13). Most international traders believe the only winners in a commercial contract dispute are the lawyers involved. It is better that the contract call out "arbitration" to be adjudicated by a commercial arbitrating body such as one administered according to the International Chamber of Commerce (ICC) Rules for Arbitration and Conciliation. Figure 7.1 shows the typical winding road from start to finish toward a contract.

Terms of sale

By terms of sale we mean the standard nomenclature (EXW, FOB, CIF, etc.) by which exporters and importers worldwide agree to the geographical location where risks and costs of the sale begin and end for each party. These terms, negotiable between buyer and seller, have been developed over hundreds of years of trading and in general are well understood by business professionals. Every nation's Commercial Code or equivalent explains a set of standard commercial terms for doing business in that nation; however, when doing business across borders domestic methods may vary. Over time a set of standard terms have evolved such that people in different countries doing business at arm's length understand. The purpose is to remove uncertainties of different interpretations of such terms in different countries and lessen misunderstandings that lead to disputes and litigation. These terms have been codified by the International Chamber of Commerce (ICC) and published in both English and French in a small soft cover book and a computer software program titled *International Commercial Terms* or INCOTERMS. The book and software can be ordered directly from the ICC.

Let's discuss a hypothetical situation. Consider you are a buyer in Germany doing business with a seller in China. The seller makes a quotation which describes the standard commercial qualities of the product in question. The price to you, the buyer, may be quoted at the factory, or on board a ship, or at some geographical place in the world. In order for you to know all the costs a specific geographical place must be specified, how else would you know the total costs involved in the transaction and whether or not a profit can be made on its sale. There may be several reasons for negotiating these terms. One side may have a better arrangement with maritime transport. The other may have a long-standing relationship with a certain shipper. We make these arrangements using "terms of sale" and there are several options.

Although there are *13* different INCOTERMS, Figure 7.2 shows six of the most common. To be on the safe side the full text as found in INCOTERMS should be reviewed.

- **EXW or Ex Works.** The seller quotes the goods at his dock (premises). This means that the buyer, in addition to paying the agreed price, is responsible for all risks and cost from the seller's place of business to the ultimate destination. In other words the seller is not responsible for loading, clearing for export or transportation. The buyer must bear all the risks and costs involved in taking the goods from the seller's premises to the eventual foreign location.
- **FAS or Free Alongside Ship.** The seller's quote includes the risk and costs related to placing the goods alongside the vessel on the quay near the named vessel in a named port. The buyer assumes all risks and costs from that point to final destination.

Figure 7.2 Terms of Sale
Where the Risks and Costs Begin and End

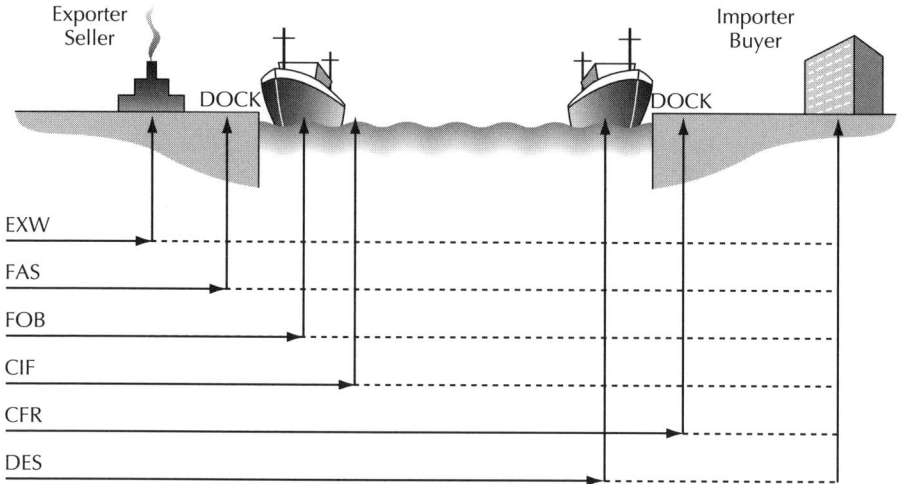

- **FOB or Free On Board.** This means that the seller's quote includes the costs and his acceptance of the risks until the goods are delivered over the ship's rail at the named port.
- **CFR or Cost and Freight.** The quotation means the seller will include payment of the costs and freight and acceptance of the risk to bring the goods to the port of destination.
- **CIF or Cost, Insurance, and Freight.** In this case the seller quotes the price to ship the goods to a named port of destination and includes the cost of maritime insurance.
- **DES or Delivered Ex Ship.** The seller offers in the quote to make the goods available to the buyer on board the ship at the named port of destination, not yet cleared for import.

Pricing

The price of your product should be high enough to generate a suitable profit but low enough to be competitive. Profit is a decision internal to the firm and varies from product to product, industry to industry, and within the market channel. Desirable profit relates to the goals of the export business. For instance, one company's objective might be to just penetrate one or two markets, another might have an aim to expand their business to eventually become a player in many foreign markets. In general, pricing should be based on long-run profit-maximizing objectives. Market share and volumes should be targeted for the long-term export commitment. If a product is entirely new to the market or has unique

Figure 7.3 Market Channel

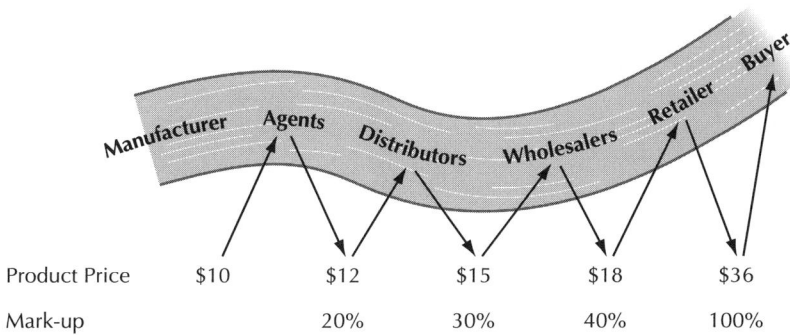

Product Price	$10	$12	$15	$18	$36
Mark-up		20%	30%	40%	100%

features, you may be able to command higher prices. On the other hand, to gain a foothold in a very competitive market, marginal cost pricing is often used.

Market channel

Each step along the market channel has a cost. Picture the channel as just that—a river running across the industry that begins with the manufacturer and ends with the buyer. In between there are agents, brokers, distributors, wholesalers, and retailers all trying to make a living off a percentage of the product's price. Figure 7.3 shows the various channel functions with hypothetical mark-ups.

Marginal cost pricing

Marginal cost pricing is the technique of setting the market entry price at or just above the threshold at which the firm would incur a loss. (Under WTO rules it is illegal to dump, that is, gain market share by incurring a loss).

Cross-border pricing

It is important that you understand not only the elements that make up your price but also those of your overseas trading associate. Remember there are no "free lunches;" everything has a cost. There are costs to produce the product, costs to sell it, and costs to move the goods.

Most new exporters simply use their domestic factory price and negotiate freight, packing, insurance, etc. using INCOTERMS. Prices may be quoted in the currency of the buyer or the seller.

Figure 7.4 illustrates how the selling price in one country becomes the buying price in the other. Typical export middleman commission

Figure 7.4 Cross-Border Pricing Model.

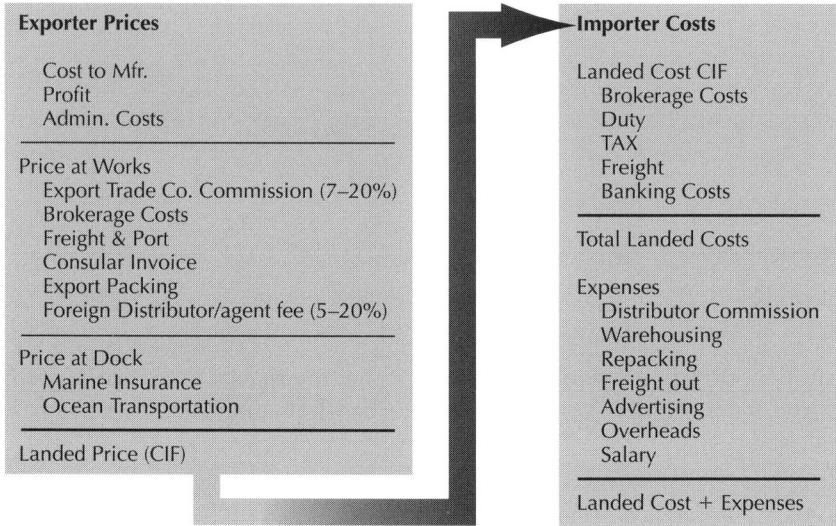

Exporter Prices	Importer Costs
Cost to Mfr.	Landed Cost CIF
Profit	Brokerage Costs
Admin. Costs	Duty
	TAX
Price at Works	Freight
Export Trade Co. Commission (7–20%)	Banking Costs
Brokerage Costs	
Freight & Port	Total Landed Costs
Consular Invoice	
Export Packing	Expenses
Foreign Distributor/agent fee (5–20%)	Distributor Commission
	Warehousing
Price at Dock	Repacking
Marine Insurance	Freight out
Ocean Transportation	Advertising
	Overheads
Landed Price (CIF)	Salary
	Landed Cost + Expenses

percentages are negotiable between seven and 20 percent. A foreign distributor or agent may ask commissions between five and 20 percent. The key commission issues are the price of the product and the number of units (sales volume) that you can sell. If, for instance, the product commands a high unit sales price the commission percentage may be quite low. Remember, a small percentage of a million dollar sale can be very good business.

Costing out and price in

Costing out and price in means calculate all your costs then compare that to the market price of the product in the country where you wish to sell it, the difference is your profit. If there is insufficient profit at the *volumes* (number of units) you wish to sell to make it worthwhile you may have to review your costs and sharpen your pencil.

Cargo insurance

Cargo insurance compensates the *owner* of goods transported by sea, air or land shipments in the event of loss that would not be legally recovered from the carrier. It can cover the goods from warehouse to warehouse or any portion between. Insurance is sometimes split between the risk takers, wherein each party covers that portion for which they are the at-risk insurable party. Great care must be taken when splitting that there are no gaps. The amount and responsibility for insurance depends on common business sense and the contract as well as INCOTERM agreed to. Traders may arrange their own insurance or have their forwarder arrange it for them. In some cases the insurance may be for a specific shipment or it may be "open" or "floating" giving "blanket" coverage for a number of shipments over a period of time.

Insurance varies in cost from the most expensive, road or rail which is sometimes as much as two percent of the value of the goods, to the least expensive, air transport at about 0.3 percent. Sea shipments are usually about 0.6 to 0.7 percent.

Recovery of loss goes to the party with insurable risk, which is usually the owner, but might be a party who has undertaken a segment of the risk of shipment. For instance two of the INCOTERMs, CIF and CIP, impose a contractual responsibility upon the exporter to insure at a minimum level regardless of ownership. Under all other INCOTERMs there is no contractual responsibility—only common business sense that you interest and the goods are protected.

Tariffs

Tariffs (synonymous with "duty") are by definition a tax at the border collected on an *ad valorem* (percentage) of the transaction value based as shown on the invoice at the time of crossing. In the vast majority of cases a tariff is collected from the importer on incoming goods, but theoretically they could be collected on outgoing (exports) as well. For instance, at one point the former Soviet Union placed heavy taxes on outgoing goods, ostensibly to control certain special materials.

■ Hot tip

Some say the word tariff comes from the Arabic term for inventory, which is *ta'rif*. On the other hand the French word, *tarif*, as well as the Spanish word *tarifa* means price list or rate book. Folklore tells us that the word originated about 700 A.D. Near Gibraltar there is a village named Tarifa. Supposedly a small band of pirates operating from there had as their prey every merchant ship passing through the narrow channel. Each ship captain had to pay a handsome sum of money before the vessel could proceed through the channel. Over time, seamen began calling the money they were forced to pay, a tariff.

Tariffs are collected for two reasons: as a deterrent to competition in order to shield home industries and to provide a share of government revenues. In most countries, tariffs serve both purposes and are a preferred method under the World Trade Organization (WTO) because tariffs are more visible and apt to be more fair than other barriers. Some countries go so far as specifying certain tariff schedule duties as "protective," others as "revenue" duties.

In as much as all countries use a border tariff it has become very transparent, that is each nation has adopted a loose-leaf book or computerized method which shows their schedule of duties to anyone. Most countries have even joined the Customs Cooperation Council (CCC) formerly known as the Brussels Tariff Nomenclature (BTN) and adopted the Harmonized Commodity Description and Coding System, thus tariffs have become even more transparent. The Harmonized System standardizes the nomenclature/numbering structure making it easier to do business across borders.

Historically, there have been conditions and historical periods when average tariffs worldwide exceeded 40–50 percent. However, after many multi-lateral rounds of the General Arrangement for Tariffs and Trade (GATT), global tariffs have been significantly reduced.

Quotas

Quotas are quantitative restrictions shown in the Harmonized Tariff Schedule which may ban or limit the volume of goods entering a given country. They are principally a method to protect certain industries, most notably textiles/apparels. Through bilateral and multilateral agreements a quota scheme exists among those nations involved in these highly competitive industries employing less-costly labor. The Multifiber Arrangement (MFA) coordinates and provides a basis against disruptive imports.

Because they are listed in the Harmonized Schedule quantitative restrictions or quotas are a very transparent means of controlling the entry of products at the border. Quotas include complete bans on the import or export of specific commodities as well as import and export quotas which limit the volume. They differ from tariffs in that they affect the quantity of goods permitted to enter the customs territory. Typically they are divided into two types: absolute and tariff-rate.

Absolute

An "absolute quota" limits the quantity of goods that enter in a specific period. Some are global while others are allocated to specific countries. Typically, because absolute quotas are filled at, or shortly after, the beginning of the quota period, they are usually opened at a specific time on the first work day of the quota so all importers have the same opportunity for simultaneous presentation of their entries. If a quantity of quota merchandise offered at entry exceeds the quota, the commodity is released on a pro rata basis (i.e. the ratio between the quota quantity and the total quantity offered for entry). If not filled at the opening, quotas are filled on a "first-come, first-served" basis. Imports in excess of quota are typically warehoused for entry during the next quota period.

Tariff-rate quotas

Tariff-rate quotas permit a specified quantity of imported merchandise to be entered at a reduced rate of customs duty during the quota period. There is no limitation on the amount of the quota product that may be entered at any time, but quantities entered during the quota period in excess of the quota for that period are subject to higher duty rates.

Export controls

The presumption of most nations is: goods are free to export unless there is an explicit, transparent statement of a need to control. However, most, if not all, nations have export control laws. Export control laws are designed to protect a country's national security and protect the domestic economy from the excessive drain of scarce materials. They generally require a license.

The history of export controls in the United States is based on the presumption that all exported goods and technical documentation are subject to licensing regulation by the government—this is fundamentally different than most countries. Therefore, the public regulation of international sales from America are often more onerous than elsewhere.

In addition to individual national controls, members of the North Atlantic Treaty Organization (NATO) are limited in their transfer of war-related technology. The exercise of controls by NATO varies from non-existent (as in the case of other members) to total embargoes (as in the cases of North Korea and Cuba).

Export controls are usually organized on a document called the Commodity Control List (CCL) according to country or by item. Some, however, focus more generally, such as those that advance human rights, or those prohibiting doing business with those who boycott for ethnic or political reasons.

Freight forwarders

There are two types of freight forwarders: ocean and air, though most freight forwarding businesses can do both. A freight forwarder is a private service company licensed to support shippers and the movement of their goods. These specialists in international physical distribution (logistics) act as an agent for the exporter (shipper) in moving cargo to an overseas destination. They are familiar with:

- the import rules and regulations of foreign countries;
- methods of shipping;

- government export regulations;
- documents connected with foreign trade.

Freight forwarders assist by advising such things as freight costs, consular fees, and insurance costs. They can recommend the degree of packing, arrange for an inland carrier, find the best airline, and even arrange for the containerization. They quote shipping rates, provide information, and book cargo space. These firms are invaluable because they can handle everything from the factory to the final destination, including all documentation, storage, and shipping insurance, as well as routing your cargo at the lowest customs charges. Often freight forwarders are called upon to help an exporter put together the final price quotation to a distributor. For example, when quoting CIF, in addition to the manufacturer's price and the commission, the forwarder can provide information on dock and cartage fees, forwarder's fees, marine insurance, ocean freight costs, duty charges, consular invoice fees, and packing charges.

Shipper

You do not have to be a licensed freight forwarder to arrange movement of goods on behalf of your own shipments. Caution; don't act as a forwarder for someone else before being issued a license. Any person whose primary business is the sale of merchandise may, without a license, dispatch and perform freight-forwarding services on behalf of their own shipments, or on behalf of shipments or consolidated shipments of a parent, subsidiary, affiliate, or associated company. You may not, however, receive compensation from the common carrier.

A large manufacturer usually has its own shipping department which serves as its own freight forwarder, but smaller manufacturing firms and small intermediaries seldom have either the staff or the time to make their own arrangements. It's not unusual (and may be quite prudent) to review a price quotation with the freight forwarder before putting it on the telex.

Customs brokers

Like the freight forwarder for exporting, the customs broker is a private service company licensed to assist importers in the movement of their goods.

Formal entries of foreign-made goods representing many billions in tariff collections are filed each year with the customs service, and virtually all of them are prepared by customs brokers on behalf of importers. Some brokers are sole proprietors with a single office at one port of entry, while others are large corporations with branches in many ports throughout the country, but all are licensed and regulated by the government.

The importer employs the customs broker as their agent and frequently is their only point of contact with the government. A broker advises on the technical requirements of importing, preparing, and filing entry documents, obtaining the necessary bonds, depositing import duties, securing release of the product(s), and arranging delivery to the importer's premises or warehouse and obtaining "drawback" refunds. The broker often consults with customs to determine the proper rate of duty or basis of appraisement and on many occasions, if dissatisfied with either rate or value, will pursue appropriate administrative remedies on behalf of the importer.

Bonds

In most countries importers must post a *surety bond* with the customs service to ensure payment of the proper amounts of duties, taxes and other charges associated with entry are paid. Bonds can be for single entry or continuous (term). Based on the value of the shipment, customs determine the value of the required bond. Often they require a bond three times the value of the shipment.

Drawback

Drawback is the refunding of tariffs paid on imported goods and their derivatives if they are subsequently exported. Some examples are: suppose you simply re-export goods that were originally imported; or you export items that contain imported merchandise; or export items that contain whole imported components. For each of these you might claim a drawback of tariffs paid when imported. The key to drawback is good inventory tracking and record-keeping procedures. Make application for drawback with your local customs port of entry office.

Physical distribution (international transport)

Physical distribution, often referred to as *logistics*, is the means by which goods are moved from the manufacturer in one country to the customer in another. Modern exporters have an extraordinary selection of means to move their goods: from multimodal, where the cargo travels sequentially aboard several modes (air, sea, road and rail) to its destination, to single modes, principally ship or airplane—and the correct selection can make the difference between a profitable venture and one that is not.

A shipper can directly arrange their own land, ocean, and air shipping of international cargo. International transportation is handled much the same as a domestic transaction, except that certain export marks must be added to the standard information shown on a domestic bill of lading and instructions to the inland carrier to notify the ocean or air carrier must also be included. Regardless of the type of carrier you use, the carrier will issue a booking contract, which reserves space on a specific ship. Unless you cancel in advance, you may be required to pay even if your cargo doesn't make the sailing.

Loading brokers

Using charter vessels is possible only when shipping very large quantities. Loading brokers, also known in some countries as non-vessel owning common carriers (NVOCC) or shippers associations, reduce costs by grouping small shipments from different companies.

Sea transportation

Maritime transportation carries the vast amount of international cargo, as much as 90 percent. Compared to air freight it is much slower but less expensive. There are three types of ocean service: conference lines, independent lines, and tramp vessels.

Conference lines

Conference lines are an association of ocean carriers that have joined together to establish common rates and shipping conditions. Conferences have two rates: the regular tariff and a lower, contract rate. You can obtain the contract rate if you sign a contract to use conference vessels exclusively during the contract period.

Independent lines (outsiders)

Independent lines accept bookings from all shippers contingent on the availability of space and are often less expensive than conference rates. An independent usually quotes rates as much as 10–15 percent lower than a conference carrier in situations where the two are in competition.

Tramp vessels

These usually carry only bulk cargoes and do not follow an established schedule; rather, they are ships for hire and operate on negotiated case-by-case charters.

Air transportation

Air freight is a popular and competitive method for international cargoes. Growth has been facilitated by innovations which improved capacity, use of very efficient loading and unloading equipment, and handling of standardized containers. Unlike ship transport, there are no conference systems for air cargo. Air freight moves under a general cargo rate or a commodity rate. A special unit load rate is available when using approved air shipping containers. The advantages of air freight are:

- speed of delivery, which gets perishable cargoes to the place of destination in prime condition;
- ability to respond to unpredictable product demands;
- rapid movement of repair parts.

Land transportation

Transportation over land has become less regulated and, therefore, more competitive and efficient. It is by far the largest transportation method with the number of trucks and lorries on roads worldwide approaching 90–100 million. Exporters look primarily to land transportation to move their goods to the nearest port of departure or as one leg of a sea, land, or air blend. Combined with *multimodalism or intermodalism* shippers can rely on this method for door-to-door delivery.

Multimodalism or intermodalism

The movement of international shipments via container using sequential transportation methods is alternately called multimodalism or intermodalism and is the system of the future. The concept makes use of the most efficient and cost-effective methods to move goods. The simplification and organization of movements of cargo has given birth to transportation specialists and an entirely new set of terms.

Containers

Containers are large boxes standardized eight feet by eight feet in cross section and 10, 20 or 40 foot lengths. Shipping volumes are measured in twenty-foot equivalent units (TEUs). The major ports of the world such as Singapore, Frankfurt, Los Angeles, handle millions of containers each year.

Load centering

This concept stimulated the sophistication of today's intermodal world. As ships grew to hold more containers, they became more expensive to

Figure 7.5 The Multimodal Concept
Source: Nelson, C. (1996) *Import/Export: How to Get Started in International Trade,*
McGraw-Hill. Reproduced with the permission of the McGraw-Hill Companies.

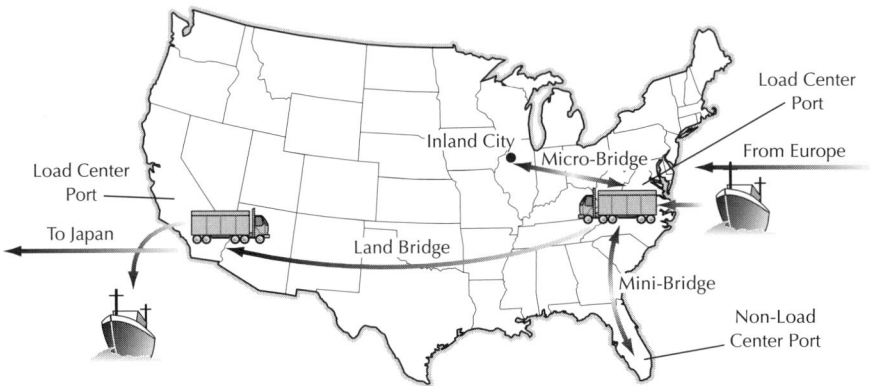

operate. One way to reduce costs was to hold down the number of port calls. In order to fill the ships at fewer ports, the cargo is funneled into these load centers.

Land bridges

A *micro-bridge* is the routing of a container to or from anywhere internal to a country, to or from any port. A *mini-bridge* moves a container that originates or terminates in a port other than the one where it enters or leaves the country. A *land bridge* off-loads a container at any port, ships it cross-country by rail, then reloads aboard a vessel for final movement to a foreign destination. *RO/RO* refers to the roll on/roll off capability of containerized cargo, which is the foundation of multimodalism.

An example of intermodalism might be a container of goods originating in Europe but destined for Japan. It could be rolled off a ship by truck then on to a train in New York (RO/RO), where it would be joined by another container trucked in from Florida (mini-bridge), also destined for Japan. The containers would then be moved across the United States (land bridge) then rolled off the train and onto a ship in Long Beach which would complete the movement to Tokyo. Figure 7.5 illustrates the multimodal concept.

Packaging and marking for overseas shipment

Your product(s) must travel thousands of miles in an undamaged condition. As much as 70 percent of all cargo loss can be prevented by proper packaging and marking. The package must protect against breakage, dampness, careless storage, rough handling, thieves, and weather.

Breakage

Ocean shipments are often roughly loaded aboard by stevedores using fork lifts, slings, nets, and conveyors. During the voyage, rough water and storms can cause loads to shift and sometimes crash into other containers. Even small packages sent through the mails can be squeezed, thrown, or crushed. Assume the worst—use stronger and heavier materials than for domestic shipments, but don't over pack—you pay by weight and volume. For large ocean shipments consider standardized containers that can be transferred from truck or rail car without opening.

Pilferage (theft)

Use strapping and seals, and avoid trademarks or content descriptions.

Moisture and weather

The heat and humidity of the tropics as well as rainstorms and rough weather at sea can cause moisture to seep into the holds of a ship. From that moisture come fungal growths, sweat, and rust. Waterproofing your shipment is essential for most ocean shipments. Consider plastic shrink-wrap or waterproof inner liners and coat any exposed metal parts with grease or other rust inhibitors.

Marking (labeling)

Foreign customers have their needs, shippers have theirs, and terminal operators have theirs. Each will specify certain marks (port, customer identification code, package numbers and number of packages) to appear on shipments. Other markings such as weight, dimensions, and regulations that facilitate clearing through customs can be specified. Figure 7.6 is a sample of markings.

Checklist for shipping

- Write your customer's name and address or shipping code on the package.
- Use black waterproof ink for the stencils.
- Include port of exit and port of entry on your label.
- Don't forget package and case number.
- Include dimensions (inches and metric).
- Mark exports: "Made in _____ (country)," etc. to get through customs in most foreign countries.
- Express gross and net weight in pounds and/or kilograms.

Figure 7.6 Markings

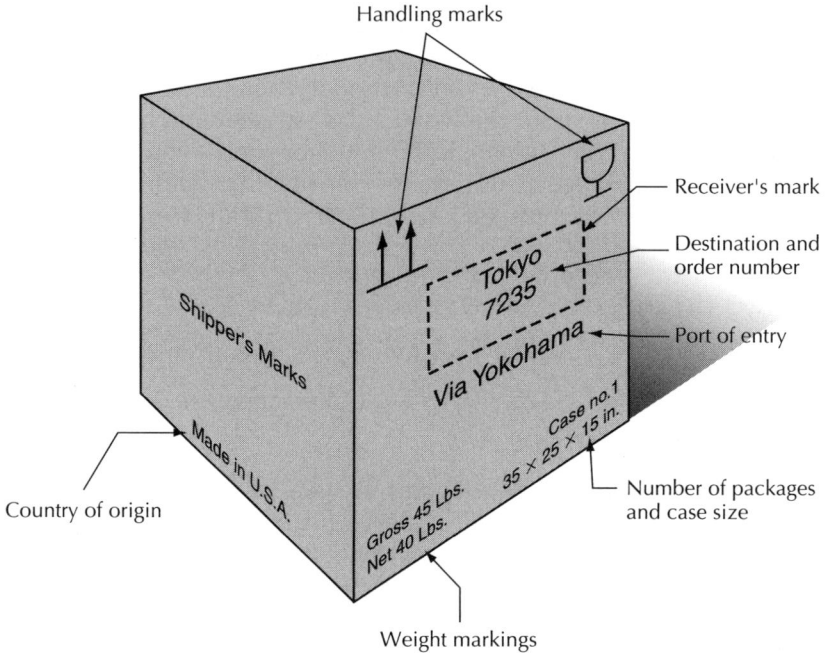

- Don't forget cautionary markings such as "this side up" or "handle with care" in *both* languages.
- Don't use brand names or advertising slogans on packages.
- Any shipments that carry explosives or volatile liquids must conform to local law and international agreements.

Documentation

Documentation falls into two categories: "shipping" and "collecting" and very often the same document is needed for both functions. The experienced trader knows that shipments can be detained on the pier for weeks because of inattention to proper documentation. You, the exporter won't get your money and the importer won't get their goods unless the paperwork is complete and accurate! Keep in mind that customs brokers and freight forwarders are specialists in documentation as well as physical distribution.

Shipping documents

Shipping documents permit an export cargo to be moved through customs, loaded aboard a carrier, and shipped to its foreign destination. These documents are:

- export licenses;
- packing lists;
- bills of lading;
- data Collection.

Bank collection documents

Collection is the procedure whereby a bank collects money for a seller against a draft drawn on a buyer abroad, usually through a correspondent bank. Bank collection documents are those needed for submission to the importer (in the case of a draft) or to the importer's bank (in the case of a L/C) in order to receive payment. Some or all of the following documents may be needed:

- commercial invoices;
- consular invoices;
- certificates of origin;
- inspection certificates;
- bills of lading;
- manufacturing certificates;
- insurance certificates;
- dock receipts;
- warehouse receipts.

Certificate of origin

The certificate of origin is a signed statement that certifies to the buyer the country in which the goods were produced. A recognized Chamber of Commerce or governmental organization usually performs the certification. Some countries require a separate certificate countersigned, and sometimes with a visa, by the resident consul. These statements are required to determine applicable tariffs as well as any preferential duties such as "most favored nation." Often, as little as 35 percent of a nations materials and/or labor can qualify it for favorable duties.

Checklist for certificates of origin

- The letter or certification form should originate from the address of the manufacturer of the product.
- An *officer* of the company must sign the letter.
- The certificate will not be accepted if it is from an outside sales office or distributor. It cannot be signed by a salesperson.
- The letter should clearly state where the product in question was manufactured.

Commercial invoice

A commercial invoice is a bill for the goods from the seller to the buyer. The bill conforms in all respects to the agreement between buyer and seller. It could have the exact terms of the pro forma invoice first offered in response to a quotation, or it could differ in those terms that were the result of final negotiations. It is one method used by governments to determine the value of the goods for customs valuation purposes and should itemize the merchandise by price per unit and any charges paid by the buyer, and specify the terms of payment and any marks or numbers on the packages.

Consular invoice

The purpose of a consular invoice is to allow clearance of your shipment into the country that requires it. Although not required by all countries, it is obtained from the commercial attaché or through the consular office in the port of export. When required, it is in addition to a commercial invoice and must conform in every respect to that document as well as the bill of lading and any insurance documents.

Certificate of manufacture

Certifies the goods ordered by the importer have been produced and are ready for shipment. For example it might be used in those cases when the manufacturer has moved ahead in production with only a down payment, thus allowing the importer to avoid allocation of the full amount too far in advance. Generally, invoices and packing lists are forwarded to the importer with the certificate of manufacture.

Export licenses

As discussed earlier, not every country requires export licenses. These apply to products that the government wants to control closely for either strategic or economic reasons such as certain natural resources, weapons, technologies, or other high-tech products.

Insurance certificates

Insurance certificates provide evidence of coverage and may be a stipulation of a contract, purchase order, or commercial invoice in order to receive payment. These indicate the type and amount of coverage and identify the merchandise in terms of packages and identifying marks. Make certain that the information on this certificate agrees exactly with invoices and bills of lading.

Inspection certificates

This document protects the importer against fraud, error, or quality performance. It is most often conducted by an independent firm, but it is sometimes carried out by the shipper. An affidavit that certifies the inspection is often required under terms of a letter of credit.

Packing lists

A packing list accompanies the shipment and itemizes the cargo in detail. It includes the shipper, the consignee, measurements, serial numbers, weights, and any other data peculiar to the shipment. When correctly completed it is placed in a waterproof bag or envelope and attached with the words: "Packing List Enclosed."

Bills of lading

A bill of lading is a contract between the owner of the goods (exporter) and the carrier. It is often negotiable and links the contract, collection documents, and the carrier, and is both evidence that the shipment has been made, and your receipt for the goods that have been shipped. When endorsed by the shipper, you can use the bill of lading for sight draft or for L/C shipments.

Straight bills of lading

These are non-negotiable bills that consign the goods to a buyer or other party named on the document. Once consummated, the seller and/or the seller's bank loses title control because the goods will be delivered to anyone who can be identified as the consignee.

Order bill of lading

Unlike the "straight" bill, it represents the title to the goods in transit, and is negotiable. The original copy must be endorsed before it is presented to the bank for collection. In other words, the "order" bill can be used as collateral in financing—as documentation to discount or sell a draft. L/C transactions specify to whom the endorsement is to be made. Typically, they are made "in blank," or to the order of a third party, a bank, or a broker. *Air bills of lading* are usually "straight" (i.e. non-negotiable). Ocean shipping companies can issue "straight" or "to order."

Clean on board

Clean on board means that the carrier accepts the cargo and will load it aboard the vessel without exception.

Foul bill

A foul bill indicates an exception, that is, some damage is noted on the bill of lading. Discuss this with your carrier or freight forwarder to make sure you have an opportunity to exchange any damaged goods and obtain a "clean" bill.

Dock receipts and warehouse receipts

In some cases where the shipper is not responsible for moving the merchandise to a foreign port, these documents may be requested.

Summary

The transaction part of cross-border business is dissimilar to a domestic transaction because of many things, including currencies, government regulations, and cultural differences, but over time, processes have been developed to smooth the way. More than anything else, precision of and agreement to terms and conditions must be negotiated prior to contract.

The next chapter reveals the dos and don'ts of international business behavior as it relates to selling your products or services across borders.

CHAPTER EIGHT

Dos and dont's of world behavior and travel

Fear and suspicion are obstacles to clear thinking especially on matters where foreigners are concerned.

Jan Pen

Business survival increasingly depends on reaching out to the people and cultures of the world to sell your goods and services. The purpose of this chapter is to relieve the anxiety about things foreign that prevent some people from exporting. It is also intended to provide suggestions that can facilitate the location and cultivation of new customers and improve relationships with foreign representatives. It is organized into two parts: Culture and Travel.

For a fuller discussion of the business implications of culture the book *Protocol For Profit: A Manager's Guide to Competing Worldwide* is recommended reading. It is a companion to this book in the Global Manager Series and offers an in-depth discussion of protocols and their implications for 135 countries.

Culture

Culture has to do with diverse groups of people—their customary beliefs, social forms and the material traits of a racial, religious group. Culture is a set of meanings or orientations for a given society, or social setting. It's a complex concept because there are often many cultures within a given nation. For you as an international business person, the definition is more difficult because a country's business culture is often different than its general culture. Thus the environment of international business is composed of language, religion, values and attitudes, law, education, politics, technology, and social organizations that are different.

Culture gives you a set of codes to deal with, sets priorities among the codes, and justifies the need for the culture, usually by means of an associated religion.

Whatever a nation's culture is, it works for them. In order to function within it, you must get on the bandwagon.

The Japanese do it very well. They don't try to change the way of life in the other country, they learn about it.

It's a country's culture that regulates such things as sexuality, child raising, acquisition of food and clothing, and the incentives that motivate people to work and buy products. All of these things are of course major factors in marketing products. Business culture is secondary to a country's general culture, but provides the rules of the business game and explains the differences and the priorities.

The ability to be successful in another culture requires an accommodating attitude and an appreciation of the following elements of culture.

Relationships

Relationships developed over a long period of time is the thing that reduces "mistrust" which is the dominant element of behavior that prevents people from doing business across borders. To meet this challenge you need to understand the countries, the people, and the cultures wherever you intend to do business.

Language

This, above all else is the thing that sets humans apart from other forms of life. It is the way we tell others about our history, and our intentions for the future. There are more than 3000 languages in the world today and probably as many as 10,000 dialects. Obviously, since there are only about 200 nations on earth, many countries have more than one language and culture. Some of the languages within a country have priority. Some are used for business, others are used for training and education. You need to have an appreciation that there are language hierarchies within nations, in order to proceed with such every day practices as contract definition. The multiplicity of languages and the accompanying cultures in the world economy is having a dynamic affect on global trade. Every time a cultural barrier is crossed there is a potential communications problem and international trade depends on communications. Speaking in the customer's language is the cardinal rule of international trade. Probably nothing deserves your attention as an international manager more than the possibility of language confusion and misunderstanding. It is not uncommon that trade is stifled simply because one or both parties to the relationship misinterpreted the meaning of a simple sentence.

Body language

Can body language affect your business dealings?

You can bet on it!

Body language is sometimes called the "silent language." It's the first form of communication we learn, and we use it every day to tell other people how we feel about ourselves and them. This language includes our posture, gestures, facial expressions, costumes, the way we walk, and even the treatment of time, material things, and space. Body language is learned the same way we learned spoken language—by observing and imitating the people around us when we were growing up. We learned gender signals appropriate to our sex by imitating our mother and father. People communicate a great deal by their gestures, facial expressions, posture and even their walks.

Religion

Nothing destroys the development of relationships more than stereotypes of religious attitudes. Religion plays a major part in the cultural similarities and differences of nations. In itself religion can be a basis of mistrust and a barrier to trade. Religion is often the dominant influence for the consumer of products. Such things as religious holidays determine buying and consumption patterns. Knowing what is forbidden and what a society expects as a result of their various religions affects market strategy.

Values and attitudes

The role of values and attitudes in international business are difficult to measure, but vital to success. Work ethics and motivation are the intangibles that affect economic performance. Values, for instance, affect how you view time and in more modern societies time has become a commodity, i.e. "time is money." Building international business and trade across national borders just doesn't happen at big-city pace. In countries that have older, more traditional values, time is often measured in the movement of the sun, phases of the moon or relative to planting seasons. Values of a society determine its attitudes toward wealth, consumption, achievement, technology, and change and you must evaluate in terms of the host culture. Researching attitudes about openness and the receptivity to new technology are the essentials of marketing America's changing products.

Legal environment

The laws of a society are another dimension of its culture. Most of the world's legal systems can be classified under the two headings of code law and common law. This does not mean all laws can be identified under those two headings because those are the only two systems. About half of the nations of the world are under a form of either code or common law, but the other half are under either Muslim, Communist or indigenous laws. In most cases none of the world's legal systems are pure. See Chapter 13 for a more complete discussion of the international legal system. Complications among national legal systems could drive the faint hearted from international trade, but international law is growing and there is a set of adjudication practices that have developed over the years. For the majority of dealings, you will be most interested in the law as it relates to contracts, but you should always consider litigation as a last resort. Settle disputes in other ways if possible. Most international commercial disputes can be solved by conciliation, mediation, and arbitration. The International Chamber of Commerce provides an arbitration service that can often be written right into a sales contract for use should the unspeakable happen.

Education

Culture shapes our thoughts and emotions. Your motivation is influenced by your education, as well as other things such as values and religion, which has already been discussed. The biggest international difference is the educational attainment of the populace. It is not unusual to find only the elite of some nations educated to the levels some countries assume for all people. The impact of education is therefore profound for marketing products as well as establishing relationships, because good communications are often based on relative education capacities and standards.

Technology

Understanding the technological gap among nations is an essential element to exporting products across borders. Wide gaps still exist between the most advanced nations and those that are still what we call "traditional societies."

Social organization

International trade cannot be conducted without understanding foreign social relationships. To develop market segmentation and target markets the social organizations of a country must be studied. Insensitivity to the customs of the consumer country will not only result in misinformed decisions but also precipitate resentment and in some cases recrimination. Social stratification is the hierarchy of classes within a society—the relative power, social priorities, privilege, and income of those classes. Each class within a system has somewhat different and distinct tastes, political views, and consumption patterns. Many countries have a socio-religious ideology that allows rank to be intrinsic and inherited biologically. This implies that different categories of humans are culturally defined as consisting of different worth and potential for performance. Regardless of how you react to such non-competitive socialization, such ideas are predictable in some countries. Faced with such a system of socio-religious rank it is essential that you learn how to deal with it—not attempt to change it.

Negotiating

Unfortunately, all too many firms wander into international bargaining situations with no plan and no idea how to proceed. For them, it's an ad-lib and ad-hoc operation all the way. For some, lack of preparation is the result of a sense of corporate superiority, but for most it's pure ignorance of the number and competence of the ferocious competitors out there scouring the world for scraps of business.

The first step in preparing for international negotiations, is to develop a complete assessment of your firm's capabilities. Analyze your strengths and weaknesses, particularly in terms of managerial skills, product delivery, technical abilities, and global resources.

Next, analyze your target—the company or country you intend to sell your product to. Keep in mind that the human and behavioral aspects of your negotiations will be vital.

- Understand the place in the world to where you will be traveling.
- Know their culture, history, and political processes.
- Play particular attention to the importance of face saving to the people of the country where you will be negotiating.
- What is the host government's role in country negotiations?
- How important are personal relations?
- How much time should you allow for negotiations?

The third step is to know your competitors. What is their financial position, their strengths and weaknesses, and what are their capabilities in terms of negotiating gambits?

The last step is to prepare and train the negotiating team. In today's increasingly competitive business world, there is no substitute for extensive advanced preparation and thought. Many companies have taken to role playing their negotiations long before the initial quote is submitted, or the actual marketing of a product begins. Teams are formed and each team is given a set of negotiating alternatives. Each team pretends to represent a product, company, or country which might be the line-up of competitors. With a chalkboard nearby on which a team presents its position, the negotiators go through sufficient rounds to get a sense of the process. Sometimes price is reduced by 10 percent, or service warranties are offered. Even specific advertising concepts are discussed. Little is left to chance.

Competence in formulating strategy and negotiating skill is seldom learned from books—both subjects are ruled by so many variables that there is no substitute for experience and knowledge. Nevertheless, preparation and role playing acts as an excellent training device and serves to sharpen the skills of even the most experienced.

Some key elements of cross-cultural negotiations

- Use the team approach. Take along financial and technical experts. Have someone take notes while the negotiators focus on the action.
- Dress for business. Show by your appearance that the event is of major importance.
- English is often the negotiating language, nevertheless take someone on your team who speaks the opponent's tongue. Rudimentary knowledge of key foreign terms and numbers might ease the process.

Knowing something of another culture helps smooth the way to adjustment and prevents unrealistic expectations. On the other hand when you understand and are conscious of your own cultural conditioning you can begin to see that your customs and ways are not "natural" for all people.

Just visiting

Most business trips are usually short term. Nevertheless, it's important to understand as much about the culture of a country as possible, even when just visiting. To begin let's look at some generalities—some ideas that will help you make a good impression no matter where you're doing business.

Rank and titles

Notwithstanding powerful ideas about democracy and individual equality, most of the societies of the world still highly prize rank and titles. This is true in business as it is in the diplomatic relations between nations. In other words the world is still rank conscious and in order to be successful you must be able to sort juniors from seniors. Failure to understand who has influence may close doors instead of opening them.

By rank we mean who has a higher status among the hierarchy of their organization, not necessarily in the world at large. There are no worldwide rules and unlike military officers or police, business people do not wear uniforms that show their rank. In the business world the only way we know relative rank is through research or by what is shown on our business cards. Very high ranking people, if they have cards at all, often have only name cards—their point is, it is your job to research who they are and it is unlikely they want to do business with you if you don't.

Titles vary in their usage. Mister (Mr.), Miss (Ms.), Missis (Mrs.), Doctor (Dr.), Colonel (Col.), Licencia (Lic.), mean essentially what they say. But President, Vice President, Manager, or Director may mean different things in different companies and countries. Be sure your research leads you to understand the rank of your foreign business partners.

Dress

Do first impressions matter? You bet they do and the clothes you wear often provide that first impression. You are always safe to project a conservative image. That is, for men: a dark suit, white shirt, and conservative tie; for women: a knee-length dress, high-cut blouse and comfortable shoes. Of course weather and culture may dictate that on certain occasions non-Western dress may be appropriate. For instance in the Philippines a *Barong Tagolog* shirt is always appropriate. Light clothes in particularly sultry climates may also make sense. On all matters related to dress don't hesitate to ask your host or business partner for advice and follow the country culture.

Business cards

Business cards have become the universal silent method of communicating such things as rank and position. Your company name and title of your position should be on the card. Many have the same information in a second language on the other side. Business cards are often the first form of communication between business people and the body language of exchanging is important. Extending the card with the right hand while bowing slightly is the standard method of presentation; however, in some Asian nations two hands are used.

Gift giving and receiving

We seldom can go wrong when we give a gift to others. In general people love to give and receive gifts. In most societies, adults, although they may not show it among company, are as enthusiastic as children when given a gift, even though in many cultures they aren't opened in front of the giver. They are often reminders of pleasant times and friendships. Years later, people look at an object and say, "that was given to me by _____ on the occasion of _____." Women must be careful of the message that a gift could convey in some cultures, but in general, gift giving shows our interest and respect. It is better often to bestow several inexpensive, well-thought-out gifts instead of lavish expenditures. The latter may apply if you have developed a long-term relationship. Often the best gift is one representative of your country, something crafted only where you come from. When presenting gifts to a group, give things of equal value, but be certain the top of the rank structure receives his or hers first. On the other hand, the kind of gift we give can get us in a whole lot of trouble.

Bribes

Be certain you don't mix up gift giving with bribery which is commonplace in many countries as a method of facilitating certain things that otherwise would be done as a routine function of employment. Called *baksheesh* in Eastern countries; *mordida* (a little bite) in Spain and Mexico; *jeito* in Brazil; *grease* in the U.S.A.; *dash* in Africa; *kumshaw* in South East Asia, these payments can become a habit and in no way equate to a friendship gift.

Cost

In general your gifts should be modest in cost yet convey the sincerity of the act. To be too expensive might be construed as naive bribery. To be too inexpensive might give the impression that it is given artlessly.

Use

To be on the safe side, gifts should either have utility, or stimulate conversation about your culture and country. CDs, cologne for the wife, a favorite book, or imported liquor are in the category of safe gifts. Handcrafted are better than mass-produced gifts.

Saving face

Saving face is not just an Asian concept, although it is particularly sensitive in those countries. Avoiding embarrassment to others, particularly ranking persons is essential wherever you are in the world.

People of any country like to talk about their own land and people. If you ask questions which show genuine interest it will cultivate their respect towards you. But no one likes critical questions such as: Why don't you do it this way? Or, how come you do it that way? Above all they don't want to hear how much better it is where you come from.

First impressions do count, and the wrong first impression can stop your business deal in its tracks. Bad first impressions are all but impossible to overcome.

1 SMILE! It's the universal business language and saves many problems.
2 But smile right. The smile in which the lips are parted in a sort of an

ellipse around the teeth comes across as phony and dishonest. Smile easy—the kind where the full teeth are exposed and the corners of the mouth are pulled up. This kind of smile says, "Hi, I'm sure pleased to meet you!"

3 Grooming is important all over the world. Studies indicate that most people are more attracted to others who are neat, well groomed, and dress crisply.

4 Flash your eyebrows. That is, in most cultures raising the eyebrows almost instinctively in a rapid movement and keeping them raised for about a half-second is an unspoken signal of friendliness and approval.

5 Lean forward. Liking is produced by leaning forward.

6 Look for similarities. People tend to like others who are like them, so common experiences and interests are often a starting point for producing liking.

7 Nod your head. People like other people who agree with them and are attentive to what they are saying.

8 Open up. A position in which your arms are crossed in front of your chest may project the impression you're resisting the other person's ideas. Open, frequently outstretched arms and open palms project the opposite.

Women in international trade

Obstacles confronting women in the international marketplace are still substantial. That bias requires them to overcome more hurdles than men. It is not surprising then that there is a diversity of views about female participation in the still overwhelmingly male-dominated business worlds of other countries.

For the most part, businesswomen figure out ways to overcome the obstacles by simply end-running the problem and going to more receptive markets. Women doing business in most Middle Eastern countries often arrange for men to handle their direct negotiations with Arab businessmen.

In spite of the difficulties, there are many success stories, and women in the international marketplace are encouraging other women to join them.

About jokes

The people of every country enjoy humor and they all have their funny stories, but explaining complicated jokes to businesspersons who don't share your culture can be very tricky. Here are a few dos and don'ts:

1 Do remember that each culture reacts differently to jokes.

2 Don't tell foreigners a joke that depends on word play or punning.

3 Do be careful of the subject of your joke. It could be taken seriously in a culture different than your own.
4 Do be informed about the sensitive issues in the country where you are visiting.
5 Do ask to hear a few local jokes. They will give you a sense of what's considered funny.
6 Do tell jokes, everyone enjoys a good laugh.

Travel

Nothing improves a business connection or for that matter any relationship more than a face to face meeting. Don't let technology overwhelm your sale. Facsimiles, the World Wide Web, and satellite televised meetings are not a substitute for the personal touch.

Planning

Your trip begins long before you actually travel. It begins two or three months in advance when you visualize why you are undertaking this voyage to other countries and what you expect to accomplish. Give some thought to your goals and their relative priorities. Begin by obtaining the names of possible contacts, confirming appointments, and checking transportation schedules. The more planning you do, the more time, opportunity, and money you will save in the long run. Double-check holidays and make sure you are not wasting your time sitting in a hotel on a foreign non-work day. Make sure you know the normal work day of the destination nations. For instance, in many Middle Eastern regions the work week typically runs from Saturday to Thursday. Another thing to take into account are potentially dangerous in-country situations such as civil unrest or a disease infestation. The State Departments of most nations have a travel alert system that can be tapped for current situations.

Itinerary

Travel is expensive; therefore, care should be taken to have a full but not overloaded schedule. Two or three definite appointments, spaced comfortably throughout the day are more productive and enjoyable than a crowded agenda that requires you to rush from one meeting to the next without allowances for concluding business. Keep your schedule flexible enough to allow for both unexpected problems and opportunities. You are reminded that time is reckoned from Greenwich, England in time zones that span the globe. Make sure you think ahead about the local time and arrange schedules accordingly.

Preparations

Travel agents can help arrange your transportation and hotel reservations and they can be helpful in planning the itinerary, obtaining the best rates and explaining such things as visa requirements.

Passports

A valid passport is normally required for all travel outside your home country. Make certain it is still valid and will remain so for your entire trip.

Visas

Visas are provided, for a small fee, by the foreign country's embassy or consulate in your country. To obtain a visa you must have a current passport. Allow several weeks to obtain visas, especially if traveling to Eastern Europe or developing nations. Some countries do not require visas for tourist travel but do require them for business travel.

Vaccinations

Health requirements vary from country to country. A travel agent or airline can advise you of the different requirements. In some cases vaccinations against typhus, typhoid, and other diseases are advisable even though they are not required.

Travel check list

- seasonal weather conditions;
- health care requirements;
- what and what not to eat;
- electrical current (do you need a transformer or plug adaptor?);
- money (currency requirements, credit cards, and travelers checks);
- in-country transportation;
- tipping (how much and who);
- customs regulations.

Assistance

Every country is attempting to help businesses to sell their goods abroad, so your first stop before leaving your country and on entry into the foreign country should be to your economic and/or foreign commercial offices. These services are free or at least very low cost so why not take advantage of them? Both often provide in-depth briefings and can arrange introductions to appropriate firms, potential clients, and government officials. Discuss your needs with the staffs of the local embassy or consulate.

Temporary import bonds

Foreign customs regulations vary widely from place to place, and the traveler is wise to learn in advance the regulations that apply to each country to be visited. If you plan to carry product samples be alert that you may be required to pay import duties. Temporary import bonds can be arranged by freight forwarders through foreign customs brokers or it is possible to take your chances and pay cash to foreign customs officials on arrival for such a bond.

Carnets

In some countries your goods can go duty-free and extensive customs procedures may be avoided if you have an ATA (Admission Temporaire) Carnet. The ATA Carnet is a standard international customs document used to obtain duty-free temporary admission of certain goods on an annualized basis into the countries that are signatories to the ATA Convention. Under the ATA Convention commercial and professional travelers may take commercial samples, tools of the trade, advertising material, and cinematographic, audiovisual, medical, scientific, or other professional equipment into member countries temporarily without paying customs duties and taxes of posting a bond at the border of each country to be visited.

Applications for ATA Carnet are made to the Council for International Business in your country. Since countries are continuously added to the ATA Carnet system the traveler should contact the Council for International Business to learn if the country to be visited is included on the list. The list of about 50 nations where the ATA carnet can be used (current as of 1998) may be found in Appendix D. The fee charged for the Carnet depends on the value of the goods to be covered. A bond, letter of credit, or bank guarantee of 40 percent of the value of the goods is also required to cover duties and taxes that would be due if goods imported into a foreign country were not paid by the carnet holder. Typical processing fees are:

Shipment value	Basic processing fee
Under $5,000`	US$120
$5,000 - 14,999	US$150
$15,000 - 49,000	US$175
$50,000 - 199,999	US$200
$200,000 - 499,999	US$225
$500,000 and over	US$250

Further information can be found in the informative book published by the Council titled: *Carnet: Move Goods Duty-free Through Customs.*

Summary

Even today in the rapidly globalizing world, some people have preconceived notions which prevent them from crossing borders to do business. To reduce any mistrust you may have of another culture, an understanding of cultural implications increases the chance of doing business and making a profit. It is essential to travel to countries where you plan to do business, to meet the people, and gain direct insight into the opportunities.

The next chapter explains how to manage your risk by using letters of credit, different types of drafts, and insurance policies.

CHAPTER NINE

Managing risk

Fortune favors the brave

Terrence

Even doing business in your own home town involves risk. By it's very nature free enterprise is like playing roulette because capitalist theory is about investing in a venture, often with only a hope for profit. Commerce is inherently risky and you should not expect cross-border business to be different. A certain amount of uncertainty is always present when doing business across international borders, but much of it can be hedged, managed, and controlled. All major exporting countries have arrangements to protect exporters and the bankers who provide their funding support. Avoiding and/or controlling risks in global trade is an everyday occurrence but understanding the instruments available, while not difficult, is *absolutely vital*.

There are five kinds of international business risks but, as shown in Table 9.1, management instruments exist for only four: payment; foreign exchange exposure; political; and shipping.

Commercial risk

The fifth kind of risk is that which is inherent to free enterprise. While there are insurance policies that shelter insolvency and protracted default by a buyer, disputes over quality, non-delivery, warranty, or loss of markets due to competition are not covered. Pick your customers and markets carefully. The key to managing or avoiding commercial risk is a good

Table 9.1 Cross-Border Risk

Payment:	The risk of not being paid.
Foreign Exchange:	The risk of foreign exchange fluctuations.
Political:	Risk of war, coup d'état, revolution, expropriation, expulsion, foreign exchange controls, or cancellation of import or export licenses.
Transportation:	Risk of damage and/or loss at sea or other transportation

contract with a clause that establishes legal recourse should things not go well.

Bad debts are more easily avoided than rectified. If there are payment problems keep communicating and working with the firm until the matter is settled. Even the most valued customers have financial problems from time to time. If nothing else works, request your department of trade or commerce or the International Chamber of Commerce to begin negotiations on your behalf. The truth is that the likelihood of a bad debt from an international customer is very low. In the experience of most international businessmen, overseas bad debts seldom exceed 0.5 percent of sales. The reason is that in overseas markets, credit is still something to be earned as a result of having a record of prompt payment. Use common sense in extending credit to overseas customers, but don't use tougher rules than for your domestic clients. Information that is current and accurate is the foundation of good financing decisions. Basically two types of international credit information exists: (1) the ability and willingness of importing firms to make payment, and (2) the ability and willingness of foreign countries to allow payment in a convertible currency. The following are several ways to obtain credit information about companies and their countries.

Information about domestic firms

- commercial banks;
- commercial credit services;
- trade associations;
- trade references.

Information about foreign firms

- foreign credit specialists in the credit departments of large exporting companies;
- commercial banks, which check buyer credit through their foreign branches and correspondents;
- commercial credit reporting services, such as Dun and Bradstreet;
- consultations with your EXIMBANK;
- your national commerce department.

Information about foreign countries

- World Bank;
- Chase World Information Corporation;
- your government commerce/trade department;
- Internet.

Payment risk

Mistrust across international borders is a natural thing; after all, there is a certain amount of mistrust even in your own culture. Payment risk includes not being paid and non delivery of goods. One key to risk management is a well-written sales contract. When gaining contract agreement between yourself and your overseas business associate be sure to include the method of payment.

Ideally an exporter would wish to deal only in cash, but in reality, few business persons are initially able or willing to do business under those terms. Because of the risk of non-payment due to insolvency, bankruptcy, or other severe deterioration, a list of methods, procedures, and documents have been developed which help to ensure that foreign buyers honor their agreements.

Payment options

The exporter wants to be certain that the importer will pay on time once the goods have been shipped. On the other hand the importer wants to be sure the exporter will deliver on time and that the goods are exactly what the buyer ordered.

Ensuring prompt payment often worries exporters more than any other factor. The methods of payment, in order, from low risk to the exporter to high risk, are: cash in advance, credit card, bank transfers, direct debit, letters of credit, foreign bank transfers, foreign bank checks, sight draft, time draft, consignment, and open account. Table 9.2 compares the various methods of payment in order of increasing risk to the exporter.

Advance payment (cash)

This method of getting paid is the most desirable for the exporter—you get payment before the goods are shipped. But the foreign buyer often objects to tying up his or her capital and assuming all the risk. On the grounds that seeing the merchandise is the best insurance, most foreign businessmen try not to pay until they actually receive the goods. Furthermore, the buyer may resent the implication that he or she may not be creditworthy. On the other hand, in cases where the buyer orders special equipment (designed to the buyer's specifications) it is not unusual to receive at least partial payment in advance.

Credit cards

There is a growing use of credit cards, especially when buying over the Internet or for direct mail marketing. By encouraging their use payment barriers are often avoided. Currency conversions are done within the

Table 9.2   Comparison of Exporter Payment Options

Method	Time of Payment	Risk to Exporter	Goods available to Buyer
Advance Payment (cash)	Immediately	Low	After payment
Credit Card	Immediately	Low	After payment
Bank Transfer	Immediately	Low	After payment
Direct Debit	Immediately	Low	After payment
Letter of Credit	After shipping	Low	After payment
Foreign Bank Checks	Upon clearance and payment of fees	Medium	After payment
Sight Draft	On presentation of draft	Medium (only if goods are returned/ disposed of)	After payment
Time Draft	On maturity of draft	Medium-High (relies on importer to pay draft)	Before payment
Consignment	When sold	High	Before payment
Open Account	As agreed	High (unless strong relationship)	Before payment

credit card company's system, using hourly exchange rates. The entire transaction can take place within a few days, thus reducing the risk of currency fluctuations. Risk of non-payment is low because the legitimacy of the account can be verified before shipping the product.

Bank transfer

For this method the foreign buyer goes to their bank and has the money transferred into the exporter's account. The burden of exchange rate fluctuations usually remains with the importer and depends on whether payment is in local currency or the seller's currency.

Direct debit

This method is becoming increasingly popular especially with direct-mail marketers and sellers over the Internet. Originally used in Europe, it permits the exporter to directly debit the importer's bank account, sometimes without prior notification (variable), as long as the buyer receives the lowest price available at the time of debit. This requires setting up a bank account in a foreign country.

Letters of credit (L/C)

Nations, companies, and individuals have engaged in trade for centuries and from the beginning have searched for the best financing alternative. A letter of credit (L/C) is an instrument issued by a bank in favor of a beneficiary, which substitutes the bank's credit worthiness for that of the applicant. By putting the bank between the importer and exporter, a letter of credit becomes the most equitable method of sharing the risks between a buyer and seller. The most common form of collection is payment against an L/C and is a method well understood by traders around the world, is simple, and is as good as your bank. Internationally the term *documentary credits* is synonymous with the term letter of credit and these are the basis of thousands of transactions worth billions of dollars every day in every part of the world. They are almost always operated in accordance with the Uniform Customs and Practice for Documentary Credits of the International Chamber of Commerce, a code of practice which is recognized by banking communities in over 160 countries. A *Guide to Documentary Operations*, which includes all of the standard forms, is available by writing to ICC Services S.A.R.L., 38 Cours Albert ler, 75008 Paris, France, telephone 33-01-49-53-28-28, fax 33-01-49-53-29-24, e-mail: iccwbo.org, or Internet: www.iccwbo.org.

The L/C is the time-tested method whereby an importer's bank guarantees that if all documents are presented in exact conformity with the terms of the L/C, they will pay the exporter. The procedure is not difficult to understand, and most cities have banks with persons familiar with L/C's mechanics.

An L/C is a document issued by a bank at the buyer's request in favor of the seller. It promises to pay a specified amount of money upon receipt by the bank of certain documents within a specified time or at intervals corresponding with shipments of goods. It is a universally used method of achieving a commercially acceptable compromise.

Once the buyer and the seller agree that they will use an L/C for payment, and they have worked out the conditions, the importer applies for the L/C to his or her international bank. Figure 9.1 is an example of a letter of credit application.

Using the application as its guide, the bank issues a document of credit incorporating the terms agreed to by the parties. Figure 9.2 exemplifies an L/C.

Think of a letter of credit as a loan against collateral, which often depends on the relationship of the buyer to the buyer's bank. Typically, if you don't already have an account the bank will want you to become a new customer but will require 100 percent collateral. For a proven account, the bank will establish a line of credit. For instance, if you have US$50,000.00 in your account and the transaction is expected to cost US$10,000.00, your account will be reduced to US$40,000.00 and the line

Figure 9.1   Request to open a letter of credit

To: *Importer's international bank*

Request to open documentary
credit (commercial letter of
credit and security agreement)

Date_____

Please open for my/our account a documentary credit (letter of credit) in
accordance with the undermentioned particulars.
We agree that, except so far as otherwise expressly stated, this credit will be
subject to the Uniform Customs and Practice for Documentary Credits,
ICC Publication #290.

We undertake to execute the Bank's usual form of indemnity.

Type of credit: *Irrevocable*, i.e. cannot be canceled without beneficiary's
agreement.
Revocable, i.e. subject to cancellation.

Method of Advice: ❑ Airmail   ❑ Cable, short details   ❑ Cable, full details.
Beneficiary's bank:_____

In favor of Beneficiary: Company name and address.

Amount or sum of:

Availability: Valid until_____in_____for negotiation/date/place acceptance/
payment.

This credit is available by drafts drawn at_____sight/accompanied by the
required documents.

Documents required: Invoice in three copies
Full set clean "on board" bills of lading to order of shipper,
blank endorsed. In case movement of goods involves more
than one mode, a "Combined Transport Document" should
be called for.
Negotiable Marine and War risk insurance for %
(usually 110%) of invoice value covering all risks.

Certificate of Inspection

Other Documents: Certificate of origin issued by Chamber of Commerce in
three copies.

Packing List

Quantity &
Description
of Goods

Price per unit:

Terms & relative port or place: C.I.F./C.&F./F.O.B./F.A.S./_____
Place_____

Figure 9.2 Sample letter of credit

Name of Issuing Bank	Documentary Credit No._____
Place and date of issue	Place and date of expiration
Applicant	Amount
	Credit available with
	❏ Payment ❏ Acceptance ❏ Negotiation
Shipment from_____ Shipment to_____	Against presentation of documents detailed herein
	❏ Drawn on_____ Bank

Invoice in three copies

Full set clean "on board" bills of lading to order of shipper, blank endorsed. In case movement of goods involves more than one mode, a "Combined Transport Document" should be called for.

Negotiable Marine and War risk insurance for_____% (usually 110%) of invoice value covering all risks.

Certificate of Inspection

Certificate of origin issued by Chamber of Commerce in three copies.

Packing List

Documents to be presented within_____days after date of issuance of the shipping document(s) but within the validity of the credit.

We hereby issue this Documentary Credit in your favor.

Issuing Bank

of credit established as US$10,000.00. Letters of credit are viewed as an extension of credit and the appropriate collateral will be negotiated between the importer and the bank. The bank may not require dollar-for-dollar collateral and may finance inventory on the water, etc.

Types of L/Cs

There are two types of letters of credit: "revocable" and "irrevocable." Revocable credit means the document can be amended or canceled at any time without prior warning or notification of the seller. Irrevocable simply means that the terms of the document can be amended or canceled only with the agreement of all parties.

The bank's involvement

Letters of credit are payable either at sight or on a time draft basis. Under a sight L/C, the "issuing" bank pays, with or without a draft, when satisfied that the presented documents conform with the L/C. An "advising" bank (most often the "confirming" or seller's bank) informs the exporter or beneficiary that an L/C has been issued. "Confirmation" means the advising bank guarantees payment by the foreign bank if documents are presented in strict compliance to terms of the L/C and the issuing bank does not pay.

Under a time (usance) L/C, once the documents are presented and found to be in exact conformity the draft is stamped "accepted" and can then be negotiated as a "banker's acceptance" by the exporter, at a discount to reflect the cost of money advanced against the draft.

Banks deal in documents not merchandise, therefore the importer is responsible for doing "due diligence" on the supplier.

Banks charge the buyer for handling commercial letters of credit. These charges vary from country to country. For an import and domestic L/C you might expect to pay ⅛ of one percent of the transaction, with a minimum (about US$150.00). Amendments might cost ⅛ of one percent with a minimum of US$100.00. Acceptance fees might be two percent of the draft with a minimum of US$75 for each draft accepted, and discrepancy fees, US$40. Export advising fees might be US$60, while confirmation fees would also be a percentage of the draft (subject to country risk conditions) with a minimum of about US$100.

Charges for assignment of proceeds and or transfers might be ¼ of one percent of the transaction with a minimum of US$150 with discrepancy fees of about US$45.00.

Standby L/Cs bring issuance fees which are often charged on an annual percentage (360-day basis) based on credit risk considerations with a minimum US$250. Amendment fees are risk-related charges usually with a minimum of US$250. They will be a flat fee if just narrative, but will be the same as the issuance fee if the value of the L/C is changed.

Figure 9.3 shows the three phases of documentary credit in their simplest form. In Phase I, your (*issuing*) bank notifies the seller through an *advising* bank that a credit has been issued. In Phase II, the seller then ships the goods and presents the documents to the bank, at which time the seller is paid if the documents are found to be in compliance and the funds have been received from the issuing bank. Phase III is the

Figure 9.3 Three phases of letters of credit

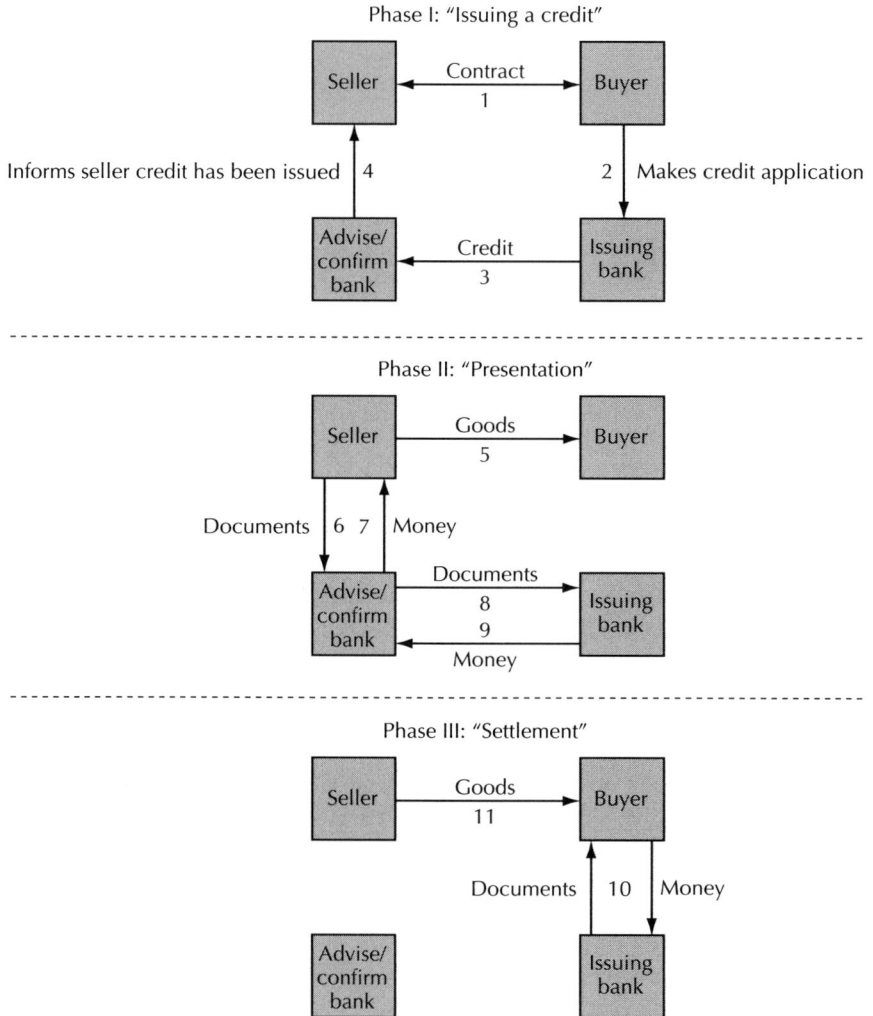

Phase I: "Issuing a credit"

Phase II: "Presentation"

Phase III: "Settlement"

"settlement" phase, wherein, the documents are then transferred to the buyer's bank, whereupon the buyer pays the bank any remaining moneys in exchange for the documents. Thus, on arrival of the goods, the buyer or importer has the proper documents for entry.

Below are the steps involved for the seller to receive payment by letter of credit.

1 "Seller" agrees to sell goods to "buyer" using a letter of credit as a means of financing the transaction.

2 "Buyer" makes application for a letter of credit with his bank, the

issuing bank, and signs the bank's letter of credit agreement form. The issuing bank approves the application and issues the actual letter of credit document.

3   Once approved, the issuing bank forwards the letter of credit to the advising bank.

4   The advising bank, after verifying the LCs authenticity, delivers the letter of credit to "seller."

5   Having received the letter of credit and being certain of the ability to comply with its terms, "seller" ships the merchandise to "buyer." If an exporter feels he is unable to comply with the terms of the letter of credit, an amendment can be requested. If and when an amendment to the letter of credit is necessary, "seller" must request it from "buyer," who will in turn request it from the issuing bank.

6   "Seller" prepares documents and draft and presents them to the negotiating bank.

7   The negotiating bank checks the documents and pays funds to "seller" upon receipt of funds from reimbursing bank and/or issuing bank in accordance with the terms of the letter of credit when all terms and conditions have been complied with. The negotiating bank then forwards the documents to the issuing bank.

8–10   The issuing bank receives the documents and checks them. If the documents are in compliance with the letter of credit, the issuing bank debits "buyer's" account and forwards the documents to "buyer" with notice of debit to his account.

11–12   "Buyer" takes the documents and picks up the merchandise from the carrier. This completes the letter of credit cycle for an export transaction.

Standby L/Cs
Sometimes when dealing in an open account, the exporter requires a "standby L/C." This means just what the name implies; the L/C is not to be executed unless payment is not made within the specified period, usually 30–60 days. Standby L/Cs are particularly useful where there are a lot of repetitive shipments. Bank handling charges for standby letters of credit are usually higher than for commercial (import) L/Cs.

Special middleman uses
There are three special uses of commercial letters of credit for the middleman: transferable, assignment of proceeds, and back-to-back L/Cs. Table 9.3 compares the risks involved with using each method.

Transferable
Figure 9.4 shows pictorially how the "transferable L/C" works. The buyer opens the L/C, which states clearly that it is transferable, on behalf

Table 9.3 Comparison of Middle Man Risks

	Assignment of Proceeds	Transferable Letter of Credit	Back-to-Back
Risk to Middleman	Supplier relies on middleman to comply with L/C	Middleman relies on supplier to comply with L/C	Supplier's performance must satisfy both L/C's
Risk to Middleman's Bank	None	Minimal	Supplier's do not comply with master L/C
Disclosure	Buyer and seller are not disclosed	Buyer and seller are disclosed	Buyer and seller are not disclosed (with third-party documents)

of the middleman as the original beneficiary who in turn transfers all or part of the L/C to the supplier(s). The transfer must be made under the same terms and conditions as the original L/C with the following exceptions: amount, unit price, expiration date, and shipping date. In this instance the buyer and supplier are usually disclosed to each other.

Assignment of proceeds
The assignment of proceeds method is shown in Figure 9.5, and Figure 9.6 shows a typical letter of assignment. It should be noted that the proceeds of all letters of credit may be assigned. In this instance, the buyer opens the L/C to the middleman who assigns all or a portion to the supplier, who is not a party to the L/C and is at risk of giving merchandise to the middleman with no assurance of payment. The buyer relies on the

Figure 9.4 Transferable letter of credit

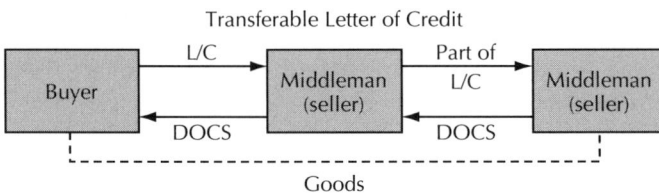

Transferable Letter of Credit

- L/C must state that it is transferable
- Original beneficiary transfers all or part of L/C to supplier(s)
- Transfer must be made under the same terms and conditions with the following exceptions:
    Amount
    Unit price
    Expiration date
    Shipping date
- Buyer and supplier usually disclosed to each other

Figure 9.5 Assignment of Proceeds

Assignment of Proceeds

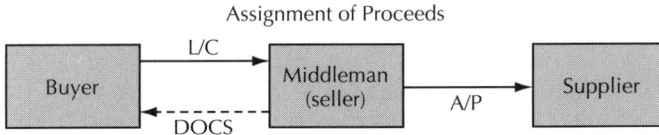

- Supplier relies on middleman to comply with L/C so that he or she can be paid. Discrepancy in middleman's documents will prevent payment under L/C
- Middleman instructs advising bank to effect payment to supplier when documents are negotiated
- Buyer and seller are not disclosed to each other
- Proceeds of all letters of credit can be assigned

middleman to comply so that he can be paid. Any discrepancy in middleman documents will prevent payment under the L/C. The middleman instructs the advising bank to effect payment to the supplier when the documents are negotiated. In this way, buyers and sellers are not disclosed to each other.

Back-to-back letter of credit
When using the "back-to-back" method shown in Figure 9.7 the middleman must have a line of credit because the middleman is responsible for paying the second (backing) L/C regardless of receipt of payment under the first (master) L/C. Great care should be exercised when using this method because discrepancies on the first L/C will result in non-payment and the middleman's ability to pay could be a substantial credit risk. Back-to-back L/Cs should be issued on nearly identical terms and must allow for third party documents.

■ Hot tip Ten Letter of Credit Checkpoints

1 The L/C has not been overdrawn.
2 The expiration date AND shipping dates have not expired.
3 The draft is error-free, signed, and matched to the invoice.
4 The invoice matches the stipulations on the letter of credit.
5 The invoice clearly indicates the nature of the merchandise, as well as shipment specifics and charges.
6 The insurance policy and certificate are enclosed.
7 The insurance document covers all risks.
8 The bill of lading is correctly assigned, endorsed, and dated, as stipulated in the L/C.
9 You have all the documents stipulated in the L/C.
10 The merchandise matches with its description on the L/C.

Figure 9.6 Typical Letter of Assignment

ASSIGNMENT OF PROCEEDS

Gentlemen:

Here is Letter of credit No._____
issued by_____in favor of_____
_____for an amount in excess of $_____
expiring _____.

Our drafts and documents in terms of this credit will be presented by us to your office, and when they are negotiated/paid, we authorize and direct you to pay to_____the sum of $_____from the proceeds of these drafts, in consideration of value received.

These instructions are irrevocable and shall continue under any extension of this Letter of Credit. Please acknowledge receipt of these instructions directly to_____ by forwarding them a copy of this letter.

Sincerely yours,

_____

Signature verified:

_____
Name of Bank

_____
Authorized Signature

The above assignment has been duly noted on our records.

_____
The Bank of San Diego International Banking Department
Authorized Signature

Bank drafts

Bank drafts (bills of exchange) are used as payment for many sales using one of two time-tested banking methods, "sight" and "time". Each useful under certain circumstances. Bank drafts are simply written orders which activate payment either at sight or at "tenor," (a future time or date).

A bank draft is a check, drawn by a bank on another bank, used primarily where it is necessary for the customer to provide funds payable at a bank in some distant location. The exporter who undertakes this payment method can offer a range of payment options to the overseas customer.

Figure 9.7   Back-to-Back Letter of Credit

Back-to-Back Letter of Credit

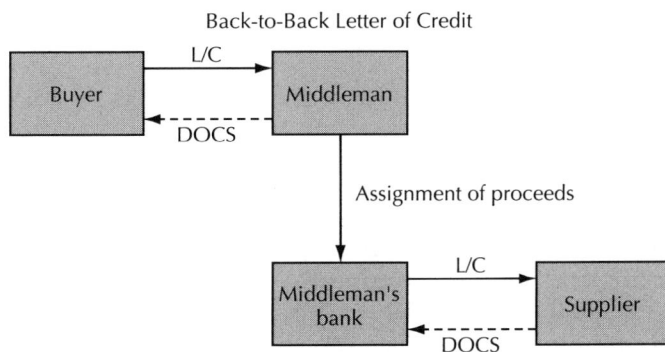

- Requires credit line for middleman
- Middleman is responsible for paying the second (backing) L/C regardless of receipt of payment under first (master) L/C
- Substantial credit risk in that discrepancies on the first L/C will result in non-payment
- L/Cs are issued on nearly identical terms
- Middleman's ability to pay is a key consideration
- L/C must allow third-party documents

Sight draft

At sight indicates that a negotiable instrument is to be paid upon presentation or demand. It can be clean (just the draft) or documentary. This is similar to the time draft except that the importer's bank holds the documents until the importer releases the funds. Sight drafts are the most common method employed by exporters throughout the world. It is nothing more than a written order on a standardized bank format requesting money from the overseas buyer. While this method costs less than the letter of credit it has greater risk because the importer can refuse to honor the draft.

Time (usance) draft

This is an acceptance order drawn by the exporter on the importer (customer), payable a certain number of days after "sight" (presentation) to the holder. Think of it as nothing more than a promise to pay in the future.

Documents such as negotiable bills of lading, insurance certificates, and commercial invoices accompany the draft and are submitted through the exporter's bank for collection. When presented to the importer at his bank, the importer acknowledges that the documents are acceptable and commits to pay, by writing "accepted" on the draft and signing. The importer normally has 30 to 180 days, depending on the draft's term, to make payments to its bank for transmittal. The bank has no financial obligation if the importer does not pay at maturity.

Consignment

The seller (*consignor*) retains title to the goods during shipment and storage of the product in the warehouse or retail store. The consignee acts as a selling agent selling the goods and remitting the net proceeds to the consignor. Like open-account sales, consignment sales can also be risky and lend themselves only to certain kinds of merchandise. Works of art are often sold on consignment. Great care should be taken in working out this contractual arrangement. Be sure it is covered with adequate risk insurance.

Open account

The *open account* is a trade arrangement in which goods are shipped to a foreign buyer without guarantee of payment. Though it is the riskiest, many firms that have a long-standing business relationship with the same overseas firm use this method. Needless to say, the key is to know your buyer and your buyer's country. You should use an open account when the buyer has a continuing need for the seller's product or service. Some experienced exporters say that they deal only in open accounts, but they always preface that statement by saying that they have close relationships and have been doing business with those overseas clients for many years. An open account can be risky unless the buyer is of unquestioned integrity and has withstood a thorough credit investigation. The advantage of this method is its ease and convenience, but with open account sales, you bear the burden of financing the shipment. Standard practice in many countries is to defer payment until the merchandise is sold, sometimes even longer. Therefore, among the forms of payment, open account sales require the greatest amount of working capital. In addition, you bear the exchange risk if the sales are quoted in foreign currency. Nevertheless, competitive pressures may force the use of this method. Using export credit insurance can mitigate the risk and the bank will discount the receivable.

Foreign exchange risk

When exporters deal in their own currency there is less foreign exchange risk; however, the strength and popularity of currencies is cyclic and there could be loss of business due to non-competitiveness due to escalating cost of goods if the foreign currency devalues. Importers must buy foreign currency to pay for products and services from risk-avoiding foreign suppliers who demand payment in their own currency. Often, an exporter is faced with the prospect of pricing products or services in currencies other than their own. There are two kinds of foreign exchange risk: transaction and translation.

Transaction

In the current era of floating exchange rates, there are risks due to exposure whenever there are cash flows denominated in foreign currencies. Exposure is the effect on a firm or an individual if there is a change on exchange rates. Hedging or covering is the use of the forward foreign exchange market to avoid foreign currency transaction risk.

The forward exchange rate is the "spot" rate that is contracted today for the delivery of a currency at a specified date in the future, at a plus or minus interest rate differential agreed upon today.

The best management decision for an exporter is to hedge or cover in the forward market when there is risk of exposure. Use the forward rate for the date on which payment is required. This avoids all foreign exchange risk, is simple, and reasonably inexpensive. The cost of a forward contract is small—the difference between the cost of the spot market (today's cost of money) and the cost of the forward market. Major international banks and brokerage houses can help you arrange a foreign exchange forward contract. Spot and forward markets are quoted daily in most major newspapers.

Translation

This is the risk related to *accounting practices* when using different denominations of currency. Between reporting periods the relative values of two currencies may change. These losses or gains have significance for investment decisions and valuation of assets.

Political risk

National policies often change when new politicians come to power, as a result, the risk of war, coup d'état, revolution, expropriation, expulsion, embargo, foreign-exchange controls, or cancellation of import or export licenses exists in some nations more than others. The level of political risk is analyzed and measured, then made available to international businesses by private organizations as well as governments. Based on these analyses, political risk insurance is also available from private as well as government sources. Of course, there is a cost in the form of premiums for this insurance so the decision whether to insure or not must be based on good business sense. A small, low-value transaction may not warrant insurance, but, it is essential to insure high value exports.

Table 9.4 Comparison chart of export credit insurance programs commercial coverage only

	Fidelity and deposit	American Credit Indemnity	CNA Insurance Company
RESTRICTIONS	Product may be 100% foreign content. No coverage to government buyers. Insolvency must occur while policy is in force.	Product may be 100% foreign content. No coverage to 100%-owned government buyers. Insolvency must occur while policy is in force, if policy is not renewed	No US content requirement. Will consider coverage on sovereign buyers. Coverage is based on the date of insolvency, however may bridge two policies.
COVERAGE	Defined insolvency and protracted default in eligible countries. Excludes insolvency due to war. Normally 85% coverage.	Defined insolvency and protracted default in eligible countries specified by country limit schedule. Excludes insolvency due to political events including war. Political coverage can be endorsed to policy for additional premium.	Defined insolvency and protracted default in eligible countries. Excludes insolvency due to war. Normally 90% coverage.
COUNTRY ELIGIBILITY	List of over 100 eligible countries, primarily developed countries.	List of over 50 eligible countries.	List of over 100 eligible countries.
CREDIT APPROVALS	F&D gathers information and establishes credit limits for each buyer.	ACI gathers information and establishes credit limits for each buyer. Supplying financial data can improve results.	Continental gathers information and establishes credit limits for each buyer. Also offers blanket coverage allowing for shipments to unnamed buyers without acquiring prior approval.

DEDUCTIBLE	No deductible.	Depending on profit margin, may be no deductible.	Aggregate per policy year deductible. Will also consider non-deductible policies.
PREMIUM PAYMENT	Prepayment, with year end adjustment. Determined as a percentage of insured sales.	Requires spread of risk, key accounts, or whole turnover. Prepayment with risk-based pricing on approved coverage.	1) Prepayment based on approved credit limits, adjusted for changes in coverage levels, or 2) Monthly determined as a percentage of insured sales.
MINIMUM PREMIUM	$1,250 per policy year.	$5,000 per policy year. If domestic policy in place with ACI, $2,500 min. per year.	$2,500 per policy year.
CLAIM FILING	Insolvency claims can be filed at any time during policy period as soon as practical after acquiring knowledge. Protracted default 180 days after due date.	Insolvency claims can be filed at any time during policy period after acquiring knowledge but no later than the account becoming 180 days past due or within 45 days after the end of the policy period whichever is earlier. Past due claims must be filed within 180 days after due date. No collection fees except uninsured portion of account if any.	Insolvency claims must be filed within 20 days after acquiring knowledge. Past due claims must be filed within 3 months after due date. Due date may be adjusted to allow for flexibility. May have collection charges.

(*Source*: Imperial Bank, USA)

Table 9.5 Comparison chart of export credit insurance programs comprehensive coverage (commercial and political)

	FCIA (Great American Insurance Company)	Export-import Bank	Trade Underwriters (Reliance Insurance Co.)	American International Underwriters (AIU)
RESTRICTIONS	No US content restriction. Product may be 100% foreign content.	Products must be 51% US content on cost basis. Military goods and/or services not eligible. Must be shipped from US.	No US content restriction. Product may be 100% foreign content.	No US content restriction. Product may be 100% foreign content.
COVERAGE	1) 95% for monthly reporting policy. 2) 90% for country limits policy with a % refund for no claims bonus.	1) 95% for both commercial and political. 2) 90% commercial and 100% political.	95% coverage; may be eligible for no claims bonus.	90% coverage with a % refund for no claims bonus.
COUNTRY ELIGIBILITY	All countries can be considered. Determined by each country's economic and political climate. Can include domestic sales. Policy endorsed for countries covered.	Dependent on US government foreign policy. Specified by country limitation schedule.	All countries can be considered. Determined by each country's economic and political climate. Can include domestic sales. Policy endorsed for countries covered.	All countries can be considered. Determined by each country's economic and political climate. Can include domestic sakes. Policy endorsed for countries covered.

CREDIT APPROVALS	Flexible Discretionary Credit Limits giving insured option to approve accounts to approved limits.	Discretionary Credit Limits giving insured option to approve accounts to approved limits.	Flexible Discretionary Credit Limits giving insured option to approve accounts to approved limits.	Flexible Discretionary Credit Limits giving insured option to approve accounts to approved limits.
DEDUCTIBLE	Per policy year deductible, based on date of shipment.	Per policy year deductible, based on date of shipment.	Per policy year deductible, based on date of shipment.	Per policy year deductible, based on date of shipment.
PREMIUM PAYMENT	Monthly or prepay, determined as a % of insured sales. Requires spread of risk, normally whole turnover.	Monthly, determined as a % of insured sales. Requires spread of risk, normally whole turnover.	Prepay determined as a % of approved country limits. Requires spread of risk or key accounts.	Prepay or quarterly installments, determined as a % of insured sales. Requires spread of risk or key accounts.
MINIMUM PREMIUM	$10,000 per policy year. Minimum insured volume of $3,000,000.	$500 per policy year.	$10,000 per policy year. Minimum insured volume of $3,000,000.	$25,000 per policy year.
CLAIM FILING	90 days after due date.	90 days after due date.	90–360 days after due date.	90–360 days after due date.

Source: Imperial Bank, USA

Private insurers cover political and commercial credit risks. Policies can be purchased that exclude commercial risk and cover country risk only and vice versa. See charts of export credit insurance programs provided by some U.S. companies in Tables 9.4 and 9.5.

Much of the political-risk insurance is tied to credit provided to foreign buyers through national export credit organizations. No two national export credit systems are identical. However, there are similarities, the greatest of which is the universal involvement of government through the export credit agency concerned and of the commercial banking sector in the workings of the system.

Most countries have export-import banks which serve by providing credit support in the form of loans, guarantees, and insurance. EXIM banks cooperate with commercial banks in providing a number of arrangements to help exporters offer credit guarantees to commercial banks that finance export sales. Commercial banks are essentially intermediaries to EXIMBANKs for export guarantees on loans.

Transportation risks

Cargo insurance is an essential business tool for the exporter. Generally, coverage is sold on a warehouse-to-warehouse basis, i.e. from the seller's factory to the receiver's platform. It is available for air, land, ocean, and the mails. Coverage usually ceases a specific number of days after the ship or plane is unloaded. Policies can be purchased on a "per shipment" or "blanket" basis. Freight forwarders usually have a blanket policy to cover clients who do not have their own policy. Most insurance companies base cargo insurance on the value of all charges of the shipment including freight handling, etc. plus 10 percent to cover unseen contingencies. Rates vary according to product, client's track record, destination, and shipping method.

Ocean cargo insurance costs about US$0.50 to US$1.50 per US$100.00 of invoice value. Air cargo is usually about 25–30 percent less.

Summary

Of course there are risks to exporting your goods and services to foreign nations, but there are risks just doing business in your own country. The good news is that over the centuries international traders have developed many ways to manage and even avoid the risks of doing international business.

The next chapter explains how to finance an export venture.

CHAPTER TEN

Financing

> The man of yesterday has died in that of today,
> that of today dies in that of tomorrow.
>
> *Plutarch*

When business people think of finance they often have in mind "long-term" requirements to start a venture or sustain the firm over the long haul, such as capital loans for real estate, buildings, equipment, and improvements. Of course, capital is the major engine of growth for free enterprise. Long-term investment is also a major stimulant for international trade and investment—with capital, businesses are able to move toward outward orientation and world competition.

But, exporters often find "short-term" financing more daunting than long-term finance. Keeping the firm afloat on a day-to-day basis requires "working capital" to produce the product, and "cash flow" for marketing costs. There is nothing worse for the business person than to have orders which cannot be filled or bills which cannot be paid simply because there are outstanding unpaid accounts receivable—cash flow.

The risk takers

At the danger of sounding elementary, recall that the availability of financial capital depends on "return" versus "risk," and for long-term financing it comes in two forms: debt (bank loans, etc.) and equity (ownership). Debt being long-term borrowing without giving up ownership and equity which requires sharing some interest with those who invest. Although not limitless, for the right return there is actually a great deal of capital available and in many forms, not necessarily currency. Over the long history of international trade, exporters have also developed mechanisms to vault them over the "short-term" problems of doing cross-border business.

Long-term sources

Much capital for long-term expansion is raised internally within the firm, but the search for external sources is an ongoing necessity. Today global businesses often look beyond their home country. At one time the only sources for long-term financing were local banks and investors. Today the sources are global. Today, financial markets all over the world are convenient. Capital is fully mobile and moves to the beat of the drum of interest rate and return on investment. A business leader in Bangkok, Thailand, can pick up the telephone and tap into global financial capital markets wherever it makes best business sense.

The sources of long-term financial capital come in many forms some of which are personal savings, bank loans, subsidies, and venture capitalists. Some nations tie loans and grants to specific projects, foreign country and supranational sources are often tactically interesting.

Savers

Savers are not an extinct breed. Much of the world's wealth is still held in the hands of ordinary people who have lead frugal lives and saved a portion of their wages for the rainy day.

What do savers look for? The "cost of capital" is the market lending (borrowing) interest rate from a nation's best banks. Many people who have excess financial capital want to do better than the cost of capital. If the bank in their country, which is generally a very conservative place to invest, is offering a seven percent return, many would risk a portion of their savings for a 10 or 12 percent return in another country even though the investment carried more risk; therefore, for the right project financial capital is very available. Even gifts and grants are available for the right project.

Bank borrowing

Bankers are semi-risk takers, that is, their purpose is to rent money and it does not earn if it is sitting in a vault; therefore to the extent you can show some competence in your endeavor, they are willing to make loans. The point is that there is a lot of money in world banks and, except for national laws requiring reserves most money must be in motion at all times. International traders now search the world for their borrowing needs—they are fickle and their appetite follows world interest rates. Loans for international trade fall into two categories: secured and unsecured.

Secured

To reduce their exposure to loss banks often ask for collateral. Financing against collateral is called *secured financing* and is the most common method of raising new money. Banks will advance funds against payment obligations, shipment documents, or storage documents. Most common of these is advancement of funds against payment obligations or documentary title. In this case, the trader pledges the goods for export or import as collateral for a loan to finance them. The bank maintains a secure position by accepting as collateral documents that convey title such as negotiable bills of lading, warehouse receipts, or trust receipts.

Unsecured

In truth, *unsecured financing* is only for those who have a sound credit standing with their bank or have had long-term trading experience. It usually amounts to expanding already existing lines of working credit. For the small importer-exporter unsecured financing will probably be limited to a personal line of credit.

Stock markets

Stock markets are also worldwide. Financial markets are no longer just London and New York. Stock markets are open 24 hours a day all over the world: Tokyo, Hong Kong, Singapore, Paris, London, New York, San Francisco. Even Taiwan is moving in the direction of becoming a major financial capital.

Venture capitalists (VCs)

These are the organizations that build a pool of funds from those who are willing to take large risks for major returns. Those that provide the funds are people who generally have excess financial capital, enough that a loss might not put them in the pauper's house. Venture Capitalists are now operating in almost every country and they are looking for projects that have high potential. VCs often work hand-in-hand with the industrial policies of governments to focus capital into those projects which have high national priority and in some way have a measure of government protection.

Short-term sources

Trade finance or discounting is the dominant method of short-term exporter financing. Banks buy or lend against time drafts from a seller that a creditworthy foreign buyer has accepted or agreed to pay at a future date. This converts the paper into immediate cash. The amount the exporter receives is, of course, less than the face value. The difference, called a "discount" represents the fees and interest the bank charges for holding the draft until maturity. The exporter has several discounting or trade finance options: banker's acceptances, confirming, borrowing against receivables, sale of receivables, factoring, forfait financing. The following section explores these options but first let's discuss the terms "draft", "recourse," and "tenor."

Draft

A draft is a written order for a certain sum of money to be transferred on a certain date from the person who owes the money or agrees to make the payment (the drawee) to the creditor to whom the money is owed (the drawer of the draft). It is the same as a "bill of exchange."

Recourse

Recourse simply means that the original party or discountee takes responsibility to make good any default related to the transfer or sale of the note, receivable or document involved in the transaction. Non-recourse means exactly that—the seller accepts no responsibility for the failure to pay. There are, of course, various negotiable positions with regard to recourse. An example of limited recourse might be the circumstance wherein the documents, notes, or receivable are flawed, fraudulent or otherwise illegal.

Tenor

Tenor is the term used to designate the number of days payment is due after sight or after a date.

Banker's acceptances

Banker's Acceptances (B/A) are the dominant form of worldwide trade (discount) finance because it is the easiest and cheapest form. It is a method whereby a bank undertakes to accept the obligation of paying a time draft at a discount rate. A "clean" banker's acceptance is one which is not backed by a letter of credit. While most are backed by L/Cs, some banks provide the clean B/A option for accounts-receivable financing to importers and exporters alike. You receive the face value of the note, less the interest and fees as of the date you present the draft. Interest is based on the bank "discount rate" which is very favorable. Fees are bank charges for lending its name and credit rating and for the trouble of performing the transaction plus whatever country political risks it perceives. Typical fees might be ½ to one percent, depending on the risk and tenor. It could be as high as two percent in the case of a politically risky country and the shorter the tenor the higher the fee. Recourse is a negotiable, which also has a cost. Once accepted, the document, note or receivable becomes a negotiable instrument which can be bought and sold in the secondary market.

How a banker's acceptance works

The banker's acceptance (B/A) is a time draft presented to a bank by an exporter. This differs from what is known as a *trade acceptance* between buyer and seller in which a bank is not involved. The bank stamps and signs the draft "accepted" on behalf of its client, the importer. By accepting the draft, the bank undertakes and recognizes the obligation to pay the draft at maturity, and has placed its creditworthiness between the exporter (*drawer*) and the importer (*drawee*). Banker's acceptances are negotiable instruments that can be sold in the money market. The B/A rate is a discount rate generally two to three points below the prime rate. With the full creditworthiness of the bank behind the draft, eligible B/As attract the very best of market interest rates. The criteria for eligibility are

1 the B/A must be created within 30 days of the shipment of the goods;
2 the maximum tenor is 180 days after shipment;
3 it must be self-liquidating;
4 it cannot be used for working capital purposes;
5 the credit recipient must attest to no duplication.

Confirming

Confirming is a financial service common to Europe in which an independent company confirms an export order in the seller's country and makes payment for the goods in the currency of that country. The items eligible for confirmation are the goods themselves, transportation costs, forwarding fees, custom brokerage fees and any duties. For the exporter, confirming means the entire transaction from production to end user can be fully coordinated, bundled, and paid for over time.

Borrowing against receivables

Not every bank will loan against your foreign receivables as collateral. Those that do usually demand they be insured and will then only loan up to as high as 80–85 percent of the value of the goods. In many instances, a credit line can be negotiated against an aging of receivables schedule. The advantage of this kind of financing is its flexibility, the disadvantage is that the non-liquid asset remains on your balance sheet.

Sale of receivables

If it is difficult to find a bank to lend against receivables, it is doubly difficult to find one that will buy them, yet they do exist and the advantage is that the asset may then be removed from your balance sheet. The costs are similar to borrowing but probably would involve higher recourse costs.

Factoring

Factoring is the discounting of a foreign account receivable that does not involve a time draft. A factor is an agent who will, at a discount (usually five to eight percent of the gross), buy receivables. Banks do 95 percent of factoring; the remainder is done by private specialists. The exporter transfers title of the goods to a factoring house for cash at a discount from face value. Exporters tend to turn to factors as a last resort because it is more expensive than other discounting practices. Yet, by its very nature is more accessible to smaller firms because it primarily deals in low-value, short-term (90–120 day) payments. Factoring often includes other services such as credit research, collection, and age analysis. The factor makes a profit on the collection and provides a source of cash flow for the seller, albeit less than if the business had held out to make the collection itself.

For example, suppose you had a receivable of US$1,000.00. A factor might offer you a US$750.00 advance on the invoice and charge you five percent on the gross of US$1,000.00 per month until collection. If the collection is made within the first month, the factor would only keep US$50.00 and return US$200.00. If it takes two months, the factor would keep US$100.00 and return only US$150.00, etc.

The importer benefits from having the cash to reorder products from overseas. For a manufacturer, the benefit can be cash flow available for increased or new production.

Forfait financing

The term "a forfait" is a French term and literally translates to "surrendering rights." And that is the case for the classical forfaiting transaction, where the buyer gives up rights when purchasing a promissory note at discount from a seller (usually an exporter). This forfaiting of rights is signified by signing on the back of the note the words "without recourse" at the time of endorsement.

All of this may seem complicated bankers talk to the average business person, but the method has been a major financial device in Europe for many years and is growing worldwide. This is particularly true when doing business with developing nations that need capital equipment and place pressures on exporters to carry term paper in addition to government supported schemes such as countertrade and off-sets (discussed next).

Strong export-oriented countries, particularly European, have used this method as a matter of course. Financing houses in Switzerland, the United Kingdom and most other major banks in Europe handle these transactions as matter-of-factly as they would handle a banker's acceptance or letter of credit.

Why use forfaiting?

You want to sell your products but don't want long-term debt. Nevertheless, through competitive pressures (such as not losing out to another seller of the same goods just because of a lack of ingenuity for financing) you have been forced to accept a debt instrument. You need cash flow for working capital or other internal business reasons. Another reason you may want the debt instrument removed from your balance sheet is the credit and country risk exposure it represents. So, you are willing to sell the debt for liquidity.

How it works

The manufacturer (exporter) who agrees to discount the promissory notes is quoted a fixed price by the forfaiter (buyer of note) which locks in an interest expense while receiving immediate cash for the transaction. The forfaiter is only involved in the financial part of the transaction and in no sense enters any part of the commercial agreement reached between buyer and seller of the merchandise. Thus, the integrity of all parties is of paramount importance.

Whereas factoring is more suited to smaller deals (less than US$10,000), forfaiting is better suited for the higher level, medium- to long-term obligation of a minimum US$250,000 and more than 180-day payment terms. This is mainly because it is generally more expensive— usually costing several points above LIBOR plus front-end fees. Keep in mind that the investor who buys the promissory note assumes not only the forfaiting risk but also the country risk exposure (in lieu of an insurance premium the exporter would otherwise pay separately).

Other trade financing options

In addition to traditional trade financing several other important tools are available to the exporter. They include buyer credit arrangements, leasing, and various government support mechanisms.

Buyer credit arrangements

Much of the world's large international transactions are backed by home governments or a consortium of banks that loan, guarantee, provide insurance. National export financing agencies make their loans direct or to participating banks that then lend forward.

Leasing

International leasing has become an important form of financing worldwide, with leasing centers being established to take advantage of tax laws. Leasing has the advantage that the buyer needs little or no down payment and can tailor the payments.

Government support

Exporting is a cross-border business function for governments because it creates jobs, and brings in foreign currency; therefore, your first stop for short-term financing is your local international trade office. Most export/import banks have programs to guarantee short-term loans to support exporter working capital needs.

Supranational lending banks

Seeing the need to create trade and stimulate growth most nations of the global economic system in concert have developed a number of supranational intergovernmental lending banks. These exist at the world level as well as at the regional level.

World Bank

The World Bank Group, born in 1944 at the same conference held at Bretton Woods, New Hampshire, as the International Monetary Fund (IMF) (discussed later), is the most prominent supranational source of long-term lending and policy advice for developing countries. It promotes economic development and works to raise living standards by investing in productive projects and promoting the adoption of sustainable economic policies. It comprises four institutions:

1 the International Bank for Reconstruction and Development (IBRD), better known as the World Bank;
2 the International Development Association (IDA);
3 the International Finance Corporation (IFC);
4 the Multilateral Investment Guarantee Agency (MIGA).

The World Bank or IBRD makes "hard loans," that is, at market rates of interest for up to 35 years. These loans must be guaranteed by the borrowing government and repaid in convertible currency. To obtain its funds, the IBRD sells bonds on the international capital markets, and by selling its loan portfolios to private investors. Loans are principally used for social capital purposes, that is, for infrastructure: agriculture, roads, electric power, water supply, transportation, communications, and education.

International Development Association (IDA)

The International Development Association (IDA) is the "soft" or no-interest agency for the many developing countries that cannot qualify for

World Bank loans. IDA extends credits for periods up to 50 years, repayable, except for a modest service charge, in easy terms after a 10-year grace period. Unlike the World Bank, the IDA does not generate its own capital. It is dependent on member countries for replenishment.

International Finance Corporation (IFC)

The International Finance Corporation (IFC) participates in private-sector industrial projects. It does not make loans to governments, but rather is a lender or investor in equity along with private investors. The IFC gains its funds from member country subscriptions to its capital stock, from sale of its own investment portfolio to private investors, and from its right to borrow from the World Bank up to four times its own unimpaired capital and surplus.

Multilateral Investment Guarantee Agency (MIGA)

Multilateral Investment Guarantee Agency (MIGA), which began operation in June 1988, insures private foreign investment in developing countries against non-commercial risks such as expropriation, civil strife, and inconvertibility.

United Nations Development Program (UNDP)

The United Nations Development Program (UNDP) is intended to assist in identification, investigation, and presentation to financial agencies those projects in developing nations that make good investment sense.

Regional development banks

In addition to the World Bank Group, nations of specific regions of the world have formed other development banks intended to serve unique development needs.

Inter-American Development Bank (IDB)

Membership in the Inter-American Development Bank (IDB) is made up of the United States and all Latin American countries except Cuba. The IDB offers three categories of funds: "hard loans" those at ordinary capital market rates; "soft-currency window" those loans which have easy terms; and a Social Program Trust Fund (SPTF) to finance low-income housing and other social projects.

Asian Development Bank (ADB)

Established in 1966, the Asian Development Bank (ADB) has 19 Asian members, 11 European members plus the United States and Canada.

African Development Bank (AFDB)

The African Development Bank (AFDB), limited to a membership of only independent African countries, authorizes financial capital for "real" or "social" capital needs.

European Bank for Reconstruction and Development (EBRD)

The European Economic Community (EEC) has formed a new supranational institution named the European Bank for Reconstruction and Development (EBRD). This multinational organization has the goal of promoting democracy, pluralism, and the rule of law in assisting the changing central and eastern European nations who divorced themselves from communism during the peaceful revolution of 1989. Its charter will require at least 60 percent of its resources be devoted to private sector projects. Of the 39 member nations, 30 sent their presidents to inaugurate its birth in April 1991. According to its first president Jacques Attali, its goal is to reunite "the two halves of Europe." To be headquartered in London, the bank will promote business training, advise governments on shifting to market economies, help rebuild infrastructures, take part in creating a banking system and capital markets, assist in privatizing state-owned companies, encourage small business and help restore the environment.

Foreign aid

Many industrialized nations, including Japan, South Korea, Taiwan, and Germany, have increased their foreign assistance programs. They dispense funds to less developed countries through special agencies much like the United States Agency for International Development (USAID). This agency was chartered in 1961 to administer economic and technical programs through grants and loans for private and public sector development projects. In recent times most American capital-dispensing assistance funds have emphasized privatization and the stimulation of industrial programs.

Countertrade

Another creative alternative to sticky sales projects which might not otherwise happen due to currency barriers is countertrade. Out of necessity, "global businesses" from all nations are engaging in this practice. It is especially growing among capital equipment manufacturers, but has application for many interesting projects. For instance Pierre Cardin agreed to serve as a consultant to China in exchange for silks and cashmeres. Coca-Cola traded its syrup for cheese from a factory it built in the Soviet Union, for oranges it planted in an orchard in Egypt, and for tomato paste from a plant installed in Turkey.

Warning! There are countless stories of warehouses filled with goods that could not be sold after doing a countertrade deal. Countertrade is not recommended for the "new" to export company.

Countertrade is an umbrella term for a variety of unconventional reciprocal trading arrangements, the basic forms of which are counterpurchase, compensation, barter, buy-back, or swap. "Offset" and "switch trade" are terms used to describe unique types of countertrade often encompassing one or more of the above forms.

In general these terms involve the direct exchange of goods for other goods, without the use of money as a medium of exchange and often without involvement of a third party. They differ from each other with respect to the length of time to complete the transaction, the type of goods involved, and the financial arrangements involved.

In 1972 there were no more than 12 countries involved in countertrade. By 1985, more than 80 countries used the process. According to a recent report by the International Trade Commission, between two and three percent of all world trade is countertrade and in 1984, 5.6 percent or $7.1 billion of U.S. sales contracts involved the process.

U.S. government position

At the outset of any discussion of countertrade, you should understand why most governments do not fully support this method of doing business. Countertrade and barter are viewed as inconsistent with an open, free-trading system and not in the best long-term interest of the contracting parties. The point is, some foreign governments mandate countertrade, offsets, and other performance requirements but this is contrary to multilateral trade and payments principles which all free-market countries support.

Reasons for countertrade

There are several reasons why businesses and countries use countertrade transactions.

1 **Credit constraints.** Some countries have international debt problems which require them to manage their foreign currency very carefully. Getting dollars out of the country to pay an exporter is often

determined by the national priority of the goods being traded. Through countertrade agreements, countries such as Brazil, Mexico, and Peru, burdened by huge foreign debts and lacking capital of their own, can acquire the imports they need to keep their industry running and boost domestic growth.

2 **Creative marketing and financing.** Developing countries, wishing to minimize outlays of hard currency, use mixes of countertrade and soft currency. They often negotiate the establishment of cash-generating projects which are independent of the original transaction thus drawing new investments into the country.

3 **Dealing with controlled (non-market) economies.** Recent attitude changes by U.S. and other Western nations toward controlled economies such as the Soviet Union bode for an increase in countertrade in order to accommodate bilateral currency clearing difficulties or transfers of technology.

Who uses countertrade?

Participation in countertrade is dominated by exchanges between developed and developing nations, but it also occurs between one developing nation and another. One such deal occurred in late 1985 when a group of Brazilian businessmen agreed to swap $600 million worth of goods instead of paying for them outright. Strapped for cash, Peru swapped non-ferrous metals such as silver, copper, and zinc, as well as agricultural and non-traditional export products for Brazilian soybeans, sugar, and diverse manufactured goods—tractors, trucks, etc.

Barter deals do occur between the developed countries, but not due to lack of currency. More often these trades are arranged as an easy way to unload surplus products. Less developed countries also countertrade their surpluses. Nigeria for instance, has traded its oil for everything from chicken to automobiles, and Iran and Iraq have swapped oil for finished steel to rebuild as a result of previous conflicts.

Aerospace companies have the most experience—trading airplanes for goods. One of the best stories is about McDonnell-Douglas. When Yugoslavia sought to purchase $35 million worth of Mac's aircraft, the country had only $26 million available for the proposed purchase. Rather than miss the sale, Douglas suggested that Yugoslavia supply "Mac-Air" with parts for the aircraft equal in value to the missing $9 million. The arrangement succeeded and Douglas Aircraft has been refining its countertrade techniques ever since.

Forms of countertrade

Countertrade is a reciprocal trading arrangement. Countertrade transactions include:

- Counterpurchase obligates the foreign supplier to purchase from the buyer goods and services unrelated to the goods and services sold, usually with a one to five-year period.
- Reverse countertrade contracts require the importer (a U.S. buyer of machine tools from Eastern Europe, for example) to export goods equivalent in value to a specified percentage of the value of the imported goods—an obligation that can be sold to an exporter in a third country.
- Buyback arrangements obligate the foreign supplier of plant, machinery, or technology to buy from the importer a portion of the resultant production during a 5–25 year period.
- Clearing agreements between two countries that agree to purchase specific amounts of each other's products over a long-term specific period of time, using a designated "clearing currency" or barter in the transactions.
- "Switch" arrangements that permit the sale of unpaid balance of a clearing account to be sold to a third party, usually at a discount, that may be used for producing goods in the country holding the balance.
- Swap schemes through which products from different locations are traded to save transportation costs (e.g. Soviet oil may be "swapped" for oil from a Latin American producer, so the Soviet oil is shipped to a country in South Asia, while the Latin American oil is shipped to Cuba).
- Barter arrangements through which two parties directly exchange goods deemed to be of approximately equivalent value without any flow of money taking place.

Counterpurchase

Companies in the industrialized countries seeking to sell their products in most less developed countries (LDCs) often discover that the LDCs will not agree to purchase contracts, unless the exporting companies agree to buy or market products of the LDC that are valued at less than those products in the original Western purchase contract. If the products offered by LDCs are unrelated to the products being sold by the company seeking to export (i.e. they do not result from the Western export of plant, equipment, technology, or products), the agreement is referred to as a "counterpurchase" arrangement.

Compensation

Sometimes referred to as "buybacks," compensation agreements entail the sale of plant, equipment, and/or technology in return for resultant products once the facilities become functional. These types of arrangements, frequently shorter-term and involving the sale of a "turnkey" facility, became popular in the mid-1960s. Most early compensation deals involved the sale of technology and machinery for large-scale petrochemical facilities and mining operations. Compensation has two classifications:

1 *Direct*. This is a counterdelivery (also known as buyback) related directly to the product being sold.
2 *Indirect*. This includes all counterdelivery (also known as counterpurchases) of products unrelated to the product being sold.

Barter

Barter is the contractual direct exchange of goods or services (usually a short-term transaction) between principals without the use of money as a medium of exchange and without the involvement of a third party. In this type of arrangement, the two contracting parties decide the value of the products (or services) to be exchanged. When the volume of the exchange, and delivery dates are agreed upon, each side fulfills its obligation and the deal is complete.

Switch

Switch trading, typically associated with East—West countertrade occurs after counterdeliveries of products begin. If the recipient of the counter-trade products cannot dispose of the goods, the products are turned over to a Western trading house specializing in switch trade. A switch operation frequently involves a series of complicated transactions before a hard currency buyer is found. Trading house experts, or switch traders, maintain a self-developed network of companies and individuals that offer ready markets for discounted countertrade products. Many of these deals take more than one year to complete and most of the switch trading organizations are located in Western Europe and deal primarily in Eastern European goods. There are advantages and disadvantages in dealing with switch traders. Obviously a company can easily dispose of countertrade obligations to a switch-trading house. This releases the companies own staff from the time-consuming tasks of marketing the goods. The disadvantage is that a switch trade is often looked on as an insincere attempt to establish a long-term trade relationship.

Offset

A final type of countertrade, the offset agreement, is mainly used for long-term defense-related sales, and other "big ticket" items. They are used by a country to help recover the hard currency drain resulting from the purchase. Offset arrangements can generally be classified into one of three categories:

1 Direct offsets include any business that relates directly to the product being sold. Generally, the foreign vendor seeks local contractors to joint venture or co-produce certain parts.
2 Indirect offsets include all business unrelated to the product being sold; generally the vendor is asked to buy a country's goods or invest in an unrelated business.
3 A combination of direct and indirect offsets.

What does countertrade cost?

The variables for a countertrade deal are time, knowledge of how to dispose of a product, and volume. Some large firm's have established their own profit or cost centers to specialize in satisfying countertrade obligations, but most smaller companies deal through agents or trading companies. Twenty-five thousand dollars plus expenses up front is not unusual for a countertrade commission. That amount should be deducted later from a success or retainer fee. The trade-off is the cost of consultant commissions against developing your own in-house capability.

Another cost might be as a result of overvaluation of products on the part of producers. Care must be given that a negative cost factor isn't borne by one party or the other due to incorrect valuation. It is not unusual that products offered for countertrade are overvalued by the producer. If the products to be received in return are urgently needed, you may be able to negotiate a lower value, one which might more closely approximate the market value. However, many countries rebel at these efforts, because they view it as an insult, lowering the prestige of the country and the producer. To avoid this type of loss, you may have to inflate the price of the primary goods to arrive at an accurate relative value.

Countertrade risks

Countertrade is fraught with horror stories, so marketing in countries that barter is not a game for amateurs. Statistics show that 50 percent of all world countertrade deals lose money or only break even. You should be aware from the beginning that there have been cases where the result was a warehouse full of goods unsalable in an intended market.

Here is a list that a firm, relatively new to export, should know about dealing with countertrade:

■ Know what goods are involved.
■ Who moves the goods.
■ What fees are involved.
■ Search out any hidden costs.

- Know the countertrade liabilities.
- Know the quality.
- Know the market value of the product today.
- Know the market value of the product in the future.
- Know the exporting procedures and get agreement on when the countertrade is complete.
- Expect to pre-sell the product in the United States or a third country.
- Get the negotiations down on paper. Write the specifications, purchase orders, and letters of credit very precisely.
- Countertrade is expensive in terms of time, and transportation, so negotiate the entire deal before moving anything.

One solution would be to hire a countertrade specialist. Why? Primarily to understand the culture of the country in which you plan to deal. On the other hand quality of the compensation product is often as important as cultural differences. A China specialist would analyze the existing industries in the Chinese province where the American product is to be built and match them with known U.S. markets. That specialist would also know that another factor in dealing with China is that their bureaucrats are not good at coordinating between Trade Organizations. They don't always talk to each other. As a result the time factor is sometimes lost or forgotten, causing excessive delays in negotiations and closing deals.

Support services

Few manufacturers have developed their own in-house countertrade organizations. Most firms and especially the smaller-sized and product-specific firms need services from third parties such as banks, brokers, traders, some law firms, or specialized end users.

Many products offered in countertrade require the skills of specialized traders because the goods come from low-tech or low-growth industries. More important, the negotiator must know end user needs. Exporters should also be cautious because some foreign products often don't measure up to world-class standards.

A manufacturer should expect the countertrade specialist to handle everything including the inventory and have the funds credited to their account. In other words, it should be hands off from start to finish. Therefore, countertrade specialists should be present with representatives of the manufacturing company during countertrade negotiations.

A list of consultants can be obtained from the International Chamber of Commerce or the local World Trade Center.

Major commercial banks supplement their export related services with countertrade services. Most of this has been an advisory kind of service by matching bank clients; however some actually manage a client's countertrade transaction.

The guidelines for countertrade

- Get professional help.
- Let a consultant or an intermediary act as principal and primary negotiator from the beginning.
- Get the consultant or intermediary involved as far in advance as possible to survey the goods, conduct a feasibility study, and get a buyer.

Summary

The world is full of money ready to be invested in cross-border ventures. The problem for most exporters is their vision is too narrow, they don't exhaust all their options. The menu of short-term financing options is long and the wise seller will explore the list for the right mechanism for their firm.

The next chapter of the book explains the tricks of international trade beginning with how to beat the tax and tariff men by organizing for special tax benefits, using bonded warehouses and foreign trade zones (FTZs).

CHAPTER ELEVEN

Tax and tariff loopholes

Plan for the future because that's where you are going to spend the rest
of your life.

Mark Twain

All nations offer schemes to encourage exporting, after all it creates jobs
and brings foreign currencies. These carrots range from tax exemption of
export goods, to recovery of value added taxes and tariffs, to business
opportunities that lessen the burdens of government. The purpose of this
chapter is to explore these techniques in order to improve the firm's
profitability.

Drawback

Drawback is the refunding of duties paid on imported goods and their
derivatives if they are subsequently exported. Suppose you re-export
goods that were originally imported; or you export items that contain
imported merchandise; or export items that contain whole imported
components. For each of these you might claim a drawback of tariffs paid
when the goods first entered for consumption. The key to drawback is
good inventory tracking and record keeping procedures. Make application for drawback with your local customs port of entry office.

VAT recovery

In as much as the Value Added Tax (VAT) must be paid on entry into
those counties that use such a system and again collected at the point of
sale, the non-member exporter may (with exceptions) recover any VAT
paid on entry.

Tax exclusions for exporting

Many countries have developed schemes to lessen the tax burden for
businesses that export. Most of these are similar, only differing slightly
from that of the United States which is explained here for example
purposes.

The United States territorial tax rules offer what amounts to about a 15 percent exclusion of the taxable income earned on international sales to the firm that organizes an off-shore office through which it passes its export documentation. Here's how it works. Under rules put into effect in January 1985, exporters who wish to take advantage of this incentive, which can be very substantial, must establish a subsidiary off-shore foreign corporation. Called a Foreign Sales Corporation (FSC) under the tax code, this subsidiary organization must maintain a summary of its permanent books of account at the foreign office, and have at least one director resident outside the United States.

Meeting these requirements isn't as difficult as it sounds. Some 23 foreign countries, those which have an agreement to exchange tax information with the United States, and all U.S. possessions like the Virgin Islands, Guam, and Saipan have already established offices capable of providing direct support as your FSC. Multiple exporters, up to 25, may jointly own an FSC and through the use of several classes of common stock divide the profits of the FSC among the several shareholders. Of course larger firms can form their own FSC.

Regional free trade areas

Free trade areas may be bilateral or multilaterally negotiated. The contents of the agreement can and do include the harmonization of many conditions that range from customs procedures, to rules of origin, to the range of products to be included (industrial, agricultural, complete exchange).

Typically the nations involved agree to reduce or abolish mutual import duties and other restrictions (these could include some non-tariff barriers (NT)), often defining a time period during which duties are gradually changed. A common internal tariff (CIT) system tends to improve the uniformity and transparency of existing interstate controls.

Free trade agreements do not go so far as to harmonize the economic policies of the negotiating nations. Nor is there a negotiated common external tariff (CXT). Each member country retains its own tariff and quota system on trade with third countries; therefore these agreements can be defective unless rules of origin are carefully enforced. Examples of free trade areas include: European Free Trade Association (EFTA), North American Free Trade Agreement (NAFTA), Latin American Free Trade Association (LAFTA), Mercorsur (formed by the Southern Cone countries of South America), Australian/New Zealand Free Trade Association (ANZFTA), and Caribbean Free Trade Association (CARIFTA).

Customs union

A customs union abolishes most protectionism inside the union and sets up a common external tariff system (CXT) with regard to outside countries. It would include common non-tariffs (CNT) as well. A union is a sophisticated level of economic integration, but it does not go so far as to harmonize the economic policy within the negotiated region. Examples include: Belgium, Netherlands and Luxembourg (BENELUX) and the Economic Community of West African States (ECOWAS).

Common Market

While having the same trade policy as a customs union, a common market also allows the free transfer of the factor endowments: capital, technology, management/know-how, labor, and intelligence as well as products between member nations. Under certain crisis situations such as massive unemployment or foreign exchange shortages, an individual nation may temporarily erect barriers to the free flow between itself and the other members. Examples are: European Economic Community (EEC), Central American Common Market (CACM), Association of South East Asian Nations (ASEAN), and Andean Common Market (ANCOM).

Economic union

This is an even greater degree of economic integration than the common market, because of the effects of harmonization of national economic policies. The major characteristic of this stage of economic integration is the surrendering of sovereignty beyond the CIT and CXT of the Customs Union to allow a supranational government (above the national governments) to be responsible for economic policy. As in the United States the economic union has a single monetary system, central bank, and a common industrial/economic policy. This is a difficult stage to attain. Unlike the U.S.A. which essentially achieved this stage from its birth, blocs such as the European Union (EU) must attempt to harmonize laws and rules that have been in place for long periods. Examples: U.S.A., and EU after 1999.

Political union

The ultimate form of multinational integration is only achieved after a supranational body is promoted to unite the political environment of an earlier stage of economic integration. It requires the subordination of national entity to that of the union's entity.

The former Union of Soviet Socialist Republics (U.S.S.R.), although disintegrated as a bloc in 1991, had been, since its founding in 1922 the world's largest economic and political union. The Council of Mutual Economic Assistance (COMECON or CMEA) which included the USSR, Bulgaria, Czechoslovakia, East Germany, Hungary, Mongolia, Poland,

Romania, Cuba, and Vietnam was formed in 1949. This Moscow-based Eastern bloc organization was an example of a coordinating group to facilitate trade among the Communist nations. In early 1991, with the disintegration of the bloc, the group changed its name to the Organization for International Economic Cooperation (OIEC).

The election of a European Parliament within the EU was the first step toward forming a European political union.

Insider

A major issue for the global enterprise is the importance of taking an insider position within the trading bloc. In order to find an export outlet for goods within, many manufacturers believe the best positioning is to own or co-own a plant inside so as to take advantage of beneficial rules of origin and be perceived as a local player.

Major trade blocs

Three major trade blocs have been formed. The "triad" as it is called includes the nations of the European Union (EU) plus any others of that region which may be approved to integrate; the North American Free Trading Area including Canada, United States, Mexico and a growing number of South American nations; and Japan and the ASEAN group which originally included Brunei, Indonesia, Malaysia, Singapore, Philippines, and Thailand, but may soon include South Korea, Taiwan and Hong Kong.

European Union (EU)

The European Union (EU) is a modern evolution of a customs union (1968) expanding to a common market then to an economic union and possibly a political union.

European Free Trade Association (EFTA)

Standing in the wings to join the EU are many nations that see benefits to the economic integration. The European Free Trade Association (EFTA) members as well as nations of central Europe are candidates. EFTA formed in 1959 includes the United Kingdom, the Scandinavian countries, Austria, Switzerland, and Portugal.

North American Free Trade Agreement (NAFTA)

The first step of this integration was an agreement in 1989 between Canada and the United States negotiated to harmonize their interstate controls and achieve a Common Internal Tariff over a ten year period. In 1991, the NAFTA began negotiations to include Mexico. Other nations edging toward joining the North American integration include: Chile, and the Southern Cone countries of Argentina, Brazil, Paraguay and Uruguay.

Japan, ASEAN, and APEC

Japan stands alone as the major trading nation of Asia; however, the Association of South East Asian Nations (ASEAN), which was formed in 1975 and included Indonesia, Malaysia, Philippines, Singapore, and Thailand, has considered expanding to include South Korea, Hong Kong, Taiwan. Should these countries join, the East Asian bloc would become the largest of the Triad with a total population of about 500 million compared to the EC with about 320 million and the NAFTA with about 365 million.

This bloc is weakened by its geography and economic gaps. Made up mainly of islands strung north and south the idea of a single bloc is difficult to grasp. The economic gap is even more formidable. For instance, Indonesia's per Capita GDP is about $500 while Singapore's is about $10,000.

Minor trade blocs

Over the past 50 years or so smaller nations have been integrating economically to form their own blocs. In terms of trade volume the minor trade blocs are:

Latin America Free Trade Agreement (LAFTA)

The Treaty of Montevideo negotiated in 1960, initiated the Latin America Free Trade Agreement (LAFTA) which includes Argentina, Bolivia, Brazil, Chile, Peru, Uruguay, Mexico, Paraguay, Columbia, and Ecuador. Intended as a free trade area to liberalize trade among the participants, it turned out to be weak because the reduction of barriers had many loopholes. In 1981, LAFTA was superseded by the Latin American Integration Association (LAIA) which changed the purpose to become an area of preferences instead of a free trade area.

Central American Common Market (CACM)

In 1962, the Central American Common Market (CACM) was formed to include Guatemala, Nicaragua, Honduras, Costa Rica, and El Salvador.

Mercosur

In 1991, the Southern Cone countries of South America framed an agreement for a regional trading bloc called Mercosur which includes: Argentina, Brazil, Paraguay and Uruguay.

East Africa Economic Community

East Africa formed their Economic Community in 1967 to include Kenya, Uganda, and Tanzania.

Economic Community of West African States

The Economic Community of West African States (ECOWAS) consists of Nigeria, Ghana, Liberia, Ivory Coast (Côte d'Ivoire), Senegal, Togo, Benin, Upper Volta, Gabon, Cameroon, Mali, Gambia.

Caribbean Free Trade Association (CFTA)

In 1968, the Caribbean Free Trade Association came together and includes Antigua, Barbados, Guyana, and Trinidad.

Andean Common Market (ACM)

Following on those footsteps of CFTA, the Andean Common Market (ACM) with Peru, Chile, Columbia, Ecuador, Bolivia, and Venezuela was formed in 1969.

Gulf Cooperation Council (GCC)

On the African continent, six Arab Gulf states, Bahrain, Oman, Qatar, Saudi Arabia, and United Arab Emirates (U.A.E.) formed the Gulf Cooperation Council (GCC) in 1981. The main objective was regional economic integration, but also to develop cooperation in the fields of economics, politics, communication, social and cultural.

Arab Economic Union (AEU)

The Arab Economic Union, consisting of Libya, Tunis, Mauritania, and Morocco was formed in the late 1980s also for purposes of regional cooperation.

Arab Cooperation Council (A.C.C.)

One of the most recent attempts at integration is the Arab Cooperation Council (A.C.C.). Formed in 1989 it includes Egypt, Jordan, Iraq, and Yemen.

British Commonwealth

The British Commonwealth was one of the earliest economic unions.

German Zollverein

Another early attempt was the German Zollverein (Federal Republic of Germany) in 1834.

Benelux

Benelux, made up of the first letters of each of the member country's names, Belgium, The Netherlands, and Luxembourg, is an economic union first formed as a customs union in 1948 with a single (common) external tariff. By 1956, more than 95 percent of trade among the nations was free of all interstate controls. It was not until 1958, that the Benelux Treaty established the economic union, which when it came into effect in 1960 established the world's first completely free labor market. The Benelux Nations eventually created a common foreign trade policy which permitted the free movement of goods, workers, services and capital.

> ## Check List
>
> ■ To what trade blocs do your target countries belong?
> ■ What are the trade bloc rules?
> ■ Should the firm take an insider position?
> ■ What are the rules-of-origin implications?
> ■ What are the market implications for your product(s) vis-à-vis the bloc?

Free trade zones (FTZ)

Special zones for free trade, sometimes called in-bond regions or export processing zones did not develop in any significant way until the 19th century. Some of the more notable zones worldwide are the port regions of Hamburg, Hong Kong, Koushieng in Taiwan, and Jurong Port in Singapore. Inland free zones also exist, most notable of which are the in-bond free zones surrounding the Mexican Maquiladoras. Most nations have established free zones to promote interchange of business with market economies.

Free zones, under legislation of the sovereign nation where they are located, are considered outside the customs territory of that country. The concept is an ancient one, dating back to Egyptian times. Goods entering the zone pay no tariff or other taxes, under a guarantee (bond) that they will not be entered into the domestic market. Should they enter the domestic market, all duties must be routinely paid. While in these free zones, typically goods can be altered, assembled, manufactured and manipulated. Thus they become areas where barriers to free trade are circumvented.

Free trade zones (FTZ) (called foreign trade zones in the U.S.A) are restricted areas considered outside the customs territory under the supervision of the local customs service.

Typically an FTZ is a large warehouse, fenced and alarmed for security reasons, which tenants lease in order to bring in merchandise, foreign or domestic, to be stored, exhibited, assembled, manufactured or processed in some way. They are usually located in or near the customs ports of entry, usually in industrial parks or in terminal warehouse facilities. The usual customs entry procedures and payment of duties are not required on foreign merchandise in the zone unless it enters the customs territory for domestic consumption. The importer has a choice of paying duties either on the original foreign material or the finished product. Quota restrictions do not normally apply to foreign merchandise in a zone.

The purpose of a free trade zone is to stimulate international trade and thus contribute to the economic growth of a region by creating jobs and income. But from the point of view of an importer-exporter it's all about PROFITS.

Multinational free zones

The investment attraction objectives of two or more countries are often best met by creating a multinational zone. This cooperation serves the interests of manufacturers and traders seeking plant sites to supply the global market and spurs the development of new industry and economic growth in the region. An example is the TransCarpathian Special Economic Zone of Hungary and Ukraine.

What are the advantages of using an FTZ?

Actually, perceived advantages are limitless, unfortunately there are many cases of firms that have begun operations in FTZs and lost money. Each operation in the zone must make business and profit sense and must be individually analyzed. Here is a list of the regulatory advantages:

1 Customs procedural requirements are minimal.
2 Merchandise may remain in a zone indefinitely, whether or not it is subject to duty.
3 Customs security requirements provide protection against theft.
4 Customs duty and internal revenue tax, if applicable, are paid when merchandise is transferred from a foreign trade zone to the customs territory for consumption.

5 While in a zone, merchandise is not subject to duty or excise tax. Tangible personal property is generally exempt from state and local ad valorem taxes.
6 Goods may be exported from a zone free of duty and tax.
7 The zone user who plans to enter merchandise for consumption in the customs territory may elect to pay either the duty and taxes on the foreign material placed in the zone or on the article transferred from the zone. The rate of duty and tax and the value of the merchandise may change as a result of manipulation or manufacture in the zone. Therefore, the importer may pay the lowest duty possible on the imported merchandise.
8 Merchandise under bond may be transferred to a foreign trade zone from the customs territory for the purpose of satisfying a legal requirement to export or destroy the merchandise. For instance, merchandise may be taken into a zone in order to satisfy any exportation requirement, or an exportation requirement of any Federal law in so far as the agency charged with its enforcement deems it advisable. Exportation or destruction may also fulfill requirements of certain state laws.

The role of the customs service

Customs is responsible for controlling the admission of merchandise into the FTZ, the handling and disposition of merchandise within the FTZ, and the removal of merchandise from it. Here are several specific customs responsibilities:

■ To collect duty and taxes when foreign merchandise is brought into the zone.
■ To control the admission of merchandise into the zone.
■ The handling and disposition within the zone.
■ Supervise, inspect and/or audit FTZ operations.

Typical free trade zone options

There are two basic ways which space in a free trade zone may be leased and three general categories of zone users. These distinctions create different options for zone use.

The first choice for a tenant is to lease space in a zone on either a short or long-term basis. The second leasing choice is whether to use the public zone portion of the zone warehouse or the private portion of the facilities.

Short-term tenants frequently use the zone for temporary storage of goods when the final destination has not been determined. Long-term tenants use it for various cost savings benefits which accrue from manipulations and manufacturing that require value added.

The public portion of a zone is most often used to take advantage of the high security an FTZ provides, to gain a financial advantage, or to store an inventory that has import quota restrictions (when the quota opens up, the product is already in the country and can be moved into the market quickly). The private lease facilities are most often used by those firms that intend to manufacture or manipulate their product.

Categories of FTZ users

The first category user is the importer/exporter/re-exporter. This user admits domestic and foreign merchandise into the zone and exports the same or a modified product.

The second category of user is the non-manufacturing importer. This user is closely related to the category one user, except that in this case the importer is only interested in the space for the cost saving benefits.

Category three user is a manufacturer producing in a free trade zone. In this case the user wishes to take advantage of inverted tariff choices (allowing duty to be set on the imported components or on the finished product) for cost savings.

What goods may be placed in an FTZ?

Any domestic goods or goods originating abroad that are not prohibited by law, whether dutiable or not, may be placed in an FTZ. Goods that may not be lawfully "imported" such as obscene and immoral films, pictures advocating treason or insurrection, and goods made by convicts or forced labor may not be entered into an FTZ. Goods that may not "enter" the customs territory, such as textiles for which the quota is closed, may be placed in an FTZ.

Merchandise falls into four "status" classifications:

Privileged foreign status

Prior to any manipulation or manufacture which would change its tariff classification, an importer may apply to the district director to have imported merchandise in the zone given privileged foreign status. The merchandise is classified and appraised and duties and taxes are determined as of the date the application is filed. Taxes and duties are payable, however, only when such merchandise or articles manipulated, manufactured or produced from such merchandise, are transferred to the customs territory.

Domestic Status

This status, which may be approved upon application to the district director, is available for merchandise which is (a) the growth, product, or manufacture of the United States on which all internal revenue taxes, if applicable, have been paid, (b) previously imported merchandise on which all internal revenue taxes have been paid, or (c) merchandise previously admitted free of duty. Domestic merchandise may be returned to the customs territory free of duty and taxes upon compliance with the Customs regulations.

Zone Restricted Status

Merchandise transferred to a zone from the customs territory for storage or for the purpose of satisfying a legal requirement for exportation or destruction is considered exported and cannot be returned to the customs territory for consumption unless the rules specify that its return is in the public interest. The status of merchandise transferred to a zone under these circumstances is "zone restricted." Zone restricted merchandise may not be manipulated, except to destroy it, or manufactured in a zone. As in the case of privileged status, the zone user must apply for zone restricted status on the appropriate foreign trade zones form.

Non-privileged Foreign Status

Non-privileged foreign status is a residual category for merchandise which does not have privileged or zone restricted status. Articles composed entirely of, or derived entirely from, non-privileged merchandise are classified and appraised in their condition at the time of legal transfer to the customs territory for consumption or for customs bonded warehousing.

Articles of Mixed Status

Since manipulation and manufacture generally are permitted in a zone, articles transferred to the customs territory may be composed in part of, or derived in part from, merchandise that is privileged and non privileged, whether foreign and/or domestic. The articles are appraised according to the status of the merchandise of which they are composed or from which derived, as explained above.

Additionally, foreign merchandise, subject to specified customs controls and conditions, may be temporarily removed from a zone without formal entry for the performance of certain limited operations and therefore returned in the same zone status to the zone from which it is removed. This procedure is designed to remove unnecessary burdens on zone inventory and accounting procedures where, in so doing, there is no danger to the revenue.

What type of business would use an FTZ and what operation would they perform?

Not all businesses may benefit from FTZ operations, and those contemplating using one must analyze their market potential and economic potential. Some that might benefit are:

- Automotive Parts—Repack, re-mark and distribute.
- Clothing—cut and sew imported fabric for import and export.
- Food stuffs—label, sample and repack for shipment.
- Liquor—affix stamps, destroy broken bottles, defer duty.
- Machinery—inspect, repair, clean and paint.
- Office equipment—inspect and distribute.
- Televisions and other electronics repackaged for shipment.
- Sporting goods—sort and repackage for shipment.

A foreign trade zone is simply a way for a business to save money, no more and no less.

A foreign or "free" trade zone (FTZ) is one of the integral elements of a complete trading system and those who work in the international arena, particularly in finance, and marketing, need to (a) understand what a Free Trade Zone is designed to do, (b) become aware of its money saving advantages, and (c) begin planning for operations.

Money saving reasons to use an FTZ

The uses of a free trade zone for money saving reasons is only limited to the creativity of the user and the trade off of the costs of leasing space in a free trade zone versus storing goods in a commercial warehouse. Here are several standard reasons:

1 *Cost of money.* Drawback is the recovery of duty already paid and is a costly and time consuming process. The Treasury Department does not expedite the repayment of duties already paid, and if they finally do, they only pay 99 percent of the original amount, keeping one percent to cover administrative costs. If the duty had not been paid in the first place that sum of money could have been earning interest. The interest and administrative cost result in a cost of money that, for companies with high inventories, could have been avoided by using a foreign trade zone.
2 *Cash flow.* The money paid to the customs service under the tariff schedule is money no longer available for other uses, even if that money is later recovered under drawback procedures. Using an FTZ to defer duty or taxes improves a cash flow position.

3 *Reclamation.* There are many examples of reclamation within an FTZ which can provide cost savings, in fact the possibilities are limited only by the imagination of the user and the legality of the operation. Consider these examples: a computer manufacturer imports chips from offshore (Asia or Mexico). Before importing them the manufacturer conducts the quality assurance (QA) check within the FTZ. The firm reclaims the gold and other materials from the failed boards, sends the recovered material back to the offshore plant and imports only the chips that pass QA, thus avoiding duty on the failed units.

4 *Inverted tariff.* A free trade zone is the only method whereby an importer can choose between paying the duty rate of material parts or the rate of a finished product. The importer would of course make the choice that provided the greatest cost savings.

5 *Lower insurance costs.* A free trade zone is required to be a secure area. It is fenced and alarmed and often guarded. For that reason and because the value of an inventory is not increased by the value added in the FTZ, the inventory stored within a zone is often charged at lower insurance rates.

6 *Transportation time savings.* Goods destined for a free trade zone (FTZ) are not delayed on the dock for customs, but rather because they are considered in-bond, are usually given priority for pierside movement. Therefore those items which have some manipulations, reclamation or need to be broken into smaller shipping amounts can be expedited by using the foreign trade zone.

7 *Reduced pierside pilferage and/or damage.* Because there are no dockside delays, there is less risk of theft, pilferage and damage to the incoming goods.

8 *Fine avoidance.* Goods imported with improper or incorrect labels are subject to fines. By checking the labels within a zone the fines can be avoided.

9 *Advantage over a bonded warehouse.* Avoid the cost of a bond—the zone operator buys the bond.

10 *Environmental protection.* Reclamation activities within an FTZ are centered within an enclosed area, using special machines and can be carefully controlled.

11 *General system of preferences (GSP).* Combining the mix of content to gain the duty-free advantage of this multilateral trade agreement.

12 *State and local taxes.* Under Federal law, tangible personal property imported into an FTZ, and tangible personal property produced in the United States and held in an FTZ for export, is exempt from state and local ad valorem taxes.

13 *Quota allocations.* Duty and charges against quota allocations can be avoided if shipments are rejected.

14 *Eliminate* duty on merchandise re-exported or destroyed in the zone.

15 *Defer* duty on foreign goods until they leave the zone.
16 *Indefinite* storage awaiting a more receptive market or more favorable sales conditions.

Generalized system of preferences (GSP)

A concept developed within UNCTAD to encourage the expansion of manufactured and semi-manufactured exports from developing countries by making goods more competitive in developed country markets through tariff preferences. This multilateral trade agreement provides duty-free treatment of certain products of designated developing countries (including Mexico, but excluding Korea, Taiwan, Singapore and Hong Kong) effective January 1, 1989. When eligible products originating in a GSP designated country are imported into the United States, they receive duty-free treatment provided certain documentary, origin, and other requirements are met. The most significant requirement is the 35 percent value criteria. To be eligible for duty-free treatment, the value of materials originating in the GSP country, plus direct costs of processing performed in the GSP country, must equal at least 35 percent of the total customs appraised value.

Case studies that saved millions of dollars

Using a Free Trade Zone is not to the advantage of every business, but those that do not take the time to do some simple calculations may find that they are paying for significantly higher costs than their competitor.

The Case of the Leather Boot/Roller Skate

An importer found very high quality boots manufactured in China but the tariff at the time was too high. Cleverly, he shipped the boots into a foreign trade zone, attached wheels to the bottoms and entered the boots as roller skates. Now at practically no duty, this business person made a ton of money.

The Case of the Maritime Sub-Zone

National Ship Building Company in San Diego, California, discovered a quirk in U.S. import laws that says a vessel is "an intangible" and not subject to tariff. The company applied and received permission to become a sub-zone of the Long Beach Foreign Trade Zone. Foreign parts were brought into the zone duty-free, incorporated into the hull of the vessel, then sailed away duty-free. More than $1,000,000 was saved due to this clever use of the law.

The Case of the Computer Chip

Computer chips were manufactured offshore in Singapore. Before they were entered into the customs territory of the U.S. they were brought into a foreign trade zone for quality assurance (QA) inspection. Those found below standards were crushed, ground and sorted. The gold used in the chips was reclaimed, but never entered into the U.S. It was shipped back to the plant in Singapore. The remainder of the waste materials were entered as trash, duty-free. Only those chips that passed QA were entered for duty purposes. This firm avoided drawback, and thus kept their money working for the company, not Uncle Sam.

Customs bonded warehouse

A bonded warehouse is a building or other secure area within the customs territory where dutiable foreign merchandise may be placed for a period up to five years without payment of duty. Only cleaning, repacking and sorting may take place. The owner of the bonded warehouse incurs liability and must post a bond with the customs service and abide by those regulations pertaining to control and declaration of tariffs for goods on departure. The liability is canceled when the goods are removed.

Types of bonded warehouses

Typically there are eight different types of bonded warehouses:

1 Storage areas owned or leased by the government to store merchandise undergoing customs inspection, under seizure, or unclaimed goods.
2 Privately owned warehouses used exclusively for the storage of merchandise belonging or consigned to the proprietor.
3 Publicly bonded warehouses used exclusively to store imported goods.
4 Bonded yards or sheds for the storage of heavy and bulky imported merchandise such as pens for animals—stables and corrals, and tanks for the storage of imported fluids.
5 Bonded grain storage bins or elevators.
6 Warehouses used for the manufacture in bond, solely for exportation, of imported articles.
7 Warehouses bonded for smelting and refining imported metal-bearing materials.
8 Bonded warehouses created for sorting, cleaning, repacking or otherwise changing the condition of imported merchandise, but not manufacturing.

Table 11.1 Comparison of FTZ to Bonded Warehouse

Function	Bonded Warehouse	Zone
Customs Entry	A bonded warehouse is within U.S. Customs territory; therefore a Customs Entry must be filed to enter goods into the warehouse.	A Zone is not considered within customs territory. Customs entry is, therefore, not required until removed from a Zone.
Permissible Cargo	Only foreign merchandise may be placed in a bonded warehouse.	All merchandise, whether domestic or foreign, may be placed in a Zone.
Customs Bonds	Each entry must be covered by either a single entry, term bond or general term bond.	No bond is required for merchandise in a Zone.
Payment of duty	Duties are due prior to release from bonded warehouses.	Duties are due only upon entry into the customs territory.
Manufacture of goods	Manufacturing is prohibited.	Manufacturing is permitted with duty payable at the time the goods leave the Zone for consumption. Duty is payable on either the imported components or the finished product, whichever carries a lower rate.
Appraisal and Classification	Immediately.	Tariff rate and value may be determined either at the time of admission into a Zone or when goods leave a Zone, at your discretion.
Storage periods	Not to exceed 5 years.	Unlimited.
Operations on merchandise destined for domestic consumption	Only cleaning, repackaging and sorting may take place and under Customs supervision.	Sort, destroy, clean, grade, mix with foreign or domestic goods, label, assemble, manufacture, exhibit, sell, repack.
Customs Entry Regulations	Apply fully.	Only applicable to goods actually removed from a Zone for U.S. consumption.

Bonded warehouse or foreign trade zone?

Table 11.1 shows the advantages of a foreign trade zone over a bonded warehouse.

Being aware of all the possibilities is a vital part of competing and winning the trade game. Not every importer/exporter will need countertrade or make use of a foreign trade zone or a customs bonded warehouse, but proper and advanced planning is essential to take advantage of the subtleties of the trade laws. An appreciation of the capabilities of each of the business tools presented in this chapter could lead to the recognition of a winning opportunity.

Summary

The list of methods to stimulate exporting is long and the opportunities for you to reduce your cost lies in understanding these schemes.

The next chapter explains how to improve profits through production sharing.

CHAPTER TWELVE

Improve profits

In a price sensitive marketplace,
the lower costs achieved by offshore
production often enhance volume. We must
integrate the labor resources of the third
world, where a tremendous number of workers
are desperately in need of jobs, with the
purchasing power of the developed countries.

Peter Drucker

Production sharing is about the integration of the strengths of an organization in one country with the strengths of a firm in another country to get the right inputs for the right output in order to vault a product into the international market place at a competitive price. Of course, if quality isn't world class, nothing happens.

Industrial nations like the United States *share* their capital, highly skilled management, and high-technology with less costly labor found in less developed countries.

The amount of physical content in the product is the determinant because it is often the cost driver and therefore the key to profitability.

Some firms move toward automation as a substitute for less-skilled human labor, but many more have neither a product that lends itself to robotics nor the capital to invest.

Smaller firms with products no longer at the cutting edge of technology and facing flat domestic sales, are interested in expanding overseas, but to sustain their competitiveness, cost adjustments are required.

This chapter explains how many organizations source lower worldwide labor costs and production-sharing opportunities in order to make these competitive adjustments and improve profitability.

To attain these cost adjustments some manufacturers transfer processes that contain high physical content off-border. Thus value is added to the product at less cost by taking advantage of the lower labor rates and highly trainable foreign workforces in other nations. Production sharing provides five advantages to these companies:

1 Production/assembly plants can be nearer the export market.
2 Lower costs of production make products more competitive in the domestic marketplace.
3 Products can be offered at more competitive prices for the export market.
4 A firm can add plant capacity without a large capital expenditure.
5 Value can be added to the product at less cost.

A rose by any other name ...

The term "production sharing" means manufacturing or assembly in a country or region, not the home base of the parent company, in order to take comparative advantage of production factors, principally to increase profits. Other names commonly used for this process are:

- captive plants
- co-production
- export platforms
- global factories
- in-bond programs
- off-border production
- non-captive plants
- value-added processing
- complementary assembly facilities
- export factories
- export processing zones
- global production zones
- maquiladoras
- offshore production
- twin-plants

Special advantages

Most, if not all, of the countries that offer less expensive labor as their share are classified as developing or least-developed nations. Because the advantages for these countries are jobs, technology transfer, economic development, and foreign exchange income, attracting production-sharing opportunities has become very competitive.

The most obvious benefit to companies from industrial nations is this surplus of labor that translates into relatively low wage rates. However there are other constants such as special tariff treatment under U.S. Customs laws.

Tariff treatment

Familiarity with the Harmonized Tariff Schedule is important when considering the best tactical advantages of production sharing.

General systems of preferences (GSP)

In order to stimulate their economic development, the United Nations General Systems of Preferences (GSP) has designated certain countries, territories and associations of countries, as "recipients" of special tariff treatment. Some 84 independent nations are eligible under the Harmonized Tariff Schedule. Twenty-eight non-independent and three associations of countries are also eligible. In order to qualify for duty-free entries under this program, it must be established that the sum of the direct cost of processing operations performed in the country, plus the materials produced in the country, are more than 35 percent of the appraised value of the product at the time of its entry into the indusrtrialized nation. Needless to say, country of origin markings (explained below) are required as an element of proof.

Country of origin markings

Every article of foreign origin entering the United States must be legibly marked with the English name of the country of origin unless an exception from marking is provided for in the law. Basically, the law requires that the "ultimate purchaser" or last person in the U.S. who receives the article in the form in which it was imported, be informed as to where the article was made.

In the case of production sharing, the parent company of the overseas organization is the ultimate consumer of the imported articles and requests a waiver from the marking requirements. Waivers are granted when the imported article is substantially transformed into a new and different product in the United States wherein the imported article is not sold or offered for sale in its imported condition either over the counter or as a replacement part.

Who are the labor exporters?

Some say production sharing is the fastest growing industry in the world today. Mexico, closest to the vast domestic market of the United States, is the fastest growing of these off-shore production sharing areas. Mexico also has the greatest market share; followed by Singapore, Taiwan, Hong Kong and Malaysia.

Even Russia is moving into the production-sharing business. Free zones have been authorized for areas ranging from Armenia and Estonia to the Port of Nakhodka in the Far East. The foreign investment incentives for these zones include: duty-free export and import; a reduction in tax and lease payment discounts; labor policies governed by the local zones; and application for free market prices. Fifty percent of the production and assembly would be ordered by the state at state prices, the remainder at market prices.

The decision

Five major factors must be considered when making the production sharing decision:

1 **Suitability**. What is the suitablility of my product for production sharing?
2 **Location**. What are the relative advantages of the various production-sharing locations for my product?
3 **Method**. What method of production sharing? Invest (long term) or shelter (short term)?
4 **Costs**. What are the comparative fully burdened costs at each location?
5 **Control**. How much must we control the production process?

Product suitability

Do you make something or process something that has a great deal of physical content? Analyze your business. Are you operating on the edge of profitability because of high labor costs? If you reduced your manufacturing costs would your product be more competitive when exported to world markets?

The electric and electronics sector has the greatest share of the value added market. This is principally because this industry has the advantage of a low ratio of weight and volume to value, making it highly profitable to transport. Many other products lend themselves to low labor rate assembly: the criteria is physical content. Such things as coupon counting, sewing, and welding are among other possibilities.

Certainly offshore production deserves serious business consideration, but it is not for every firm.

Labor savings

It is not for the company with a product that has less than 25% labor content in the cost of goods sold.

Product maturity

It is an excellent method to achieve high volume assembly, but it is not for the company that does not have a mature product and market for that product. Don't try to make an offshore assembler your engineering laboratory. An offshore location is not an efficient place to prototype or do custom manufacturing. Do your Research and Development (R&D) work in the home plant, prototype and get the product into the market before you go offshore. Languages, distances, and cultures get in the way of engineering changes and before you know it you will be bogged down in production, and not meeting sales goals. It just doesn't work.

Location

Compared with other offshore centers, the distances from Mexico to most marketplaces in the United States are shortest. While it usually takes from three to four weeks to transport goods from the Far East, it takes only three or four days from Mexico. The high cost of Pacific Ocean transportation stands between the labor intensive offshore production capability of Taiwan, China, India, and Malaysia.

On the other hand, Asian, West African, and Central American locations often provide advantages when the target market is Asia, Europe, or South America.

What about labor productivity? In some countries the high degree of manual dexterity, trainability, and motivation often exceeds the averages in unit output of industrial nations. Large populations, together with substantial histories of manufacturing, and impressive "soft" infrastructures of technical institutes, business schools, and universities, provide a fertile technical environment in many less-developed lands.

Method

Nations with an abundance of lower cost labor, market their production sharing programs as "investment" opportunities, but investment is not the only offering. Private companies have ingeniously developed processes which provide for the sheltering of risk of foreign companies by contracting through an intermediary to rent space and employees, or subcontract for piece rate assembly/production.

Investment negotiables

A foreign firm can invest in most production-sharing countries. You can own and operate a plant, or enter into a joint venture to do so. In addition to low labor rates, each competing country offers significant investment incentives and concessions. Some of these negotiables include:

1 Duty-free import of capital goods, equipment, and raw materials in one or more free zones.
2 Tax holidays, i.e. exemptions from tax on profits.
3 Rent-free land.
4 Waivers of import licensing for imported capital goods and other production materials.
5 100 percent ownership for export-oriented enterprises.
6 Free remittance of profits and dividends after payment of taxes.
7 Personal tax exemptions.
8 Accelerated depreciation.
9 Investment tax credits.

10 Increased deductions for business entertainment in connection with export sales.
11 "Double deduction" of export promotion expenses.
12 Special financial assistance such as grants for research, feasibility studies, and export marketing development.
13 Provisions for employee training.

Risk sheltering

Some of the countries that offer production sharing have unstable political systems and a history of nationalizing industries on a whim. Thus the savings brought about by investment is often outweighed by reasons to shelter the risk.

Two sub-methods have sprung up over the years which allow firms to avoid the risk of overseas investment yet take advantage of lower labor rate opportunities.

Subcontracting

Driven by local investors who offer specialized assembly and manufacturing processes on a piece rate basis; this method has grown at a natural pace. The contractee can have the entire product manufactured or provide the molds, raw materials, and/or semi-assembled parts and the contractor returns the product to the parent country having supplied only the labor.

Subleasing

This method differs from subcontracting by offering space and employee rental computed at an average hourly rate instead of a per unit basis. With this method, the contractee usually provides the materials, machinery, equipment, and the management.

Control

Global factories can be characterized as "captive" or "non-captive." A captive facility would be one that is dedicated and controlled for the assembly or production for a single parent company. A non-captive plant is typically owned by a native of the country where it may be located, and operated to serve many foreign companies on a contractual basis.

Think of investment as a movement toward autarky (self sufficiency), with the plant at an overseas location. On the other hand, subcontracting is a movement away from vertical integration. Each has its advantages and disadvantages.

Table 12.1 provides a comparison of the methods in terms of cost and

Table 12.1 Comparison chart of production sharing costs and commitment

Method	Production cost	Commitment	Investment cost	Control
Own/Joint	Least	Most	Major	Complete
Sub-Cont.	Most	Least	None	Little
Sub-lease	Less	Less	Minor	Some

Figure 12.1 Production-sharing options

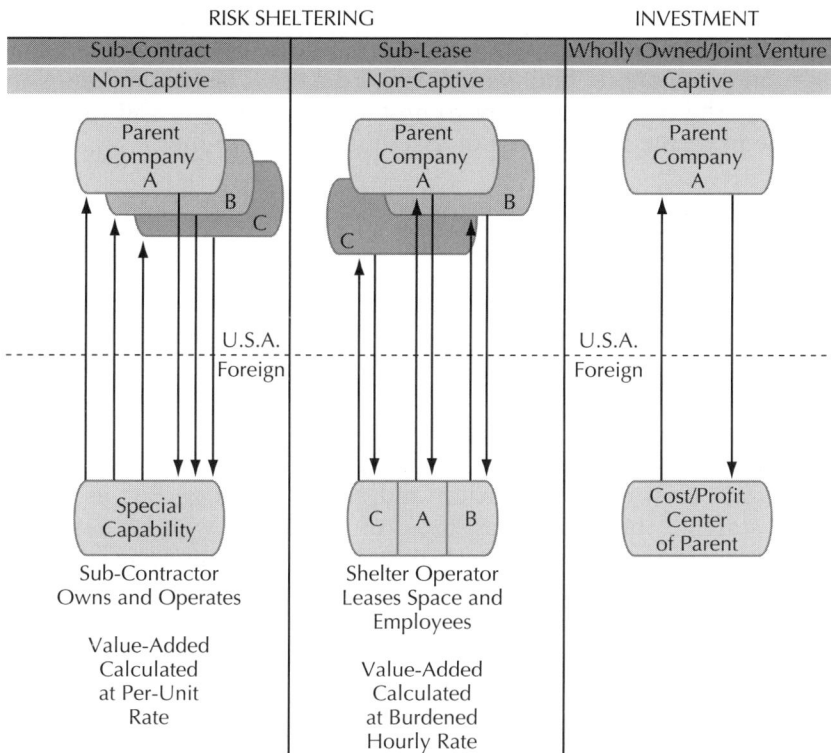

RISK SHELTERING		INVESTMENT
Sub-Contract	Sub-Lease	Wholly Owned/Joint Venture
Non-Captive	Non-Captive	Captive

Parent Company A / B / C

U.S.A. / Foreign

Special Capability

Sub-Contractor Owns and Operates

Value-Added Calculated at Per-Unit Rate

C A B

Shelter Operator Leases Space and Employees

Value-Added Calculated at Burdened Hourly Rate

Cost/Profit Center of Parent

commitment to the offshore production country. Figure 12.1 shows pictorially how they function in terms of options.

How to use them

Plants that are in-bond can be 100 percent foreign owned. These are called twin plants or "captive plants" of the parent. Of course this means buying or leasing a building, hiring and training a work force, and putting a management team in place, all of which takes time and commitment.

Joint venturing with a plant already in being can lessen that start-up time.

Another way to get started is to contract with one of the many "shelter" companies that have sprung up along the border. This is attractive to the U.S. manufacturer who knows the product but doesn't yet understand doing business in Mexico. These shelter firms offer to take on the entire interface. They provide a service to lease a building, hire a workforce, manage the operation, and take care of the nitty-gritty of accounting, paying tariffs, and coordinating transportation. The foreign firm essentially pays only a burdened hourly (value added) rate to the shelter company.

Subcontracting directly with a non-captive export platform, one that is privately held, already has the existing production capability and is making similar products, is one way to avoid delays. These companies usually require the parent company to provide all materials and machinery and quote in terms of unit cost of assembling the product.

The problems

Production sharing is not without problems. The growth of the process has brought a definite increase in management complexity. Process sophistication and competition has put pressure on the labor force as well as the technical and administrative staffs. Many of the workers are members of unions; however, strikes are rare because while the out-of-work employee in an industrial nation receives unemployment benefits, their off-border counterparts get nothing. In some areas there is a high turnover due to wage competition and skill shortages, But as one top manager stated, "the employees, most of whom are women, respond as much to modern management techniques, fair treatment and respect for cultural differences, as they do to higher wage incentives."

Unsuccessful twin plants have been, with few exceptions, the result of not doing adequate homework. For success, it is essential to be familiar with the laws, language and customs. Selection of a qualified counterpart is the most critical decision.

Summary

In truth, production sharing is about exchanging less expensive labor for the transfer of management, and technology. Less-developed nations have the labor and developed nations have the products and technology.

The next chapter explains laws and how to get help from government.

CHAPTER THIRTEEN

The laws and how to get help

... By Uniting We Stand,
By Dividing We Fall.

The Liberty Song 1768
John Dickinson

For purposes of exporting, there are two kinds of legal disputes: those related to company-to-company commercial contract disagreements and those that are government-to-government.

This chapter is organized into three sections. The first part deals with *transactional disagreements*. The second discusses the grounds for various problems related to unfair trade practices which may warrant *government-to-government intervention*. The last section lists who to contact to *make your "beef" known*, the various organizations involved in monitoring interstate controls and negotiating illegal or unfair trade practices.

Transactional disagreements

There is no body of law to which all foreign trade is subject. Each country has its own laws. Most are based in the three major thesis: common, code, or Islamic; however, there are many other minor codes of law found in various smaller states. Common law is derived from English law and found in England, United States, Canada, and other countries that have come under the influence of England. Code law is derived from Roman law and is found in the majority of all other nations of the world. Islamic law (*Shari'a*), as its name implies, is found in those Muslim nations that practice the teachings of the prophet Mohammed. Common law has its basis in tradition, past practices, and legal precedent. Code law is, in general, based on a system of written rules (codes) of law. Islamic law gains its basis in historical sources. In spite of their apparent complexities, the three legal systems are not dramatically different in so far as business is concerned.

When negotiating the contract for your exporting project you should specify a country or arbitration body where a dispute, heaven forbid, would be litigated. Lawsuits between companies or citizens of different countries are expensive, frustrating and take far longer than any other legal matter. Most experienced international business persons suggest these three steps:

1 placate the injured party;
2 if that doesn't work, arbitrate;
3 only when every other method has failed, litigate.

The best advice is to always seek a settlement through arbitration, rather than sue.

> ### ■ Hot tip
> *Always* include a jurisdictional or arbitration clause in contracts.

The decision to take legal action is essentially a business decision. Let's say you have a contract dispute that involves US$1,000. You could pursue the thousand dollars in a court, the cost of which might be US$40,000, or you could suggest to your trade partner that the thousand be split, each taking $500, and get on with doing business. Alternatively, the sum might be extremely small in comparison to your annual business volume. No one likes to give up money, but in this case you could refer the matter to arbitration or you might say, "OK, you win. Keep the thousand. In any case, I won't take you to court, but if you want to do business with me in the future we will have a sharper pen when drafting the next contract." On the other hand if the sum in question is US$1,000,000 ... that's a different business decision.

Government-to-government intervention

Now let's discuss the situations that affect your ability to compete fairly on an international basis, such as patent, copyright, or trademark infringement, violation of antitrust laws, unfair trade practices, misappropriation of trade secrets, or passing off and false advertising. If it affects only your own firm's opportunity to compete in your own country it is unlikely that your government will help you fight your individual legal battles with another government. However, your government may assist with those problems which affect an entire industry—and most of those are brought before government bodies by industry associations. That is not to say that your individual situation cannot be fought government-to-government, it just means that you should have exhausted other means and have built a very strong case.

If the problem affects other companies or an entire industry then your government is more likely to become involved. The only way this can be known is if you bring your problem to the attention of your country's department of commerce and industry.

International law, at best, is a collection of treaties, conventions and agreements between nations which have, more or less, the force of law. Don't be confused by the existence of the World Court at the Hague, and the International Court of Justice, the principal judicial organ of the United Nations. These courts apply only to disputes between sovereign nations, not between private citizens or companies.

This area of international trade can be complex because it includes such matters as balance of payments, the maneuverings of politicians, and negotiations between sovereign nations. Nevertheless, smaller firms can have an impact by making their positions known to the right people in government. In fact, most countries have a government office that provides trade remedy assistance.

Do you need a lawyer to do something about these activities?

The answer is yes and no.

As the manager/leader of the business, your job is to keep your eye on the donut—to know where the business is going, to pull it together, and manage the entire organization. It is impossible for anyone to know all the domestic, international, and foreign laws involved in a given business project. There are often corresponding domestic laws, some antedating the international agreement, some enacted to implement foreign agreements. Therefore, more than one law or rule often applies. You could probably research these matters as well as anyone, but your time is better spent looking after your business. An attorney or other consultant who specializes in international trade matters is a valuable resource and every business should include such a contact on its international trade team.

Trade laws and their application

Most international trade agreements (principally the World Trade Organization (WTO) rules and codes) provide for a variety of procedures that allow a signatory to take protective or compensatory measures wherein there are unfair competitive trade practices which cause or threaten injury to its commercial or other interests.

The first step is to specifically identify the illegal or unfair trade activity in terms of its injury to your firm and if possible, its potential injury to your industry. In every instance, proof must be made that the injury is "material."

The second step is to determine if the activity is an import which is affecting your domestic market or an activity which is affecting your ability to export.

> ### ■ Hot tip
> Material injury is defined to be harm which is not inconsequential, immaterial, or unimportant.

Having done that, link the injury to one or more existing laws, Friendship, Commerce and Navigation (FCN) agreements, or WTO rules you feel have been violated. In many cases more than one law, agreement, or rule will apply. You may not know all the legal implications, unilateral trade agreements and rules that are applicable, and you need not—that is what lawyers and government investigators are paid to do.

Next, submit your grievance, in the form of a letter of petition for relief to your appropriate government (department of commerce or trade). Here are some of the unfair trade practices you may encounter:

Recourse from unfair importing practices

These are products that enter commerce and unfairly affect domestic business.

Selective export subsidies (countervailing duty)

Suppose a subsidy is provided by a foreign country, or person or organization of that country, to certain merchandise which is then exported to your country. If the result of the subsidy can be shown to materially injure or threaten material injury by reason of imports of that merchandise, you may ask for help from the your government. You may also seek assistance if you believe the introduction of the merchandise might also materially threaten the establishment of an industry for that merchandise.

Antidumping practices

This is the practice of penetrating markets to gain rapid market share through the technique of pricing goods under fair value, such as below the price charged for the same or like product in their home market or below its cost of production. Again, material injury or threat of material injury must be established.

Investigations of costs of production

Assume you manufacture a product for $X and a company in country B manufactures and exports that same product into your country for $X minus 50 percent. In this situation, the foreign manufacturer's price is not artificial, as was the case with dumping, but by reason of wages and other factors of production the costs of production cause material injury to your company in your market and warrant investigation by your government.

Illegal practices

Earlier in the chapter there was mention of the action necessary to remedy such matters as: patent, copyright, trademark infringement, violation of antitrust laws, misappropriation of trade secrets, passing off, and false advertising. In addition to taking your own legal action you may petition your government for assistance.

An example of a recent problem were allegations that certain foreign companies were infringing on the patents of Erasable Programmable Read-only Memories (EPROM) made by an American domestic company. That company brought the matter to the United States International Trade Commission and subsequently it was brought before an administrative law judge for determination.

Investigations of injury from increased imports

This is the case where articles are imported in such increased quantities as to be a substantial cause of serious injury, or the threat thereof, to the domestic industry producing an article like or directly competitive with the imported article. You must focus on the adjustment objective by defining "positive adjustment." Industries are encouraged to submit a plan with their petition for remedy that outlines the steps they are prepared to make. These positive adjustments are:

1 Explanation of how the affected domestic industry will compete after the relief has been terminated or the transfer of resources to other productive endeavors.
2 Methods of transferring dislocated workers to productive pursuits.

General investigations of trade and tariff matters

Think of the situation where you believe and have evidence that a customs law or the relationship between your country and a foreign country relative to tariffs, bounties, preferential treatment, and almost any other trade matter has gone amuck and you want it investigated.

Escape clause/import relief

As a rule the "escape clause" is a provision included in all international trade agreements. It permits a party to the agreement to withdraw or modify a previously agreed trade concession. In this instance you are aware that your country and another nation has incurred an obligation as signatories to WTO or other agreement; nevertheless, products of a company(s) from that nation are causing "substantial cause of serious injury" or threat of injury to producers of a like or directly competitive product.

Relief from export barriers

These are interstate (government) controls which impede, block or otherwise restrict your ability to fairly compete in a foreign market.

Enforcement of trade-agreements rights and response to foreign unfair trade practices.

You expect companies from other countries to respect bilateral or multilateral agreements entered into in good faith, just as you do. Suppose however, in attempting to market in a foreign country you find a trade practice that does not give the same fair business opportunity that your country provides under the same agreement. You can ask your government to enforce the trade agreement or foreign practice which restricts or discriminates.

Unreasonable trade practices

Specifies certain "unreasonable" trade practices such as :

1 Export Targeting. A government measure that gives a domestic industry an unfair competitive advantage in trade.
2 Denial of worker rights such as collective bargaining and the right to strike.
3 Denial of market opportunities because of foreign government toleration of anti-competitive activities.

Discriminatory foreign exchange rates

Relative currency fluctuations are widely viewed as an important factor in trade flows and a major cause of large current-account deficits. As a result, stability has become a major international goal. You may ask your government to better coordinate policies multilaterally and negotiate bilaterally regarding fluctuating exchange rates.

Imports threatening national security

This activity needs little explanation. You should ask your government to provide a remedy for those goods introduced into your country which threaten national security.

Making your "Beef" known

Great emphasis is placed by state, provincial, and federal governments to stimulate international trade. Therefore, the first place to look for help or to make your disagreement known is your local or central governmental international trade organization. Americans and Japanese, for instance, have offices throughout the world organized as a part of their foreign commercial service. Almost every American state also has offices that support exporting. For instance the state of California keeps offices in Tokyo, London, Paris, and Mexico City. Through these offices a potential exporter can learn about the assistance offered by their government or lodge complaints.

Exporters of other countries would follow the same logical pattern to learn about assistance available from their nation.

Much of the current information about export opportunities can only be gained by having your own intelligence representation in a target market area in order to keep close touch with decision makers; however, there are many public sources. This part of the chapter offers a partial list of suggested organizations and publications which provide help, information, or contacts for exporting. Appendix E offers a list of abbreviations for international organizations, while appendix F shows which countries belong to these organizations.

World trade organization (WTO)

Unlike the General Agreement on Tariffs and Trade (GATT), its predecessor, the WTO has a stature commensurate with that of the Bretton Woods financial institutions, the World Bank, and International Monetary Fund. As shown in Figure 13.1, the WTO encompasses the former GATT structure and extends to it new disciplines that have not been adequately covered in the past. It facilitates the implementation of the trade agreements reached in the previous rounds by bringing them under one institutional umbrella, requiring full participation of all countries in the new trading system and providing a permanent forum to address new issues facing the international trading system. A fuller treatment of this section can be found in the Global Manager Series book *International Trade: A Manager's Guide to Strategy in the Age of Globalism*.

WTO guiding principals or "Rules of the trade game"

- Most Favored Nation Treatment (MFNT) or reciprocity is the cornerstone.
- The exception to MFNT are regional unions which do not have to offer to the whole world treatment agreed to internally.
- Tariffs are not forbidden, but increases of existing tariffs are. Once a tariff is fixed by "binding" or lowering, then binding cannot be raised, only lowered.

- Except in agriculture, quotas are forbidden.
- Maximum levels of tariffs are fixed.
- Settlements are to be negotiated by consultation and conciliation.
- Must meet the needs of developing nations. Essentially this means assisting countries ignite the growth-development process through preferences.
- Contracting parties must agree to abide by principals of WTO.
- Countries that break the rules are called to order.
- Disputes are to be brought before a WTO panel.
- Provides for Appeals and Escape Clauses
- Appeals (a temporary departure) may be made for Balance of Payments problems and in some cases under the Infant Industry Argument.
- Escape Clauses (more permanent departure) may be asked for: Economic Development; Balance of Payments; National Currencies; Infant Industry Arguments; Retaliation; Technical Transfer; Industrial Policy.

The objective of the WTO is to promote the use of multilateral rules and disciplines and limit the resort to unilateral measures for solutions of conflicts. By bringing together disciplines on government practices affecting trade in goods and services and the protection of intellectual property rights under one institutional umbrella, the WTO Agreement also facilitates the "cross-retaliation" mechanism of the integrated dispute settlement understanding.

In addition, the WTO helps to resolve the "free rider" problem in the world trading system. The WTO system is available only to countries that are contracting parties, agree to adhere to all of the Round Agreements, and submit schedules of market access commitments for industrial goods, agricultural goods, and services. This eliminates the shortcomings of the former system in which, for example, only a handful of countries voluntarily adhered to disciplines on subsidies under the 1979 Tokyo Round agreement.

Dispute settlement

The Dispute Settlement Understanding (DSU) creates new procedures for settlement of disputes arising under any of the Round Agreements. It significantly improves the existing system by providing strict time limits for each step in the dispute settlement process. The effectiveness of the system is also improved through provisions guaranteeing a right to a panel, adoption of panel reports unless there is a consensus to reject the report, appellate review of the legal aspects of a report on request, time limits on when a member must bring its laws into conformity with panel rulings, and recommendations and authorization of retaliation in the event that a member has not brought its laws into conformity with its

Figure 13.1   The structure of the WTO
The World Trade Organization, established Jan. 1, 1995, sets rules for most of the world's trade in goods and services through its committees. Small companies that follow the development of these rules could have a substantive edge in their overseas market dealings.
Source: Global Trade Information, Columbia, S.C.

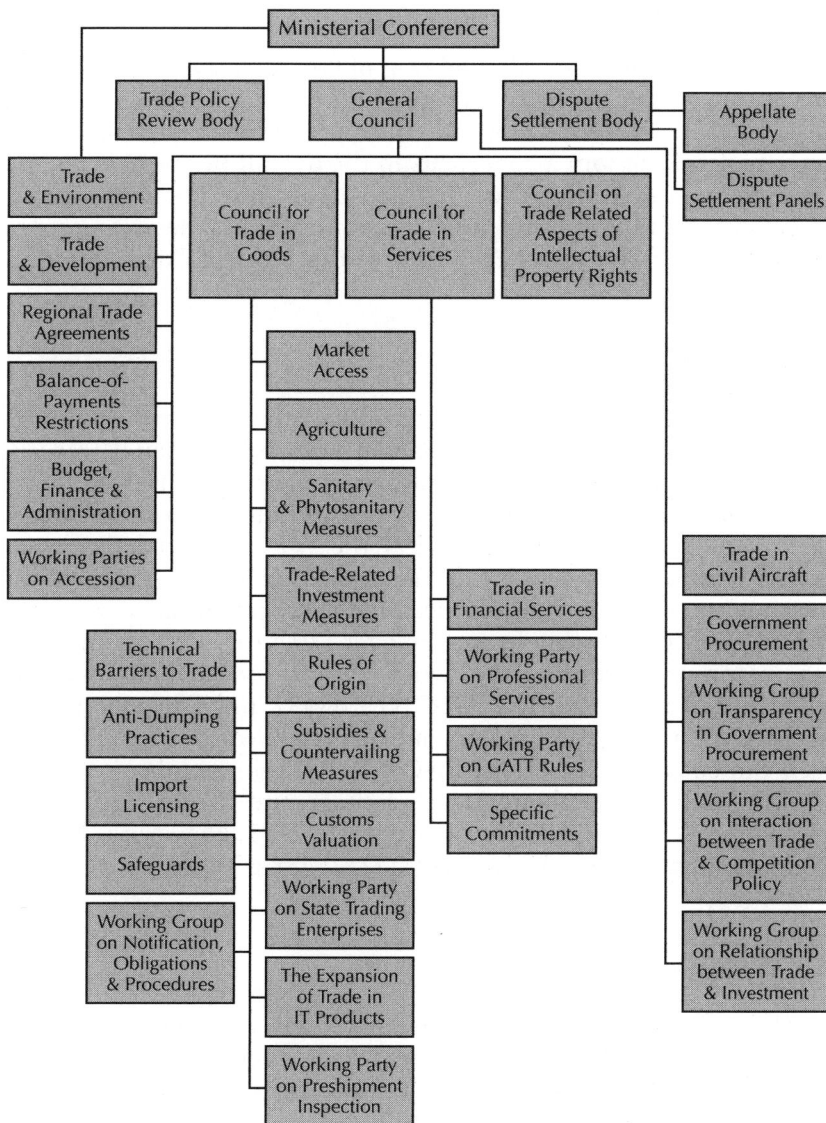

obligations within that set period of time. There would be a single system that would apply the strengthened rules and procedures to all disputes with only minor exceptions. A single panel would now be able to address all issues raised under any of the covered agreements. Public access to information about disputes is increased.

How the WTO takes decisions

The WTO continues the long tradition of GATT in seeking to make decisions not by voting but by consensus. This procedure allows members to ensure their interests are properly considered even though, on occasion, they may decide to join a consensus in the overall interests of the multilateral trading system. Where consensus is not possible, the WTO Agreement allows for voting. In such circumstances, decisions are taken by a majority of the votes cast and on the basis of "one country, one vote."

World trade centers

A World Trade Center (WTC) is an apolitical and unaligned shopping center that puts all the services associated with international trade under one roof. It is the first stop for your export venture. WTCs complement and support the existing services of private and government agencies. Some of the services you will find at the WTC are: trade information, communications services, World Trade Center Clubs, trade education programs, trade mission assistance and display facilities.

World Trade Centers are located in over 170 cities with about 100 more in the planning stages. In other words they are in virtually every major trading city in the world. The WTC NETWORK links, by electronic trading, the Centers and their clients and affiliates worldwide. Offers to buy or sell can be advertised on NETWORK's Bulletin Board.

To find out more about WTC contact the World Trade Centers Association, One World Trade Center, suite 7701, New York, NY 10048, USA, Telephone: (212) 432-2626; Fax: (212) 488-0064; WTC NETWORK: WTCA.

United Nations

The United Nations' system of organizations represents a vast global market for potential suppliers. Required products and services cover a wide spectrum, from expert input or consulting assistance on economic and engineering feasibility studies to preparation of contract documents complete with designs, specifications, and cost estimates. Key members of the system are as follows:

World Intellectual Property Organization (WIPO)

One of the 15 "specialized agencies" of the United Nations' system of organizations. WIPO, located in Geneva, is responsible for the promotion of the protection of intellectual property (copyrights, trademarks, patents) throughout the world through cooperation among states, and for the administration of various "Unions," each founded on a multilateral treaty and dealing with the legal and administrative aspects of intellectual property.

United Nations Development Program (UNDP)

The world's largest channel for multilateral technical and pre-investment cooperation. United Nations Development Programme, One United Nations Plaza, New York, NY 10017, U.S.A. Telephone: (212) 906-5000.

United Nations Industrial Development Organization (UNIDO)

A vehicle for technology transfer between developed and less developed nations. United Nations Industrial Development Organization, P.O. Box 707, A-1011, A-1070, Vienna, Austria.

Department for Technical Cooperation for Development (DTCD)

Funds surveys and feasibility studies. Department for Technical Cooperation for Development, United Nations, Tel: (212) 754-8947.

Food and Agriculture Organization (FAO)

Contact at: Food and Agriculture Organization, Via delle Tenne di Caracalla, 00100 Rome, Italy.

International Telecommunications Union (ITU)

Contact at: International Telecommunications Union, 1211 Geneva 20, Switzerland.

Inter-Governmental Maritime Consultative Organization (IMCO)

Contact at: Inter-Governmental Maritime Consultative Organization, 101-104 Piccadilly, London, WIV OAE, England.

International Fund for Agriculture Development (IFAD)

Contact at: International Fund for Agriculture Development , Via Del Serafico 107, 00142 Rome, Italy.

International Atomic Energy Agency (IAEA)

Contact at: International Atomic Energy Agency, Vienna International Centre, P.O. Box 100, A-1400 Vienna, Austria.

The World Health Organization (WHO)

Employs consulting firms that specialize in education, environment, health, and water supply. Contact at: The World Health Organization, 1211 Geneva 27, Switzerland.

World Customs Organization (WCO)

Established as the Customs Cooperation Council. A multilateral body located in Brussels through which participating countries seek to simplify and rationalize customs procedures. The mission of the WCO is to enhance the effectiveness and efficiency of customs administrations in the areas of compliance with trade regulations, protection of society and revenue collection, thereby contributing to the economic and social wellbeing of nations. The WCO is an intergovernmental organization established by a convention on December 15, 1950. Contact at: World Customs Organization, rue de l'Industrie 26-38, B-1040 Brussels Belgium, (Tel: (32 2) 508 42 11; Fax: (32 2) 508 42 40).

The Inter Agency Procurement Services Unit (IAPSU)

This is the inter-agency unit which helps the UNDP and its partner agencies procure essential project inputs. No less than 12 member organs and 16 specialized agencies use the IAPSU. Inter-Agency Procurement Services Unit (IAPSU), Palais des Nations, CH-1211 Geneva 10, Switzerland.

Development Forum Business Edition (DFBE)

The primary source of information on business opportunities in the United Nations system is Development Forum Business Edition (DFBE) which is published 24 times a year. Enquiries regarding subscriptions should be directed to: *Development Forum*, Business Edition, United Nations, Palais des Nations, CH-1211 Geneva 10, Switzerland or Development Forum Liaison Unit, Room E-1055, World Bank, 1818 H

Street N.W., Washington, DC 20433, U.S.A. Yearly subscriptions are approximately U.S. $250.00.

World Bank Group

The World Bank Group consists of the International Bank for Reconstruction and Development (IBRD), the International Development Association (IDA), and the International Finance Corporation (IFC).

The World Bank's clients are developing countries which borrow about $11–12 billion annually. Although the Bank loans money but does not award bids, it does require transparency, that is, public visibility of the bidding process. Each program and project is a discreet investment by the bank, but can represent a large number of contracts or business opportunities.

International Bank for Reconstruction and Development (IBRD)

Promotes economic development by extending loans for high-priority programs and projects.

International Development Association (IDA)

Extends loans to member countries with per capita GNP of about $700.

International Finance Corporation (IFC)

Encourages growth of productive private enterprise by extending loans.

Information about the various projects are advertised in: *Development Business* , United Nations, G.C.P.O. Box 5850, New York, NY 10163-5850, U.S.A., or *The Monthly Operational Summary*, The Johns Hopkins University Press, Journals Division, 701 W. 40th Street, Suite 275, Baltimore, MD 21211, U.S.A.

Subscriptions to the Monthly Operational Summary are $95 a year.

International Monetary Fund (IMF)

Provides short and medium-term financial aid to countries in external deficit. Tel: (202) 477-2945.

Asian Development bank (AsDB)

Provides conventional and concessional loans, technical assistance, and investment promotion to developing Asian countries. Contact at:

Consultants Services Division, Asian Development bank, P.O. Box 789, Manila, Philippines 2800.

Inter-American Development Bank (IDB)

Contributes to the accelerated development of member countries by providing loans. Contact at: Inter-American Development Bank, 808-17th Street,, NW, Washington, DC 20577, U.S.A.

African Development Bank (AfDB)

Helps formulate projects and loan applications to promote investment in public and private capital in Africa. Contact at: Information Office, African Development Bank, B.P. 1387, Abidjan, Ivory Coast.

Other sources

Firms should also always search the private sector in their area of specialization. The best informed are quite often those companies and organizations competing in similar work areas.

Trade show information

Lists of worldwide trade shows and international conferences are available from most large airlines such as Lufthansa and American Airlines as well as from your department of commerce and the local chamber of commerce. Your industry association will also know when and where the appropriate trade shows take place.

Electronic Data Interchange (EDI)

The use of computers to exchange information holds great benefits for international transactions. Help can be obtained from a number of sources including the American Standards Institute at (212) 643-4900; EDIT (703) 8342; or the NCITD (2120 925-1400.

Trade and professional associations

Trade and professional associations are often the most valuable source of not only information but contacts through networking. There seems to be an infinite number of associations—at least one for every endeavor, and many of those have international affiliations.

National Chambers of Commerce Abroad

The primary role of these overseas organizations is to promote business. They can be very helpful, particularly for business leads, advice, and referrals.

Summary

Throughout this book the author has proposed an offensive worldwide export strategy with focus on the positive business applications and fair international trade. By making maximum use of a mix of available tools, businesses can expand their international presence and make a contribution to global welfare.

■ APPENDICES ■

The ten most common exporting mistakes

Exporting is not without its pitfalls, especially for the inexperienced. You can benefit from the misfortunes of others, and share in the wisdom of hindsight. The following is a list of the ten most common mistakes that exporters have made over the years:

1 Failing to obtain qualified export counseling and to develop a master international marketing plan before starting an export business. Remember: first, define goals and objectives; then, develop a definite plan.
2 Insufficient commitment by top management to overcoming the initial difficulties and financial requirements of exporting. It may take more time and effort to establish yourself in a foreign market than in a domestic one. Although the early delays and costs may seem difficult to justify when compared to your established domestic trade, you must be patient! You should look to the long term, and shepherd your international marketing efforts through any early difficulties.
3 Insufficient care in selecting overseas distributors. The complications involved in overseas communications and transportation require international distributors to act with greater independence than their domestic counterparts. Since a new exporter is usually unknown, your foreign customers will buy on the strength of your distributor's reputation.
4 Chasing orders from around the world instead of establishing a basis for profitable operations and orderly growth. Exporters should concentrate their efforts in one or two geographical areas until there is sufficient business to support a company representative.
5 Neglecting export business when the local market booms. Such neglect can seriously harm the business and that of the overseas representatives.
6 Failing to treat international distributors on an equal basis with their domestic counterparts. Often companies carry out institutional

advertising campaigns but fail to make similar assistance available to their international distributors. This is a mistake that can destroy the vitality of your overseas marketing efforts.

7 Unwillingness to modify products to meet regulations or cultural preferences of other countries.

8 Failing to print services, sales and warranty messages in locally understood languages. Without a clear understanding of sales messages or service instructions, personnel will be less effective in performing their functions.

9 Failing to consider using an export management company.

10 Failing to consider licensing or joint-venture agreements. Other reasons, such as import restrictions in some countries, insufficient personnel and financial resources, or a limited product line cause many companies to dismiss international marketing as a possible option.

A short form of agency agreement

Short Contract

This Agreement by and between_____, known as the Company, and _____, known as the Manufacturers' Agent; in accordance with and subject to, the following:

1 The products which the Manufacturers' Agent is authorized to sell, and the prices and terms, are as shown on the addenda to this Agreement, or as specified in subsequent price books, bulletins, and other authorized documents.

2 The prices of sale at which the Manufacturers' Agent is to sell such products, shall be those currently in effect and established from time to time in the Company's price books, bulletins and in other authorized releases.

3 Said Manufacturers' Agent further agrees to abide and comply with all sales policy and operating regulations of the Company, as issued from time to time and will not obligate or contract on behalf of the Company without first having received written authority to do so from an Executive of the Company.

4 The territory in which the Manufacturers' Agent is to work is as follows:

_____

This territory is exclusive unless otherwise stated in writing. The Manufacturers' Agent shall be credited with all orders accepted by the Company from this territory, as long as this Agreement remains in force.

5 Commissions due to the Manufacturers' Agent shall be payable before the 15th day of the month following (date of shipment by the Company) OR (date of payment by the purchaser) OR (date of acceptance by the Company). If orders are returned to and accepted by the Company for credit, commissions paid or credited to the Manufacturers' Agent for such orders shall be deducted from the amount of other commissions due to the Manufacturers' Agent, if that amount is sufficient; otherwise, commissions paid on such returned-for credit orders shall be refunded to the Company

by the Manufacturers' Agent within 30 days of written request by the Company.

6 The Company reserves the right at all times to reject any and all orders because of unsatisfactory credit rating of the purchaser. On sales of unrated new accounts, the Manufacturers' Agent may be required to furnish local credit information and submit full information with orders. The Manufacturers' Agent will also assist in the collection of past due accounts owing the Company by customers located in said Manufacturers' Agent's territory.

7 When an order originates in one agent's territory for shipment into another agent's territory, or in any case when the commission is divided between two or more of the Company's agents, the commission shall be divided according to the schedule shown on the addendum to this Contract, with no part of the commission being retained by the Company.

8 During the first year, this Agreement may be terminated for any reason by either party upon 30 days' notice to the other by registered mail. After this Agreement has been in force for one full year, it may be terminated by either party, for any reason upon six months' notice to the other by registered mail. The Manufacturers Agent shall be paid commissions on all orders from his territory accepted by the Company prior to the effective termination date, even though such orders may be shipped or paid for after the effective termination date.

COMPANY APPROVAL:

By _____

Signature

_____

Title

_____

Date

_____

Manufacturers' Agent

International exclusive distribution agreement

This agreement made and entered into this _____day of _____, by and between_____ (Your city, state, zip code, country) (hereinafter referred to as_____ of the first part), and _____ (city, country) (hereinafter referred to as _____ of the second part).

WITNESSETH

1 WHEREAS, _____ is the manufacturer of the (name of product) listed in schedule A attached hereto (hereinafter together referred to as PRODUCTS).

WHEREAS, _____ wishes to sell the products in _____ (names of countries) (hereinafter referred to as TERRITORY).

NOW THEREFORE, in consideration of the premises and mutual covenants herein contained, the parties hereto agree as follows:

_____ (name of company) hereby appoints _____ the exclusive distributor of the products in the TERRITORY and hereby undertakes as follows:

A) To supply the PRODUCTS to _____ in finished package form ready for resale by _____ to users and other customers.

B) To ship the PRODUCTS to _____ within thirty (30) days from the manufacturing dates of the PRODUCTS, subject to receipt of the letters of credit opened by _____ well in time for the shipments and also subject to _____ delivery of the PRODUCTS as provided for in the following article 2 hereof.

2 _____ hereby undertakes as follows:

A) To ensure that the PRODUCTS are of such quality as shall meet the specifications to be agreed in writing between _____ and _____.

B) To supply to _____ adequate information on storage, transportation, and handling as well as technical data on the usage, expiry dates and other available and useful scientific information relating to the PRODUCTS.

C) Not to deliver to _____ any lot of the PRODUCTS which has a remaining life period of less than eleven (11) months up to its expiry date, subject to the receipt of orders as stipulated in Article 3 hereof.

D) To package and label the PRODUCTS into finished form ready for resale by _____ to users or other customers in the proper way in consideration of the information provided to _____ by _____. The finished packages shall be made in _____ company layout and shall bear the trademarks or product names determined by _____ as well as the language indicating _____ as manufacturer and _____ as distributor.

E) To indemnify and hold _____ harmless against any liability to any other third party caused by infringement of patent or trademark rights resulting from _____ sale of the PRODUCTS hereunder, provided that (i) _____ shall discontinue the sale of the PRODUCT or assume liability for any further such sale of other third party patents (s) of trademark(s), (ii) the provisions of this paragraph shall not apply unless _____ promptly gives notice to _____ (name of company) of the claim of such other third party. _____ shall, upon request by _____ cooperate with_____ in any act or thing necessary or desirable to solve any such infringement problem.

3 _____ (name of company) hereby undertakes as follows:

A) To actively sell and promote the PRODUCTS in the TERRITORY, at least using the same distribution and promotion channels and methods, exercising the same diligence and adhering to the same standards which _____ employs in marketing other products in the same or similar fields.

B) To sell or otherwise distribute only those of the PRODUCTS which are in good condition and capable of use by final users, and to destroy all the quantities which are in defective or unsuitable condition for use either due to their life expiry or otherwise.

C) To ensure that the PRODUCTS shall be stored, transported, and handled in proper way in consideration of the information to _____ by _____.

D) To make such tests of the PRODUCTS supplied by _____ as _____ (company name) may consider necessary to insure compliance with the specifications mutually agreed between _____ and _____. Failure of _____ to reject any shipment of the PRODUCTS within thirty (30) days of its arrival at destination port or airport shall constitute acceptance of the shipment and shall be conclusive evidence, as between the parties, that the shipment has met the specifications. If _____(name of company) rejects a particular shipment of the PRODUCTS, _____ and _____ shall promptly discuss to determine the conformity or non-conformity of the shipment with the specifications. Each party shall bear and pay the costs and expenses incurred on the side of such party in connection with this determination. In case of the non-conformity, _____ shall, and within three (3) months from the date of the determination of the non-conformity, either replace such shipment at no cost to _____ or refund to _____ the landed cost of the shipment, in accordance with the choice of _____.

E) To place with _____ a formal purchase order which shall reach _____ at least forty-five (45) days before the desired shipping time the minimum order quantity specified in Schedule A attached hereto or the multiples of such minimum quantity.

F) To provide _____ with a quarterly order forecast at least ninety (90) days prior to the beginning of each calendar quarter.

G) To send quarterly reports to _____ of the units and value of sales and stock of the PRODUCTS together with relevant market information of interest if any.

H) To treat all information received from _____ in connection with this agreement (including all the information disclosed by _____ before the execution of this agreement) as confidential and not to be disclosed to any other person, company or firm (except to the competent authorities in order to obtain the permits or approvals and except as far as necessary for marketing the PRODUCTS) either before or after the termination or cancellation of this agreement, except the following information.

   i) information which at the time of disclosure is part of the public knowledge;

   ii) information which, after disclosure, becomes part of the public knowledge by publication or otherwise, except by breach of this agreement by _____;

   iii) Information which _____ can establish by competent proof was in _____ possession at the time of disclosure by _____ was not acquired directly or indirectly from _____ under secrecy obligation; and

   iv) information which _____ lawfully receives from a third party; provided, however, that such information was not obtained by said third party directly or indirectly from _____ under a secrecy obligation.

I) To obtain all necessary authorities' permits or approvals for importation and marketing of the PRODUCTS in the TERRITORY.

J) To bear and pay all costs and expenses, if any, involved in this Article 3 unless otherwise stipulated therein.

4 The prices of the PRODUCTS supplied by _____ to _____

shall be those stated in Schedule A attached hereto, which prices shall be valid until _____ (date). Prices applicable to remaining period(s) of this agreement shall be agreed between _____ and _____ . If an agreement cannot be reached on prices for any applicable period prior to its starting date, either party hereto shall be entitled to cancel, with thirty (30) days' prior written notice given to the other parties, this agreement with respect to PRODUCT(S) for which the price(s) could not be agreed.

5 For the purchases of the PRODUCTS from _____, _____ shall make full payments by irrevocable letters of credit payable at sight in _____'s favor, or by such other method as the parties may agree upon.

6 This agreement shall remain in force until _____ (date) and shall be automatically renewed for successive periods of two (2) years each unless terminated at the end of the initial term or of any renewal term by at least six (6) months' prior notice in writing by either party.

7 Without prejudice to any remedy or claims it may have against the other party for breach of non-performance of this agreement, either party shall be entitled to terminate this agreement by giving the other party at least thirty (30) days prior notice in writing if the other party should violate any of the provisions or conditions of this agreement and if after having been given a written warning the other party should fail to discontinue or should fail to make good such violation within sixty (60) days after receipt of the warning.

8 In the event of insolvency or bankruptcy of either party or appointment of a trustee or receiver for either party, it shall immediately notify the other party to that effect. In any such event, any of the party so notified shall have the right to terminate this agreement at any time.

9 Upon termination or cancellation of this agreement, _____ shall surrender to _____ all written information relating to the PRODUCTS, and shall not thereafter use or disclose for use any confidential information disclosed to it by _____.

10 Upon termination or cancellation of this agreement, _____ or its nominee shall have the optional right to take over all the residual salable stocks of the PRODUCTS in the warehouses and factories of _____ at such prices as may be agreed between _____ and _____ or in the absence of agreement, at the landed cost of the PRODUCTS. _____ shall not thereafter manufacture, use or sell any product covered by this agreement using the confidential information set forth as per Article 3 hereof. However, in case _____ or its nominee does not exercise the right to take over any part of the stocks of the PRODUCTS pursuant to this Article, _____ shall be entitled to continue to sell the remaining stocks of the PRODUCTS which are in salable condition.

11 Upon termination or cancellation of this agreement, _____

shall, upon _____ request, assign and transfer to _____ or its nominee free of charge the authorities' permits or approvals for importation and marketing of the PRODUCTS in the TERRITORY as well as the rights pertaining thereto.

12 Neither party shall be responsible for failure or delay in performance of any of its obligations hereunder due to force majeure such as war, insurrection, strikes, acts of God, governmental action or any other contingency beyond its control.

13 Any right or obligation under this agreement shall be assignable or transferable by either party to any other third party only with the prior consent in writing of the other party hereto. However, this agreement shall insure to the benefit of and be binding upon the parties' successors.

14 Any and all notices required to be given under this agreement shall be made by registered airmail, cable or telex and shall be addressed to the parties at their respective offices first above referred to, except that either party may change such office by notice in accordance with this article.

15 The parties hereto recognize that it is in their mutual interests to protect themselves against claims by third parties that the PRODUCTS covered by this agreement are in some way defective or have caused damage to such third parties (which in American law is referred to as "Product Liability"). Therefore, it is agreed that during the term of this Agreement, _____ and _____ will obtain and keep in force Product Liability Insurance in an amount and with an insurance company mutually acceptable to them, which insurance shall name _____ and _____ as insureds or additional insureds. Any such liablity, loss or expense arising from third parties' claims as will not be covered by the Product Liability Insurance will be borne and paid by the party whose negligence or mistake has caused such claims.

16 All disputes, controversies, or differences which may arise between the parties, out of or in relation to or in connection with this agreement, or for the breach therof, shall be finally settled by arbitration pursuant to the then obtaining commercial arbitration rules of the United States Arbitration Association, by which each party hereto is bound. In connection with any such arbitration, it is agreed that each party shall appoint one arbitrator and the two arbitrators so appointed shall select a third arbitrator who shall act as chairman. Such arbitration shall be conducted in English languages. In arriving at their decision, the arbitration shall apply United States law with respect to any dispute, controversy, or difference regarding the performance (or failure to perform) by _____ and shall apply the law of the State of California, United States of America, with respect to any dispute, controversy or difference regarding the performance (or failure to perform) by _____. The parties shall, however, attempt in good faith to amicably settle the dispute, controversy or difference by negotiation before having recourse to the arbitration procedure.

17 This agreement is entered into in the English language. In the event of any dispute concerning the construction or meaning of this agreement, reference shall be made only to the agreement as written in English and not to any translation into any other language.

IN WITNESS WHEREOF, the parties hereto have caused this agreement to be duly executed by their respective officers on the day and year first above written.

_____   _____

_____   _____

Schedule A

Name of product:_____

Description of product_____

Technical details of product _____

_____

_____

Minimum order quantity_____

Prices_____

ATA carnet countries (1998)

Algeria	Germany	Netherlands
Australia	Gibraltar	New Zealand
Austria	Greece	Norway
Belgium	Hong Kong	Poland
Britain	Hungary	Portugal
Bulgaria	Iceland	Romania
Canada	India	Senegal
China	Ireland	Singapore
Côte d'Ivoire	Israel	South Africa
Croatia	Japan	Spain
Cyprus	Korea	Sri Lanka
Czech Republic	Lebanon	Sweden
Denmark	Luxembourg	Switzerland
Estonia	Malaysia	Thailand
Finland	Malta	Turkey
France	Mauritius	

Abbreviations for international organizations

AfDB	African Development Bank
APEC	Asia-Pacific Economic Cooperation
AsDB	Asian Development Bank
ASEAN	Association of Southeast Asian Nations
CACM	Central American Common Market
CARICOM	Caribbean Community and Common Market
COMESA	Common Market for Eastern and Southern Africa
EBRD	European Bank for Reconstruction and Development
ECOWAS	Economic Community of West African States
EEA	European Economic Area
EFTA	European Free Trade Association
EMS	European Monetary System
EU	European Union
GCC	Gulf Cooperation Council
IADB	Inter-American Development Bank
IBRD	International Bank for Reconstruction and Development
ICC	International Chamber of Commerce
IDB	Islamic Development Bank
IFC	International Finance Corporation
IMF	International Montetary Fund
ISO	International Organization for Standardization
LAIA	Latin American Integration Association
MERCOSUR	Southern Cone Common Market
NAFTA	North American Free Trade Agreement
OAS	Organization of American States
OECD	Organization for Economic Cooperation and Development
OPEC	Organization for Petroleum Exporting Countries
SACU	Southern African Development Community
EAC	Central African Customs & Economic Union
UN	United Nations
UNCTAD	United Nations Conference on Trade and Development
WCO	World Customs Organization
WIPO	World Intellectual Property Organization
WTO	World Trade Organization

Who belongs?

Arab League
Established March 22, 1945.
Members: (21) Algeria, Bahrain, Comoros, Djibouti, Egypt, Iraq, Jordan, Kuwait, Lebanon, Ubya, Mauritania, Morocco, Oman, Qatar, Saudi Arabia, Somalia, Sudan, Syria, Tunisia, United Arab Emirates, and Yemen.

Asia-Pacific Economic Cooperation (APEC)
Established November 7, 1989.
Members: (18) Australia, Brunei, Canada, Chile, China, Hong Kong, Indonesia, Japan, South Korea, Malaysia, Mexico, New Zealand, Papua New Guinea, Philippines, Singapore, Taiwan, Thailand, and the United States.

Association of South East Asian Nations (ASEAN)
Established August 9, 1967.
Members: (6) Brunei, Indonesia, Malaysia, Philippines, Singapore, and Thailand.
Observers: (3) Laos, Papua New Guinea, and Vietnam.

Caribbean Community and Common Market (CARICOM)
Established July 4, 1973; Effective August 1, 1973.
Members: (14) Antigua and Barbuda, the Bahamas, Barbados, Belize, Dominica, Grenada, Guyana, Jamaica, Montserrat, St. Kitts and Nevis, St. Lucia, St. Vincent and the Grenadines, Surinam, and Trinidad and Tobago.
Observers: (9) Anguilla, Bermuda, Cayman Islands, Dominican Republic, Haiti, Mexico, Netherlands Antilles, Puerto Rico, and Venezuela.

Central African Customs Union (UDEAC)
Established December 8, 1964; Effective January 1, 1966.
Members: (6) Cameroon, Central African Republic, Chad, Congo, Equatorial Guinea, and Gabon.

Economic Community of West African States (ECOWAS)
Established May 28, 1975.
Members: (16) Benin, Burkina Faso, Cape Verde, Côte d'Ivoire, The

Gambia, Ghana, Guinea, Guinea-Bissau, Liberia, Mali, Mauritania, Niger, Nigeria, Senegal, Sierra Leone, and Togo.

European Union (EU)
Evolved from the European Community (EC); Established February 7, 1992; Effective November 1, 1993.
Members: (15) Austria, Belgium, Denmark, Finland, France, Germany, Greece, Ireland, Italy, Luxembourg, Netherlands, Portugal, Spain, Sweden, and the United Kingdom.

Gulf Cooperation Council (GCC)
Established May 25, 1981.
Members (6) Bahrain, Kuwait, Oman, Qatar, Saudi Arabia, and the United Arab Emirates.

Organization for Economic Cooperation and Development (OECD)
Established December 14, 1960; Effective September 30, 1961.
Members: (29) Australia, Austria, Belgium, Canada, Czech Republic, Denmark, Finland, France, Germany, Greece, Hungary, Iceland, Ireland, Italy, Japan, Korea, Luxembourg, Mexico, Netherlands, New Zealand, Norway, Poland, Portugal, Spain, Sweden, Switzerland, Turkey, the United Kingdom, and the United States.

Organization of American States (OAS)
Established April 30, 1948; Effective December 13, 1951.
Members: (35) Antigua and Barbuda, Argentina, the Bahamas, Barbados, Belize, Bolivia, Brazil, Canada, Chile, Colombia, Costa Rica, Cuba (participation suspended), Dominica, Dominican Republic, Ecuador, El Salvador, Grenada, Guatemala, Guyana, Haiti, Honduras, Jamaica, Mexico, Nicaragua, Panama, Paraguay, Peru, St. Kitts and Nevis, St. Lucia, St. Vincent and the Grenadines, Surinam, Trinidad and Tobago, the United States, Uruguay, and Venezuela.

Southern African Development Community (SADC)
Evolved from the South African Development Coordination Conference (SADCC); Established August 17, 1992.
Members (10) Angola, Botswana, Lesotho, Malawi, Mozambique, Namibia, Swaziland, Tanzania, Zambia, and Zimbabwe.

Southern Cone Common Market (MERCOSUR)
Established March 26, 1991.
Members (5) Argentina, Brazil, Chile, Paraguay, and Uruguay.

World Intellectual Property Organization (WIPO)
Established July 14, 1967; Effective April 26, 1970.
Members: (140) Albania, Algeria, Andorra, Argentina, Armenia, Australia, Austria, Azerbaijan, the Bahamas, Bahrain, Bangladesh, Barbados, Belarus, Belgium, Benin, Bhutan, Bolivia, Bosnia & Herzegovina, Brazil, Brunei, Bulgaria, Burkina Faso, Burundi, Cambodia,

Cameroon, Canada, Central American Republic, Chad, Chile, China, Colombia, Congo, Costa Rica, Côte d'Ivoire, Croatia, Cuba, Cyprus, Czech Republic, Denmark, Dominican Republic, Ecuador, Egypt, El Salvador, Estonia, Fiji, Finiand, France, Gabon, The Gambia, Georgia, Germany, Ghana, Greece, Guatemala, Guinea, Guinea-Bissau, Guyana, Haiti, Holy See, Honduras, Hungary, Iceland, India, Indonesia, Iran, Iraq, Ireland, Israel, Italy, Jamaica, Japan, Jordan, Kazakstan, Kenya, North Korea, South Korea, Laos, Latvia, Lebanon, Lesotho, Liberia, Libya, Liechtenstein, Lithuania, Luxembourg, Macedonia, Madagascar, Malawi, Malaysia, Mali, Malta, Mauritania, Mauritius, Mexico, Moldova, Monaco, Mongolia, Morocco, Namibia, Netherlands, New Zealand, Nicaragua, Niger, Nigeria, Norway, Pakistan, Panama, Paraguay, Peru, Phillipines, Poland, Portugal, Qatar, Romania, Russia, Rwanda, St. Kitts and Nevis, St. Lucia, San Marino, Saudi Arabia, Senegal, Sierra Leone, Singapore, Slovenia, Somalia, South Africa, Spain, Sri Lanka, Sudan, Surinam, Swaziland, Sweden, Switzerland, Tajikistan, Tanzania, Thailand, Togo, Trinidad and Tobago, Tunisia, Turkey, Uganda, Ukraine, United Arab Emirates, the United Kingdom, the United States, Uruguay, Uzbekistan, Venezuela, Vietnam, Yemen, Yugoslavia (suspended), Zaire, Zambia, and Zimbabwe.

World Trade Organization (WTO)
Evolved from the General Agreement on Tariff and Trade; Established January 1, 1995.
Members: (130) Angola, Antigua and Barbuda, Argentina, Australia, Austria, Bahrain, Bangladesh, Barbados, Belgium, Belize, Benin, Bolivia, Botswana, Brazil, Brunei, Dar es Salaam, Bulgaria, Burkina Faso, Burundi, Cameroon, Canada, Central African Republic, Chad, Chile, Colombia, Costa Rica, Côte d'Ivoire, Cuba, Cyprus, Czech Republic, Denmark, Djibouti, Dominica, Dominican Republic, Ecuador, Egypt, El Salvador, European Union, Fiji, Finland, France, Gabon, The Gambia, Germany, Ghana, Greece, Grenada, Guatemala, Guinea, Guinea-Bissau, Guyana, Haiti, Honduras, Hong Kong, Hungary, Iceland, India, Indonesia, Ireland, Israel, Italy, Jamaica, Japan, Kenya, Korea, Kuwait, Lesotho, Liechtenstein, Luxembourg, Macau, Madagascar, Malawi, Malaysia, Maldives, Mali, Malta, Mauritania, Mauritius, Mexico, Mongolia, Morocco, Mozambique, Myanmar, Namibia, Netherlands, New Zealand, Nicaragua, Niger, Nigeria, Norway, Pakistan, Paraguay, Papua New Guinea, Peru, Phillipines, Poland, Portugal, Qatar, Romania, Rwanda, St. Kitts and Nevis, St. Lucia, St. Vincent and the Grenadines, Senegal, Sierra Leone, Singapore, Slovak Republic, Slovenia, Solomon Islands, South Africa, Spain, Sri Lanka, Surinam, Swaziland, Sweden, Switzerland, Tanzania, Thailand, Togo, Trinidad and Tobago, Tunisia, Turkey, Uganda, United Arab Emirates, the United Kingdom, the United States, Uruguay, Venezuela, Zaire, Zambia, and Zimbabwe.

A basic glossary of the most commonly used export terms

International trade, like other specialized fields, has developed its own distinctive vocabulary which can mystify laymen. Many business people stumble over the commonly used terms and acronyms that guide, regulate, and facilitate trade. Lack of precision in the language impedes communication, causes misunderstandings, and delays transactions. Undoubtedly, it loses sales for global companies.

Arranged alphabetically, this glossary of terms frequently used in global trade was sourced from the: U.S. Information Agency, U.S. Departments of Commerce, State, and Treasury, the U.S. International Trade Commission, the Office of the U.S. Trade Representative, the World Trade Organization and the UNCTAD Secretariats in Geneva. It also includes other terms researched by the author and particularly applicable to the scope of this book.

Acceptance. A bill of exchange accepted by the drawee, as evidenced by the drawee's signature on the face of the bill. The drawee commits to pay the bill at maturity. (The payee of the bill must be sure that the drawee has the means and the will to do this.)

Acceptance Draft. A sight draft document against acceptance. See Sight Draft, Documents Against Acceptance.

Acceptance Letter of Credit. An L/C available by acceptance calling for a *time draft* (or *usance draft* in international parlance). Drawn on an intermediate accepting bank, these L/Cs are popular where both buyer and seller need interim finance to facilitate cash flow.

Ad Valorem (According-to-value). See Duty.

Advance Payment. The buyer delivers cash to the seller before the seller releases the goods. Some sellers ask for this in part payment to show good faith on the part of the buyer and also to enhance their cash flow related to the sale of a particular custom-made item. May not mean exactly the same as *payment in advance*.

Advising Bank. The bank, usually in the country of the exporter, that notifies the availability of the *letter of credit* to the exporter. The advising bank is responsible for authenticating and forwarding the L/C but makes no commitment to pay unless it agrees to act as confirming bank. See also Negotiating Bank.

Advisory Capacity. A term indicating that a shipper's agent or representative is not empowered to make definitive decisions or adjustments without approval of the group or individual represented. Compare Without Reserve.

Affreightment (Contract of). An agreement between steamship line (or similar carrier) and an importer or exporter in which cargo space is reserved on a vessel for a specified time and at a specified price. The importer/exporter is obligated to make payment whether or not the shipment is made.

After Date. A phrase indicating that payment on a draft or other negotiable instrument is due a specified number of days after presentation of the draft to the drawee or payee. Compare After sight, At sight.

After Sight. A phrase indicating that the date of maturity of a draft or other negotiable instrument is fixed by the date on which it was drawn a specified number of days after presentation of the draft to the drawee or payee. Compare with After date, At sight.

Agent. See Representative.

Air Waybill. The carrying agreement between shipper and air carrier which is obtained from the airline used to ship the goods. Technically, it is a non-negotiable instrument of air transportation which serves as a receipt for the shipper, indicating that the carrier has accepted the goods listed therein and obligates itself to carry the consignment to the airport of destination according to specified conditions. Compare Inland Bill of Lading, Ocean Bill of Lading, Through Bill of Lading.

All Risks Clause. An insurance provision which provides additional coverage to an Open Cargo Policy usually for an additional premium. Contrary to its name, the clause does not protect against all risks. The more common perils it does cover are theft, pilferage, non-delivery, fresh water damage, contact with other cargo, breakage and leakage, inherent vice, loss of market, and losses caused by delay are not covered.

Alongside. A phrase referring to the side of a ship. Goods to be delivered "alongside" are to be placed on the dock or lighter within reach of the transport ship's tackle so that they can be loaded aboard the ship.

Amendment—Letter of Credit. A change in the terms, amount or expiration date of a letter of credit usually in the interest of the beneficiary. (Exporters should check Art. 9.d.iii of *UCP 500* very carefully especially regarding adverse amendments.)

Applicant. Party applying to *issuing bank* to issue the *letter of credit,* usually an importer.

Arbitrage. The process of buying foreign exchange, stocks, bonds, and other commodities in one market and immediately selling them in another market at higher prices.

Assignment of Proceeds. Document signed by the *beneficiary* under a *letter of credit* assigning the rights to proceeds from an L/C drawing to a third party. From the perspective of the assignee, an assignment differs radically from a *transferable letter of credit.* The latter conveys a right to the transferee to present documents under an L/C, the former does not.

ATA. Admission Temporary Admission.

ATA Carnet. A customs document which enables one to carry or send goods temporarily into certain foreign countries without paying duties or posting bonds.

At Sight. A phrase indicating that payment on a draft or other negotiable instrument is due upon presentation or demand. Compare After Date, After Sight.

Authority to Pay. A document comparable to a revocable letter of credit but under whose terms the authority to pay the seller stems from the buyer rather than from a bank.

Baby Letter of Credit. Second of two letters of credit in a *back-to-back L/C* arrangement.

Back-to-back Letter of Credit. A "baby" *letter of credit* in which the *issuing bank* is secured by a *master L/C.* The *applicant* of the baby will be the *beneficiary* of the master, and the terms of the two L/Cs will be such that documents presented under the baby can obtain payment under the master. "Back-to-backs" are popular among middlemen wanting to protect their position between the buyer and manufacturer.

Balance of Trade. The balance between a country's exports and imports.

Bank Affiliate Trade Association. A trade association partially or wholly owned by banking institution.

Banker's Acceptance. A *draft* bearing the *acceptance* of a *drawee* bank thus qualifying for financing in the liquid U.S. dollars banker's acceptance market. (A useful vehicle for fixed-term, fixed rate financing especially for banks without access to low-cost U.S. dollars funds.)

Banker's Bank. A bank that is established by mutual consent by independent and unaffiliated banks to provide a clearing house for financial transactions.

Bank Holding company (BHC). Any company which directly or indirectly owns or controls, with power to vote, more than five percent of voting shares of each of one or more other banks.

Barratry. Negligence or fraud on the part of a ship's officers or crew resulting in loss to the owners. See Open Cargo Policy.

Barter. Trade in which merchandise is exchanged directly for other merchandise without use of money. Barter is an important means of trade with countries using currency that is not readily convertible.

Beneficiary. The person in whose favor a letter of credit is issued or a draft is drawn, usually an exporter.

Bill of Exchange. A written, unconditional demand, signed by the drawer and addressed to the drawee, to pay a sum of money "at sight" or at some future date (x days after "sight" or x days after "bill of lading date") to the order of the payee, or to the bearer. Frequently known as a *draft* or as a bill. See Draft.

Bill of Lading. A document which provides the terms of the contract between the shipper and the transportation company to move freight between stated points at a specified charge. A receipt for goods delivered to carrier for shipment, a contract of carriage and a document of title issued by a carrier to the shipper. This *transport document* is the primary evidence of shipment of goods and the exporter's key to prompt payment. See also Charter Party B/L. Usually prepared by the shipper on forms issued by the carrier, it serves as a document of title, a contract of carriage, and a receipt of goods.

Blanket Policy. See Open Policy.

Blocked Currency. Exchange which cannot be freely converted into other currencies. Cash deposit which cannot be transferred to another country because of local regulations or a shortage of foreign exchange.

Bonded Warehouse. A building authorized by customs authorities under bond or guarantee of compliance with revenue laws for the storage of goods without payment of duties until removal.

Booking. An arrangement with a steamship company for the acceptance and carriage of freight.

Broker. See Export Broker.

Brussels Tariff Nomenclature. See Nomenclature of the Customs Cooperation Council.

Buying Agent. An agent who buys in this country for foreign importers, especially for such large foreign users as mines, railroads, governments, and public utilities. Synonymous with "purchasing agent."

Carnet. A customs document allowing special categories of goods to cross international borders without payment of duties.

Carrier. A transportation line that hauls cargo.

Cash Against Documents (CAD). Payment for goods in which a commission house or other intermediary transfers title documents to the buyer upon payment in cash.

Cash in Advance (CIA). Payment for goods in which the price is paid in full before shipment is made. This method is usually used only for small purchases or when the goods are built.

Cash with Order (CWO). Payment for goods in which the buyer pays when ordering and in which the transaction is binding on both parties.

Certificate of Free Sale. A certificate, required by some foreign governments, stating that the goods for export, if products under the jurisdiction of the U.S. Federal Food and Drug Administration, are acceptable for sale in the United States, i.e. that the products are sold freely without restriction, FDA will issue shippers a "letter of comment" to satisfy foreign requests or regulations.

Certificate of Inspection. A document in which certification is made as to the good condition of the merchandise immediately prior to shipment. The buyer usually designates the inspecting organization, usually an independent inspection firm or governmental body.

Certificate of Manufacture. A statement by a producer sometimes notarized, which certifies that manufacture has been completed and that the goods are at the disposal of the buyer.

Certificate of Origin. Certificate stating origin of goods, usually signed by the embassy in the country of the exporter which represents the country of the importer.

Chamber of Commerce. An association of businessmen whose purpose is to promote commercial and industrial interests in the community.

Charter Party. A written contract, usually on a special form, between the owner of a vessel and a "charterer" who rents use of the vessel or a part of its freight space. The contract generally includes the freight rates and the ports involved in the transportation.

Charter Party Bill of Lading. A bill of lading issued subject to a charter party arrangement. Note also that charter party B/L's are not acceptable under letters of credit unless allowed explicitly (UCP 500 Art. 25.a. refers).

C&I (Cost and Insurance). A pricing term indicating that these costs are included in the quoted price.

CIF (Cost, Insurance and Freight). Incoterm indicating that these costs are included in the quoted sale price. Includes all costs of shipment and insurance and freight up to the port of destination. The seller must insure the cargo as far as the port of delivery, for if the cargo is lost the seller will bear the consequence. Incoterms were updated in 1989 and published in *ICC 460* (Incoterms 1990).

CIF&C (Cost, Insurance, Freight, and Commission). A pricing term indicating that these costs are included in the price.

CIF&E. (Cost, Insurance, Freight, and (Currency) Clean Bill of Lading). A bill of lading signed by the transportation company indicating that the shipment has been received in good condition with no irregularities in the packing or general condition of all or any part of the shipment. See Foul Bill of Lading.

Clean Draft. A draft to which no documents have been attached.

Collection. The procedure involved in a bank's collecting money for a seller against a draft drawn on a buyer abroad, usually through a correspondent bank.

Collecting Bank. Bank in the importer's country involved in processing a collection.

Collection Papers. The documents submitted, usually with a draft or against a letter of credit, for payment of an export shipment.

Combined Transport B/L. A bill of lading used when more than one carrier is involved in a shipment, for example when a consignment travels by rail and by sea. Sometimes referred to as a multi-modal bill of lading.

Commercial Attaché. The commercial expert on the diplomatic staff of his country's embassy or large consulate in a foreign country.

Commercial Invoice. Seller's itemized list of goods shipped with descriptions, details, prices, costs addressed to buyer. This should represent a complete record of the business transaction between the exporter and the foreign importer with regard to the goods sold. It is also a document of content and therefore, must fully identify the overseas shipment as well as serve as the basis for the preparation of all other documents covering the shipment. In addition, some countries may require further documentation such as quality certificates, certificates of origin, certificates of free sale, and customs invoices.

Commercial Letter of Credit. Common parlance in the U.S. for *documentary letter of credit*, or "DC," as it is known elsewhere. See Letter of Credit.

Commission Agent. See Purchasing Agent and Foreign Sales Representative.

Commission Representative. See Foreign Sales Representative.

Commodity Credit Corporation. A government corporation controlled by the Department of Agriculture to provide financing and stability to the marketing and exporting of agricultural commodities.

Common Carrier. An individual, partnership, or corporation which transports persons or goods for compensation.

Compensation. A form of countertrade in which the seller agrees to take full or partial payment in goods or services generated from the sale.

Conference Line. A member of a steamship conference. See Steamship Conference.

Confirmation. The act of a bank to add its commitment to that of the issuing bank to pay the beneficiary for compliant documents. Under article 9.b. of *UCP 500*, confirming banks must be requested or authorized by the issuing bank to "add their confirmation" to the L/C. Note that the act of confirmation does not relieve the issuing bank of its obligation to the beneficiary.

Confirmed Letter of Credit. Issued by a bank abroad whose validity and terms are confirmed to the beneficiary in the home bank. A letter of credit bearing the confirmation, or commitment to pay, of a second bank, most often in the country of the exporter. Confirmations are the exporter's insurance against non-payment by the *issuing bank* for most reasons other than a *discrepancy*.

Confirming Bank. Bank adding its commitment to pay for compliant documents to that of the issuing bank, usually at the request of same. Confirming banks are very often *correspondents* of issuing banks. *L/C beneficiaries* should understand clearly how soon the confirming bank will pay after presentation of conforming export documents.

Consignee. The person, firm or representative to whom a seller or shipper sends merchandise and who, upon presentation of the necessary documents, is recognized as the owner of the merchandise for the purpose of the payment of customs duties. This term is also used as applying to one to whom goods are shipped, usually at the shipper's risk, when an outright sale has not been made. See Consignment.

Consignee Marks. See Marks.

Consignment. A term pertaining to merchandise shipped to a consignee abroad when an actual purchase has not been made, under an agreement by which the consignee is obligated to sell the goods for the account of the consignor, and to remit proceeds as goods are sold.

Consolidator's Bill of Lading. B/L issued by consolidator (forwarder) to a shipper as a receipt for goods to be consolidated with other cargoes prior to shipment.

Consul. A government official residing in a foreign country who is charged with the representation of the interests of his country and its nationals.

Consular Declaration. A formal statement, made to the consul of a foreign country, describing goods to be shipped.

Consular Invoice. A detailed statement regarding the character of goods shipped, duly certified by the consul of the importing country at the port of shipment.

Consulate. The official premises of a foreign government representative.

Contingency Insurance. Insurance taken out by the exporter complementary to insurance bought by the consignee abroad.

Control of Goods. Of vital interest to all parties involved in trade, control of goods is exercised through the *transport document.* It determines whether the buyer will be able to clear an inbound shipment without the *transport document,* (and thus without paying for the documents held at the bank).

Correspondent Bank. A bank overseas with which a local bank has a relationship. Relationships between banks are just one factor that determine appetite for *confirmation* and thus have relevance to importers and exporters.

Cost and Freight (C&F). Former Incoterm indicating that the sale price includes all costs of shipment and freight up to the port of destination. The buyer must insure the cargo from the port of loading, for if the cargo is lost the buyer will bear the consequence. Note that C&F is an archaic terminology replaced by CFR since Incoterms were updated in 1989 and published in *ICC 460* (Incoterms 1990).

Counterpurchase. One of the most common forms of countertrade in which the seller receives cash but contractually agrees to buy local products or services as a percentage of cash received and over an agreed period of time.

Countertrade. International trade in which the seller is required to accept goods or other instruments of trade, in partial or whole payment for its products.

Countervailing Duty. An extra duty imposed by the Secretary of Commerce to offset export grants, bounties, or subsidies paid to foreign suppliers in certain countries by the government of those countries as an incentive to export.

Country of Origin. The country in which a particular commodity is manufactured, as determined by the amount of work done on the product in the country and attested by a *certificate of origin.*

Credit Risk Insurance. A form of insurance which covers the seller against loss due to non-payment on the part of the buyer.

Customs. The duties levied by a country on imports and exports. The term also applies to the procedures and organization involved in such collection.

Customs Broker. Firm representing the importer in dealings with customs responsible for obtaining and submitting documents for clearing merchandise through customs, arranging inland transport and paying related charges.

Customs Cooperation Council Nomenclature (CCCN). The customs tariff used by many countries worldwide, including most European nations. It is also known as the Brussels Tariff Nomenclature. Compare Standard Industrial Classification, Standard International Trade Classification, and Tariff Schedule.

D/A. See Documents Against Acceptance.

Date Draft. A draft drawn to mature on a specified number of days after the date it is issued, with or without regard to the date of acceptance.

DC. Popular acronym outside the Americas for *documentary letter of credit*. The equivalent in the U.S. is the L/C, or more properly the *commercial L/C*.

Deferred Payment L/C. A letter of credit available "by deferred payment" calling for a *time draft* (or *usance draft* in international parlance) drawn on the issuing bank. Popular in cases of supplier credit.

Delivery Point. See Specific Delivery Point.

Demurrage. Storage fee for inbound merchandise held beyond the free time allowed by the shipping company. Excess time taken for loading or unloading a vessel as a result of a shipper. Charges are assessed by the shipping company.

Department of Commerce. An agency of government whose purpose it is to promote commercial industrial interests in the country. See United States Department of Commerce.

Devaluation. The official lowering of the value of one country's currency in terms of one or more foreign currencies. Thus, if the U.S. dollar is devaluated in relation to the French franc, one dollar will "buy" fewer francs than before.

DISC. See Domestic International Corporation.

Discount (Financial). A deduction from the face value of commercial paper in consideration of cash by the seller before a specified date.

Discrepancy. An instance in which documents presented do not conform to the L/C. Article 13.a. of *UCP 500* states that "banks must examine all documents stipulated in the credit with reasonable care". In fact banks exercise extreme care, and international standard banking practice dictates that exporters must exercise detailed vigilance in preparing documents under *letters of credit* if they are not to be frustrated by delays in obtaining payment.

Discrepancy—Letter of Credit. When documents presented do not conform to the terms of the Letter of Credit, it is referred to as a discrepancy.

Dishonor. Refusal on the part of the *drawee* to accept a draft or pay upon maturity.

Dispatch. An amount paid by a vessel's operator to a charterer if loading or unloading is completed in less time than stipulated in the charter party.

Distributor. A firm that sells directly for a manufacturer, usually on an exclusive contract for a specified territory, and whom maintains an inventory on hand.

Dock Receipt. A receipt issued by an ocean carrier or its agent, acknowledging that the shipment has been delivered, or received at the dock or warehouse of the carrier.

Documentary Collection. An order written by the seller to the bank to deliver *documents against payment,* or to *deliver documents against acceptance,* to the buyer. The seller's bank will act on the instruction of the seller in a principal/agent relationship and remit the documents to a branch, or a *correspondent,* in the country of the buyer, with instructions for collection. A key factor in the effectiveness of such collections is the *control of goods* exercised through the *transport document.*

Documentary Credit. See Letter of Credit (Commercial).

Documentary Draft. A draft to which documents are attached.

Documentation/Documents. See Shipping Documents.

Documents Against Acceptance (D/A). A type of payment for goods in which the documents transferring title to the goods are not given to the buyer until he has accepted the draft issued against him.

Documents Against Payment (D/P). A type of payment for goods in which the documents transferring title to the goods are not given to the buyer until he has paid the value of a draft issued against him.

Domicile. The place where draft or acceptance is made payable.

D/P. See Documents Against Payment.

Draft. The same as a "bill of exchange." A written order for a certain sum of money to be transferred on a certain date from the person who owes the money or agrees to make the payment (the drawee) to the creditor to whom the money is owed (the drawer of the draft). See Date Draft, Documentary Draft, Sight Draft, Time Draft.

Drawback (Import). The repayment, up to 99 percent of customs duties paid on merchandise which later is exported, as part of a finished product, is known as a drawback. It refers also to a refund of a domestic tax which has been paid upon exportation of imported merchandise.

Drawee. One on whom a draft is drawn, and who owes the stated amount. See Draft.

Drawer. One who "draws" a draft, and receives payment. See Draft.

Dumping. Exporting merchandise into a country at prices below the prices in the domestic market.

Duty. The tax imposed by a government on merchandise imported from another country.

Electronic Data Interchange (EDI). The exchange between computers of trade documentation. EDI can take two forms, financial and documentary, and suffers from a curse common in the world of computers; at least two message format standards. They are ANSI (popular in the U.S.) and EDIFACT (popular elsewhere).

EMC. Export Management Company.

ETC. Export Trading Company.

Eurodollars. U.S. dollars on deposit in any branch of any bank located outside the United States. Likewise, euroyen are Japanese yen on deposit in banks outside Japan, and may be outside of Europe, too. Any "eurocurrency" is a foreign currency deposit and should be treated with care if offered as a form of payment. For example, a U.S. exporter offered U.S. dollars to be delivered in some countries may face a challenge to convert these eurodollars to U.S. dollars.

Evergreen Clause. A provision in the letter of credit for the expiration date to extend without requiring an amendment.

Exchange. A pricing term indicating that these costs are included in the price.

Exchange Permit. A governmental permit sometimes required of an importer to enable him to convert his own country's currency into foreign currency with which to pay a seller in another country.

Exchange Regulations/Restrictions. Restrictions imposed by an importing country to protect its foreign exchange reserves. See "Exchange Permit."

Exchange Rate. The price of one currency in terms of another, i.e. the number of units of one currency that may be exchanged for one unit of another currency. Exchange rates may be quoted spot, for delivery within two working days, or forward, for delivery at some future time. Apt to fluctuate. Any international trader with a eye for profit will be aware of the currency circumstances affecting a partner.

Excise Tax. A domestic tax assessed on the manufacture, sale or use of a commodity within a country. Usually refundable if the product is exported.

EX "From" (Point of Origin). A pricing term ("Ex factory," "Ex warehouse," etc.) under which the seller agrees to place the goods at the buyer's disposal at the agreed place, with costs from that point being paid by the buyer.

Eximbank. An export-import bank.

Expiration Date. The final date upon which the presentation of documents and drawing of drafts under a letter of credit may be made.

Export. To send goods to a foreign country or overseas territory.

Export Broker. One who brings together the exporter and importer for a fee and then withdraws from the transaction.

Export Declaration. A formal statement made to the collector of customs at a port of exit declaring full particulars about goods being exported.

Export License. A governmental permit required to export certain products to certain destinations.

Export Management Company (EMC). A firm which acts as local export sales agent for several non-competing manufacturers. (Term synonymous with Manufacturer's Export Agent).

Export Merchant. A producer or merchant who sells directly to a foreign purchaser without going through an intermediate such as an export broker.

Export Trading Company. Firm buying domestic products for sale overseas taking title to the goods (which an export-management company usually does not).

Factor. A finance company willing to purchase a receivable at a discount, either with recourse to the seller or without. In exchange for immediate payment, the seller will transfer title to the receivable to the factor. Convenient but expensive alternative to other methods of converting receivables to cash.

Factoring. A method used by businesses including trading companies to obtain cash for discounted accounts receivables or other assets.

FCIA. Foreign Credit Insurance Association.

FI. Free In. A pricing term indicating that the charterer of a vessel is responsible for the cost of loading goods into the vessel.

FIO. Free in and Out. A pricing term indicating that the charterer of a vessel is responsible for the cost of loading and unloading goods from the vessel.

Floating Policy. See Open Insurance Policy.

FO. Free Out. A pricing term indicating that the charterer of a vessel is responsible for the cost of loading goods from the vessel.

Force Majeure: The title of a standard clause in marine contracts exempting the parties for non-fulfillment of their obligations as a result of conditions beyond their control, such as earthquakes, floods or war.

Foreign Credit Insurance Association (FCIA). An association of 50 insurance companies which operate in conjunction with the Eximbank to provide comprehensive insurance for exporters against nonpayment. FCIA underwrites the commercial credit risks. Eximbank covers the political risk and any excessive commercial risks.

Foreign Currency Account. An account maintained by a bank in foreign currency and payable in that currency.

Foreign Distribution. See Distributor.

Foreign Exchange. A currency or credit instruments of a foreign country. Also, transactions involving purchase and/or sale of currencies.

Foreign Freight Forwarder. An agent who assists his exporter client in moving cargo to a foreign destination.

Foreign Sales Agent. An individual or firm that serves as the foreign representative of a domestic supplier and seeks sales abroad for the supplier.

Foreign Sales Corporation. An American territorial tax scheme whereby a corporation within a U.S. possession, such as the Virgin Islands, or within a qualifying jurisdiction, such as Barbados, may exempt 15 per cent to 30 per cent of export profits from U.S. corporate tax. To qualify for special tax treatment, an FSC must be a foreign corporation, maintain a summary of its permanent books of account at the foreign office, and have at least one director resident outside of the U.S. A portion of the foreign sales corporations income (generally corresponding to the tax deferred income of the DISC) would be exempt from U.S. tax at both the FSC and the U.S. corporate parent levels. This exemption is achieved by allowing a domestic corporation that is an FSC shareholder a 100 percent deduction for a portion of dividends received from an FSC attributable to economic activity actually conducted outside the U.S. customs territory. Interest, dividends, royalties, or other investment income of an FSC would be subject to U.S. tax.

Foreign Sales Representative. A representative or agent residing in a foreign country who acts as a salesman for a U.S. manufacturer, usually for a commission. Sometimes referred to as a "sales agent" or "commission agent." See Representative.

Foreign Trade Zone. An American term for a site sanctioned by the authorities in which imported goods are exempted from duties until withdrawn for domestic sale or use. Can be used for commercial warehousing, assembly plants and re-export.

Forfait. The sale of a term debt against a discounted cash payment in which the seller forfeits the right to future payments by the debtor. A popular method for exporters of capital equipment to dispose of long-term overseas debt.

Forwarder's Bill of Lading. B/L issued by forwarder to shipper, a receipt for merchandise to be shipped.

Foul Bill of Lading. A receipt for goods issued by a carrier bearing a notation that the outward containers or goods have been damaged. See Clean Bill of Lading.

Fraud. All too common in international trade, especially transactional deals handling commodities and a perfect reason why any sensible importer, exporter or middleman will develop a relationship with a competent trade bank.

Free Alongside Ship (FAS). Incoterm indicating that the sale price includes cost of transport to the port of embarkation, but not the costs of loading, export clearance, ocean freight or insurance. The buyer must insure the cargo as far as the port of delivery, for if the cargo is lost the buyer will bear the consequence. Incoterms were updated in 1989 and published in *ICC 460* (Incoterms 1990).

Free of Particular Average (FPA). The title of a clause used in marine insurance, indicating that partial loss or damage to a foreign shipment is not covered. (Note: Loss resulting from certain conditions, such as the sinking or burning of the ship, may be specifically exempted from the effect of the clause.) Compare with WPA.

Free On Board (FOB). Incoterm indicating that the sale price includes the cost of transport to and loading at the port of embarkation, but not the costs of export clearance, ocean freight or insurance. The buyer must insure the cargo as far as the port of delivery, for if the cargo is lost the buyer will bear the consequence. Incoterms were updated in 1989 and published in *ICC* 460 (Incoterms 1990).

Free Port. An area generally encompassing a port and its surrounding locality into which goods may enter duty-free or subject only to minimal revenue tariffs.

Free Sale. See Certificate of Free Sale.

Free Trade Zone. A term used by all countries (except the U.S.A.) for a site sanctioned by the authorities in which imported goods are exempted from duties until withdrawn for domestic sale or use. Can be used for commercial warehousing, assembly plants and re-export. (See Foreign Trade Zone).

Freight Forwarder. A company that books shipment of goods, often as an agent for an airline. Usually, many small shipments are combined to take advantage of bulk discounts. Forwarders also may provide other services, such as trucking, warehousing and document preparation.

General Agreement on Tariffs and Trade (GATT). The General Agreement on Tariffs and Trade, a Geneva-based organization that governed world trade until the formation of the World Trade Organization (WTO) in 1995. Formed by 23 countries at a conference in Geneva in 1947 to increase trade by lowering duties and quotas. The General Agreements on Tariffs and Trade is a multilateral trade treaty among governments, embodying rights and obligations. The detailed rules set out in the Agreement constitute a code which the parties to the Agreement have agreed upon to govern their trading relationships.

General License (Export). Government authorization to export without specific documentary approval.

Gross Weight. Total weight of goods, packing, and container, ready for shipment.

Guarantee Letter. Commitment popular outside the U.S. functionally similar to *standby letters of credit*.

Handling Charges. The forwarder's fee to his shipper client.

Harmonized Code. Harmonized commodity description and coding system, an international classification system that assigns identification numbers to specific products. The code ensures all parties use a consistent classification for purposes of documentation, statistical control and duty assessment.

Horizontal Trade Association. A trade association which exports a range of similar or identical products supplied by a number of manufacturers or other producers. Webb-Pomerene Associations, trade-group organized ETCs and an ETC formed by an association of agricultural cooperatives are the prime examples of horizontally organized ETCs.

ICC. See International Chamber of Commerce.

INCOTERMS 1990. Terms of sale indicating costs and responsibilities included in the price under a sales contract (i.e. EXW FOB, CFR, CIF, DDP). Defined under *ICC Publication No. 460*, these are worldwide standardized terms that transcend borders and should be clearly understood by all parties negotiating an international sales contract. The year 1990 refers to the date of the last revision to the Incoterms.

Import. To bring merchandise into a country from another country or overseas territory.

Import License. A governmental document which permits the importation of a product or material into a country where such licenses are necessary.

In Bond. A term applied to the status of merchandise admitted provisionally into a country without payment of duties. See Bonded Warehouse.

Inconvertibility. The inability to exchange the currency of one country for the currency of another.

Inherent Vice. Defects or characteristics of a product that could lead to deterioration without outside influence. An insurance term. See All Risk Clause.

Inland Bill of Lading. A bill of lading used in transporting goods overland to the exporter's international carrier. Although a through bill of lading can sometimes be used, it is usually necessary to prepare both an inland bill of lading and an ocean bill of lading for export shipments. Compare Air Waybill, Ocean Bill of Lading, Through Bill of Lading.

Inland Carrier. A transportation line which handles export or import cargo between the port and inland points.

Insurance Certificate. Where the seller provides ocean marine insurance, it is necessary to furnish insurance certificates, usually in duplicate. The certificates are negotiable documents and must be endorsed before submitting them to the bank. The seller can arrange to obtain an open cargo policy that the freight forwarder maintains.

International Chamber of Commerce. Known as ICC for short, the International Chamber of Commerce is a non-governmental organization serving world-wide business. Members in 123 countries represent tens of thousands of business organizations and companies and promote world trade and investment based on free and fair competition. ICC Publishing SA, based in Paris, produces many publications, some of which are de facto standards in global commerce, i.e. Uniform Customs and Practices for Documentary Credits (*UCP 500*), Uniform Rules for Collections *(URC 522)* and Incoterms 1990 *(ICC 460)*. ICC Publishing SA has a sales office in New York, NY.

International Freight Forwarder. See Freight Forwarder.

Invoice. See Commercial Invoice.

Irrevocable. Adjective attached to *letter of credit* to denote an instrument that cannot be amended or canceled without the agreement of all parties to the L/C (including the beneficiary). The adjective is popular and redundant: Article 6 of *UCP500* states that credits should indicate whether they are revocable or irrevocable and that, in the absence of such indication, credits shall be deemed to be irrevocable. In most circumstances, revocable L/Cs are worthless and, as a consequence, they are very rare. Yet the initiated still refer to "irrevocable letters of credit" as if they are the exception, which they were prior to *UCP 500*, rather than the rule, which they are now.

Joint Venture. A commercial or industrial arrangement in which principals of one company share control and ownership principals of other.

Latest Shipment Date. Last day on which goods may be shipped (as evidenced by "on board" date on bill of lading, or flight date on airway-bill).

Legal Weight. The weight of the goods plus immediate wrappings which go along with the goods, e.g. contents of a tin can together with its can. See Net Weight.

Letter of Credit. An undertaking written by the *issuing bank* to pay the *beneficiary* a stated sum of money, within a certain time, against the presentation of conforming documents. Other parties to a letter of credit may be the *advising bank*, the *confirming bank*, the *negotiating bank*, the *paying bank* and the *reimbursing bank*, but the main contract of payment is between the issuing bank and the beneficiary. Since the issuing bank is very often located in a separate country from the beneficiary, the latter relies on the advising bank, locally, to notify of the arrival L/C and to authenticate it. "Documents" in the definition above may comprise of various export documents, as in a *documentary letter of credit*, or a simple statement by the beneficiary, as in a *standby letter of credit*. Under Article 13c. of *UCP 500*, conditions expressed in a letter of credit without stating the document to may be ignored.

Letter of Credit (Commercial) (L/C). A document issued by a bank at buyer's request in favor of a seller, promising an agreed amount of money on receipt by the bank of certain documents within a specified time.

License. See Exchange License, Export License, Import License, Validated License.

Licensing. The grant or technical assistance service and or the use of product rights, such as a trademark in return for royalty payments.

Lighter. An open or covered barge towed by a tugboat and used mainly in harbors and inland waterways.

Lighterage. The loading or unloading of a ship by means of a barge, or lighter which because of shallow water permits the ship from coming to shore.

Manufacturer's Export Agent (MEA). See Export Management Company.

Marine Bill of Lading. B/L for shipment by sea.

Marine Insurance. An insurance which will compensate the owner of goods transpored on the seas in the event of loss which cannot be legally recovered from the carrier. Also covers air shipments.

Marks. A set of letters, numbers and/or geometric symbols, generally followed by the name of the port of destination, placed on packages for export, for identification purposes.

Master Letter of Credit. First of two *letters of credit* in a *back-to-back* L/C arrangement.

Maturity Date. The date upon which a draft or acceptance becomes due for payment.

Most-favored Nation Status. All countries having this designation receive equal treatment with respect to customs and tariffs.

Multi-modal bill of Lading. A bill of lading used when more than one mode of transport is involved in a shipment, for example when a consignment travels by rail and by sea. Sometimes referred to as a combined transport bill of lading.

Named Point. See Specific Delivery Point.

Negotiable Bill of Lading. B/L consigned to the order of, and endorsed in blank by, the shipper. Whoever carries a negotiable bill of lading in their hand carries the document of title to the goods. That is why banks often call for a "hill set" of bills of lading under their L/Cs (see Section 7 on control of goods.) See also Straight Bill of Lading.

Negotiating Bank. The bank that checks the exporter's documents under the letter of credit and advances cash to the exporter, at a small discount, in the expectation of *reimbursement* by the issuing bank.

Net Weight. Weight of the goods alone without any immediate wrapping, e.g. the weight of the contents of a tin can without the weight of the can. See Legal Weight.

Nomenclature of the Customs Cooperation Council. This was known as the Brussels Classification Nomenclature prior to January 1, 1975. It is the customs tariff adhered to by most Europen countries and many other countries throughout the world, but not by the United States.

Ocean Bill of Lading. A bill of lading (B/L) indicating that the exporter consigns a shipment to an international carrier for transportation to a specified foreign market. Unlike an inland B/L, the ocean B/L also serves as a collection document. If it is a "Straight B/L," the foreign buyer can obtain the shipment from the carrier by simply showing proof of identity. If a "Negotiable B/L" is used, the buyer must first pay for the goods, post a bond, or meet other conditions agreeable to the seller. Compare Air Waybill, Inland Bill of Lading, Through Bill of Lading.

Offset. A variation of countertrade in which the seller is required to assist in or arrange for the marketing of locally produced goods.

On Board Bill of Lading. A bill of lading in which a carrier acknowledges that goods have been placed onboard a certain vessel.

Open Account. A trade arrangement in which goods are shipped to a foreign buyer without guarantee of payment. The obvious risk this method poses to the supplier makes it essential that the buyer's integrity be unquestionable.

Open Cargo Policy. Synonymous with Floating Policy. An insurance policy which binds the insurer automatically to protect with insurance all shipments made by the insured from the moment the shipment leaves the initial shipping point until delivered at destination. The insuring conditions include clauses naming such risks insured against as perils of the sea, fire, jettison, forcible theft, and barratry. See Perils of the Sea, Barratry, All risks Clause.

Opening Bank. Common terminology among bankers for *issuing bank* in the *letter of credit* process.

Open Insurance Policy. A marine insurance policy that applies to all shipments made by an exporter over a period of time rather than to one shipment only.

OPIC. Overseas Private Investment Corporation. A wholly owned government corporation designed to promote private investment in developing countries, by promoting political risk investment in developing countries, by providing political risk insurance, and some financing assistance.

"Order" Bill of Lading. A bill of lading, negotiable made out to the order of the shipper.

Packing Credit. Common parlance internationally, especially in Asia, for *pre-export finance* provided against a *letter of credit*.

Packing List. A list prepared by the seller itemizing goods shipped, quantities, sizes, weights and packing marks. Very common in trade finance, the packing list should be prepared so as to be consistent with other documents especially under a *letter of credit*.

Parcel Post Receipt. The postal authorities' signed acknowledgement of delivery to them of a shipment made by parcel post.

Paying Bank. The bank nominated in the L/C to pay out against conforming documents, without *recourse*. Exporters interested in their cash flow should understand whether the paying bank is in their own country, or that of their customer, the importer.

Payment in Advance. The buyer delivers cash to the seller before the seller releases the goods. Can be referred to as "cash in advance," or CAD and may not mean exactly the same as *advance payment*.

Perils of the Sea. A marine insurance term used to designate heavy weather, straining, lightning, collision, and sea water damage.

Phytosanitary Inspection Certificate. A certificate, issued to satisfy import regulations of foreign countries, indicating that a shipment has been inspected and is free from harmful pests and plant diseases.

Piggybacking. The assigning of export marketing and distribution functions by one manufacturer to another.

Port Marks. See Marks.

Pre-Export Finance. Terminology of U.S. bankers for a loan to an exporter to finance the accumulation of materials, the manufacture, assembly, production, packaging and transport of physical goods to fulfill an export order. Commonly guaranteed by Ex-1m or SBA Working Capital Guarantee programs.

Presentation Period. Time allowed after issue of transport document to present documents under L/C.

Presenting Bank. Bank in a documentary collection process presenting export documents to the *drawee* for payment. The exporter and the presenting bank behave in a principal/agent relationship and it is therefore wise of the uncertain exporter to ensure that the collection is presented by some bank other than the importer's bank.

Procuring Agent. See Purchasing Agent.

Proforma Invoice. Following negotiations, the exporter issues this document which confirms product details, prices, shipping, and payment terms. This is the starting point for further documentation.

Purchasing Agent. An agent who purchases goods in his/her own country on behalf of large foreign buyers such as government agencies and large private concerns.

Quota. The total quantity of a product or commodity which may be imported into a country, imposed by governments. Usually quotas protect a domestic market. In the U.S., sugar, wheat, cotton, tobacco, textiles and apparel are governed by quotas.

Quotation. An offer to sell goods at a stated price and under stated terms.

Rate of Exchange. The basis upon which money of one country will be exchanged for that of another. Rates of exchange are established and quoted for foreign currencies on the basis of the demand, supply and stability of the individual currences. See Exchange.

Received for Shipment B/L, Bill of Lading indicating goods received for shipment (but not "onboard"). Unacceptable B/L unless specifically allowed by the letter of credit or unless it is marked "onboard" with a date and signature.

Recourse. Payment with recourse means that the paying party retains the right to the funds in the event that reimbursement (from another party) is not forthcoming. An important concept in trade finance.

Red Clause Letter of Credit. An L/C with a "red clause" in it, allowing the *beneficiary* to draw down an *advance payment* prior to shipment, usually against presentation of a simple receipt. So called because traditionally it was written in red ink, the purpose of this clause is to finance the seller during the preparation of the export order. The applicant will be liable for any drawings even if goods are never shipped. This is one reason why importers should expect red clause L/Cs to be collateralized differently from plain import L/Cs.

Reimbursing Bank. The bank empowered by the issuing bank (i.e. with a bank balance) to charge the account of the issuing bank and pay to the bank collecting funds under a letter of credit.

Remitting Bank. Exporter's bank in a documentary collection process taking export documents and sending them to a *correspondent* in the country of the importer (the drawee in the collection process).

Representative. The word "representative" is preferred to the word "agent" in writing. Since "agent" in an exact legal sense, connotes more binding powers and responsibilities than "representative." See Foreign Sales Representative.

Revocable. Applied to letters of credit. A revocable letter of credit is one which can be altered or cancelled by the buyer after he has opened it through his bank. See Irrevocable.

Revolving Letter of Credit. L/C that reinstates automatically. May revolve in relation to time or value, the latter being cumulative or non-cumulative.

Royalty Payment. The share of the product or profit paid by a licensee to his licensor. See Licensing.

SA (Société Anonymé)—French expression meaning a corporation.

S/D. See Sight Draft.

Sales Agent. See Foreign Sales Representative.

Sales Representative. See Foreign Sales Representative.

Sanitary Certificate. A certificate which attests to the purity or absence of disease or pests in the shipment of food products, plants, seeds, and live animals.

Shipper's Document. Commercial invoices, bills of lading, insurance certificates, consular invoices, and related documents.

Shipper's Letter of Credit. The exporter issues this to the freight forwarder. It covers key details of the transaction, shipping terms and other applicable instructions which the freight forwarder must follow.

Ship's Manifest. A true list in writing of the individual shipments comprising the cargo of a vessel, signed by the captain.

SIC: See Standard Industrial Classification.

Sight Draft (S/D). A draft so drawn as to be payable upon presentation to the drawee or at a fixed or determinable date thereafter. See Documents Against Acceptance, Documents Against Payment.

SITC. See Standard International Trade Classification.

Specific Delivery Point. A point in sales quotations which designates specifically where and within what geographical locale the goods will be delivered at the expense and responsibility of the seller; e.g. FAS named vessel at named port of export.

Spot Exchange. The purchase or sale of foreign currency, usually against an equivalent amount of local currency, for delivery within two working days after the agreement.

Standard Industrial Classification (SIC). A numerical system developed by the U.S. Government for the classification of commercial services and industrial products. Also classifies establishments by type of activity.

Standard International Trade Classification (SITC). A numerical system developed by the United Nations to classify commodities used in international trade and for reporting trade statistics.

Standby Letter of Credit. An L/C popular in the U.S. issued with the purpose of guaranteeing payment in the event of non-performance by *applicant*. Similar in method to *commercial letters of credit* and subject to *UCP 500* but different in three significant aspects: (1) beneficiary's statement or claim of default suffices to draw (in contrast to a pile of detailed export documents under commercial L/C), thus (2) discrepancy rate is between low and zero, therefore (3) expect banks to collateralize standby L/Cs somewhat differently to commercial L/Cs (i.e. 100 per-cent).

State-Controlled Trading Comapny. In a country with a state trading monopoly, a trading entity empowered by the country's government to conduct export business.

Steamship Conference. A group of vessel operators joined together for the purpose of establishing freight rates. A shipper may receive reduced rates if the shipper enters into a contract to ship on vessels of Conference members only.

Steamship Guarantee. A guarantee issued by a bank to a steamship line against financial loss arising from the release of a consignment without the appropriate *transport document*. Popular because goods frequently arrive at the port of discharge before documents are available to clear them.

Stocking Distributor. A distributor who maintains an inventory of goods of a manufacturer.

Straight Bill of Lading. A B/L consigned directly to a party (as opposed to *negotiable bills of lading* issued "to order" of shipper) who holds title to the goods. Discomforting to bankers if the consignee party is not the bank. A straight B/L cannot be endorsed to another party.

Swap Arrangements. A form of countertrade in which the seller sells on credit and then transfers the credit to a third party.

SWIFT. Society for Worldwide Interbank Financial Telecommunication. A cooperative owned by a consortium of banks designed to carry formatted messages between them in a secure environment. The messages all relate to financial transactions between banks and their customers.

Switch Arrangements. A form of countertrade in which the seller sells on credit and then transfers the credit to a third party.

Tare Weight. The weight of packing and containers without the goods to be shipped.

Tariff Schedule. A schedule or system of duties imposed by a government on goods imported or exported, the rate of duty imposed in a tariff.

Tenor. The time fixed or allowed for payment, as in "the tenor of a draft."

TEU. Twenty-foot equivalent unit. A measurement of cargo based on a standard ocean shipment container, which is 20 feet in length.

Through Bill of Lading. A single bill of lading covering both the domestic and internatinal carriage of an export shipment. An air waybill, for instance, is essentially a through bill of lading used for air shipments. Ocean shipments, on the other hand, usually require two separate documents—an inland bill of lading for domestic carriage and an ocean bill of lading for international carriage. Through bills of lading, therefore, cannot be used. Compare Air Waybill, Inland Bill of Lading, Ocean bill of Lading.

Time Draft. A draft so drawn as to mature at a certain fixed time after presentation or acceptance.

Trade Acceptance. A *time draft* where the drawee signs the word "accepted" across the face and thus commits to pay the holder upon maturity. The instrument will be as valuable as the creditworthiness of the accepting party allows.

Trade Development Program (TDP). This program is designed to promote economic development in the Third World and the sale of U.S. goods and services to these developing countries. It operates as part of the International Development Cooperative Agency.

Trade Mission. A mission to a foreign country organized to promote trade through the establishment of contracts and exposure to the commercial environment. They are frequently organized by Federal, State, or local agencies.

Tramp Steamer. A ship not operating on regular routes or schedules.

Transport Document. A bill of lading, an air waybill, a truck receipt, any other document acting as a receipt for goods and a contract of carriage. Of all these transport documents, only a bill of lading is a document of title.

Transshipment. Shipment of merchandise to destination abroad on more than one vessel. Liability may pass from one carrier to the next, or it may be covered by a *through bill of lading* issued by the first carrier.

Trust Receipt. Release of merchandise by a bank to a buyer in which the bank retains title to the merchandise. The buyer, who obtains the goods for manufacturing or sales purposes, is obligated to maintain the goods (or the proceeds from their sale) distinct from the remainder of his/her assets and to hold them ready for repossession by the bank.

Turnkey. A method of construction whereby the contractor assumes total responsibility from design through completion of the task.

UCP 500. Uniform Customs and Practice for Documentary Credits, Publication No. 500 of the International Chamber of Commerce. The indisputable authority on letters of credits recognized internationally UCP 500 serves as the self-regulation of the L/C industry and renders L/Cs a more reliable form of payment. Copies of this crucial document (and of URC 522) can be obtained from the ICC Publishing Inc., 156 Fifth Avenue, Suite 820, New York, NY 10010 (Telephone (212) 206-1150) at the time of writing or, perhaps, from a bank that specializes in international trade finance. ICC has a whole range of interesting publications dealing with many aspects of international trade. *Be particularly careful of any L/C which does not clearly state it is subect to UCP 500. Usually in the final paragraph.*

Unconfirmed Letter of Credit. A *letter of credit* that does not carry any *confirmation* by a second bank, usually located in the country of the *beneficiary*. Exporters intent on collecting payment under such L/Cs should hold a view as to risk of non-payment for various reasons.

URC 522. Uniform Rules for Collections, Publication No. 522 of the *International Chamber of Commerce.* An internationally recognized code for the handling of collections, clean or documentary.

Usance. Banker's terminology, in use more commonly overseas than in the U.S., indicating time allowed for payment of a bill of exchange (contrast with Sight Above).

Usance Draft. More often referred to in the U.S. as a *time draft.* See also Documents Against Acceptance.

Usance Letter of Credit. Sometimes referred to in the U.S. as a time L/C.

Validated Licence. A government document authorizing the export of commodities within limitations set forth in the document.

Vertical ETC. An ETC that integrates a range of functions taking products from suppliers to consumers.

Visa. A signature of formal approval on an entry document. Obtained from a Consulate.

Warehouse Receipt. A receipt issued by a warehouse listing goods received for storage.

Wharfage. Charge assessed by carrier for the handling of incoming or outgoing ocean cargo.

With Average (WA). A marine insurance term meaning that a shipment is protected from partial damage whenever the damage exceeds three percent (or some other percentage).

Without Reserve. A term indicating that a shipper's agent or representative is empowered to make definitive decisions and adjustments abroad without approval of the group individual represented. Compare Advisory Capacity.

Bibliography

Axtell, Roger E., (ed. and compiler) (1985) *Do's and Taboos Around the World: A Guide to International Behavior*, The Parker Pen Company, USA.

Becker, Tom (ed.) (1981) "Proposed Export Trading Company Legislation: A Panacea for Expanding Exports and Transfer of Appropriate Technology to Latin America in Center for Strategic and International Studies." *The Export Performance of the United States: Political and Economic Implications*, Praeger, New York, NY.

Becker, Tom, and Porter, James (1983) "How You Can Use The New Export Trading Companies", *Industrial Marketing*, New York, NY, USA.

Bilkey, Warren J. and Tesar, George (1977) "The Export Behavior of Smaller Sized Wisconsin Manufacturing Firms," *Journal of Industrial Business Studies*, Spring/Summer, pp. 93–98.

Breen, George (1982) *Marketing Research*, 2nd edn, McGraw Hill, New York, NY, USA.

Boone and Kurtz (1980) *Contemporary Marketing*, 3rd edn, The Dryden Press, New York, NY, USA.

Brooks, Mary R., and Rosson, Philip J. (1982) "A Study of Export Behavior of Small- and Medium-size Manufacturing Firms in Three Canadian Provinces," in Michael R. Czinkota, and George Tesar, (eds) *Export Management: An International Context*, Praeger, New York.

California State World Trade Commission and the California European Trade and Investment Office (1989) *Europe: 1992, Implications for California Businesses, A Guidebook*, Office of the Government, State of California.

Cao, A. D. (1981) "U.S. Export Trading Companies—The Time is Now.", *Business*, New York, NY.

Cassell, Clark C. and Delphos, William A., (ed.) (1990) *The World is Your Market: An Export Guide For Small Business*, Braddock Communications, Washington, DC, USA.

Cateora, Philip R. (1983) *International Marketing*, 5th edn, Richard D. Irwin, Inc., New York, NY.

Cavusgil, S. Tamer (1981) "Some Observations on the Relevance of Critical Variables for Internationalization Stages," in Michael R. Czinkota, and George Tesar, (eds) *Export Management: An International Context*, Praeger, New York, NY.

Chung, Dr. Sunny (1989) "Here's Help in Understanding International Culture Shock," *Currents*, the Newsletter of United States International University, San Diego, CA. USA.

Cronin, Steven (1982) *Problems of the Export Management Company in Southern California*, Thesis, San Diego State University, USA.

Dodge, H. Robert (1982) Fullerton, Sam D., Rink, David R., and Merrill, Charles E., *Marketing Research*, Bell & Howell Companies, Chicago, IL, USA.

Enen, Jack, Jr. (1991) *Venturing Abroad: International Business Expansion Via Joint Ventures*, Liberty Hall Press, Blue Ridge Summit, Penna., USA.

Goldsmith, Howard R., (1989) *Import/Export: A Guide to Growth, Profits, and Market Share*, Prentice Hall, Englewood Cliffs, New Jersey, USA.

Green Memo (1982) "The Export Trading Company Act of 1982. P.L. 97–290." Washington D.C. General Council's Office, National Association of Manufacturers, 3, November.

Harris, Philip and Moran, Robert (1982) *Managing Cultural Differences*, Intercultural Press, Inc. Washington, DC.

Hills, Ambassador Carla A. (1989) "Statement of", Office of the United States Trade Representative, Executive Office of the President, Washington, D.C.

Hoffheinz, Roy Jr., and Calder, Kent E. (1982) *The Eastasia Edge*. New York: Basic Books Inc., New York, NY.

Horowitz, Rose A. (1989) "Soviets Design Incentives for New 'Free Zones'", *The Journal of Commerce*, New York, NY.

Jimenez, Guillermo (1997) *Export–Import Basics: The Legal, Financial and Transport Aspects of International Trade*, International Chamber of Commerce, Paris, France.

Johnson, Wesley J. and Czinkota, Michael R. (1982) "Managerial Motivation as Determinants of Industrial Export Behavior," in Michael R. Czinkota, and George Tesar, (eds), *Export Management: An International Context*, Praeger, New York, NY.

Joynt, Pat (1982) "An Empirical Study of Norwegian Export Behavior," in Michael R. Czinkota, and George Tesar, (eds), *Export Management: An International Context*, Praeger, New York, NY.

Lowe, Janet (1985) "It's Just a Matter of Manners," *The San Diego Tribune*, San Diego, CA.

Marotta, George (1989) "Europe, Inc.," *San Diego Union*, San Diego, CA.

McKay, Edward S. (1972) *The Marketing Mystique*, American Management Association, Inc., New York, NY.

Meissner, Frank (1982) "U.S. Export Trading Companies: is the Japanese Success Story Reproducible, Adoptable, or Improvable?" In Michael R. Czinkota, and George Tesar, (eds), *Export Policy: A Global Assessment*, Praeger, New York, NY.

Morrison Ann V. and Layton, Robin (1986) "GATT: A Look Back," Office of Multilateral Affairs, International Trade Administration, June 23, *Business America*, Washington, DC.

Morrison Ann V. and Layton, Robin (1986) "GATT's Seven Rounds of Trade Talks Span More Than Thirty Years," Office of Multilateral Affairs, International Trade Administration, July 7, *Business America*, Washington, DC.

Morrison Ann V. and Layton, Robin (1986) "Tokyo Round Agreements Set Rules for Non-tariff Measures," Office of Multilateral Affairs, International Trade Administration, July 7, *Business America*, Washington, DC.

Nelson, Carl A. (1984) *The Relationship of Export Obstacles to the Export Trading Company Act of 1982*, Dissertation, United States International University, San Diego, CA.

Nelson, Carl A., Commander, U.S. Navy (1971) "Student notes for Cross-cultural survival," U.S. Navy, Pre-Vietnam duty, San Diego, CA.

Nelson, Carl A., Dr. (1990) *Global Success: International Business Tactics for the 1990s* Liberty Hall Press, Blue Ridge Summit, Penna., USA.

Nelson, Carl A. (1995) *Import/Export: How to Get Started in International Trade*, 2nd edn., McGraw-Hill, New York, NY.

Nothdurft, William E. (1992) *Going Global: How Europe Helps Small Firms Export*, The Brookings Institute, Washington, DC, USA.

Office of the United States Trade Representative (1989) "Fact Sheet: Special 301 on Intellectual Property," Washington, DC.

Offitzer, Karen, (ed.), (1992) *The Learning Annex Guide To Starting Your Own Import–Export Business*, Citadel Press, New York, NY, USA.

Oberg, Dr. Kalervo (1955) "Culture Shock," *Anthropologist*, Health, Welfare and Housing Division, U.S. A.I.D., Brazil.

Pasquinelli Jr., Arthur (1982) *Services: How to Export, A Marketing Manual*, Northern California District Export Council, San Francisco, CA.

Pavord, William C., and Bogart, Raymond G. (1975) "The Dynamics of the Decision to Export," *Akron Business and Economic Review*, 6, No. 1 (Spring): 6–11, Akron, OH.

Pregelj, Vladimir N. (1985) "Trade Remedies Available to the United States Under International Agreements and Corresponding Domestic Laws," The Library of Congress, Report No. 85–1008 E, October 18, Washington, DC.

Pregelj, Vladimir N. (1987) "Import Relief: A Brief Historical Survey of Presidential Discretion in Providing a Remedy in Escape Clause/

Import Relief Investigations," June 26, The Library of Congress, Washington, DC.

Reed, John S. (1989) "The Service Sector: The Key to America's Economic Future," *Analysis, Reports and Briefings from the Congressional Economic Leadership Institute*, Washington, DC.

Reishauer, Edwin O. (1964) *Japan Past and Present*, 3rd edn, Japan: Charles E. Tuttle Inc., New York, NY.

Ried, Stan, (1982) "The Impact of Size on Export Behavior in Small Firms," in Michael R. Czinkota, and George Tesar, (eds), *Export Management: An International Context*. Praeger, New York, NY.

Sek, Lenore (1989) "Unfair Foreign Trade Practices: Section 301 of the Trade Act of 1974," The Library of Congress, Washington, DC.

Seligman, Scott D. (1983) "A Shirt-sleeve Guide to Chinese Corporate Etiquette," January–February, *The Chinese Business Review*, Los Angeles, CA.

Superintendent of Documents (1987) *Foreign Trade Barriers*, U.S. Government Printing Office, Washington, DC.

Sweeney, Paul and Dierks, Carsten (1988) *Europe 1992: The Removal of Trade Barriers in the Common Market in 1992 and the Implications for American Businesses*, a research paper, Department of Marketing, College of Business Administration, Texas A&M University, Dallas, TX.

Terpstra, Vern (1983) *International Marketing*, 3rd edn, The Dryden Press, New York, NY.

U.S. Department of Commerce and UNZ&CO (1998) *A Basic Guide to Exporting*, UNZ&CO, New Providence, NJ, USA.

U.S. Small Business Administration (1979) *Export Marketing for Smaller Firms*, 4th edn., Washington D.C.

U.S. Department of Commerce (1989) *The Services Industries Development Program*, Report by the Secretary of Commerce, Washington, DC.

U.S. Department of Commerce (1988) *U.S. National Study on Trade in Services*, a Submission by the United States Government to the General Agreement on Tariffs and Trade, Washington, DC.

U.S. Department of Commerce (1984) *The Export Trading Company Guidebook*, International Trade Administration, Washington, DC.

U.S. Department of Commerce (1985) International Trade Administration, *Foreign Business Practices: Materials on Practical Aspects of Exporting, International Licensing and Investing*, Superintendent of Documents, GPO, Washington, DC.

U.S. International Trade Commission (1988) "Proposed Rules Governing Trade Remedy Assistance", International Trade Commission, 19 CFR Part 213, Federal Register, Vol. 53, No. 245, Wednesday, December 21, Washington, DC.

United States International Trade Commission (1984) *Rules of Practice and Procedure,* 19 CFR Chap II, Revised through November 30, Washington, DC.

United Nations Office at Geneva (1986) *UNCTAD at a Glance,* UNCTAD Information Unit, TAD/INF/PUB/86–1, Printed at U.N. Geneva, GE. 86–57083–November, Geneva.

Verzariu, Pompiliu (1984) *International Countertrade: A Guide for Managers and Executives,* U.S. Department of commerce, ITA, Washington, DC.

Wells, L. Fargo and Dulat, Karin B. (1989) *Exporting From Start To Finance: A Comprehensive Guide to Organizing for Export Marketing, Operation, Documentation, Legal Issues, Financing, Government Assistance, Sources of Information and More,* McGraw-Hill, New York, NY, USA.

Weiss, Kenneth D. (1987) *Building an Import Export Business,* John Wiley & sons, Inc., New York, NY, USA

Young, Alexander K. (1979) *The Sogo Shosha: Japan's Multinational Trading Companies.* Westview Press, Colorado.

Index